TM

References for the Rest of Us! ®

BESTSELLING BOOK SERIES

Do you find that traditional reference books are overloaded with technical details and advice you'll never use? Do you postpone important life decisions because you just don't want to deal with them? Then our *For Dummies®* business and general reference book series is for you.

For Dummies business and general reference books are written for those frustrated and hard-working souls who know they aren't dumb, but find that the myriad of personal and business issues and the accompanying horror stories make them feel helpless. *For Dummies* books use a lighthearted approach, a down-to-earth style, and even cartoons and humorous icons to dispel fears and build confidence. Lighthearted but not lightweight, these books are perfect survival guides to solve your everyday personal and business problems.

> *"More than a publishing phenomenon, 'Dummies' is a sign of the times."*
>
> — *The New York Times*

> *"A world of detailed and authoritative information is packed into them..."*
>
> — *U.S. News and World Report*

> *"...you won't go wrong buying them."*
>
> — *Walter Mossberg, Wall Street Journal, on For Dummies books*

Already, millions of satisfied readers agree. They have made For Dummies the #1 introductory level computer book series and a best-selling business book series. They have written asking for more. So, if you're looking for the best and easiest way to learn about business and other general reference topics, look to For Dummies to give you a helping hand.

Cooking With Spices

FOR DUMMIES®

by Jenna Holst

Cooking With Spices For Dummies®

Published by:
Wiley Publishing, Inc.
909 Third Avenue
New York, NY 10022
www.hungryminds.com
www.dummies.com

Library of Congress Control Number: 2001092897

ISBN: 0-7645-6336-X

10 9 8 7 6 5 4 3 2 1

1B/RQ/RQ/QR/IN

Distributed in the United States by Wiley Publishing, Inc.

Distributed by CDG Books Canada Inc. for Canada; by Transworld Publishers Limited in the United Kingdom; by IDG Norge Books for Norway; by IDG Sweden Books for Sweden; by IDG Books Australia Publishing Corporation Pty. Ltd. for Australia and New Zealand; by TransQuest Publishers Pte Ltd. for Singapore, Malaysia, Thailand, Indonesia, and Hong Kong; by Gotop Information Inc. for Taiwan; by ICG Muse, Inc. for Japan; by Intersoft for South Africa; by Eyrolles for France; by International Thomson Publishing for Germany, Austria and Switzerland; by Distribuidora Cuspide for Argentina; by LR International for Brazil; by Galileo Libros for Chile; by Ediciones ZETA S.C.R. Ltda. for Peru; by WS Computer Publishing Corporation, Inc., for the Philippines; by Contemporanea de Ediciones for Venezuela; by Express Computer Distributors for the Caribbean and West Indies; by Micronesia Media Distributor, Inc. for Micronesia; by Chips Computadoras S.A. de C.V. for Mexico; by Editorial Norma de Panama S.A. for Panama; by American Bookshops for Finland.

For general information on Wiley's products and services please contact our Customer Care department; within the U.S. at 800-762-2974, outside the U.S. at 317-572-3993 or fax 317-572-4002.

For sales inquiries and resellers information, including discounts, premium and bulk quantity sales and foreign language translations please contact our Customer Care department at 800-434-3422, fax 317-572-4002 or write to Wiley Publishing, Inc., Attn: Customer Care department, 10475 Crosspoint Boulevard, Indianapolis, IN 46256.

For information on licensing foreign or domestic rights, please contact our Sub-Rights Customer Care department at 212-884-5000.

For information on using Wiley's products and services in the classroom or for ordering examination copies, please contact our Educational Sales department at 800-434-2086 or fax 317-572-4005.

Please contact our Public Relations department at 212-884-5163 for press review copies or 212-884-5000 for author interviews and other publicity information or fax 212-884-5400.

For authorization to photocopy items for corporate, personal, or educational use, please contact Copyright Clearance Center, 222 Rosewood Drive, Danvers, MA 01923, or fax 978-750-4470.

About the Author

Jenna Holst is the author of *Stews,* (Wiley, 1998) and *Cooking Soups For Dummies,* (Wiley, 2001). Her work has been featured in many national magazines, including *Food & Wine, Weight Watchers,* and *Redbook*. She has worked for many years as a food writer, culinary instructor, and consultant. Her clients have included several book publishers as well as PBS and cable television programs. Formerly a resident of New Jersey, she currently lives in South Africa.

Dedication

For Ginny and Marsh.

Author's Acknowledgments

Thanks to Michelle Carr, Guillaume Steyn, Linda Ingroia, Tim Gallan, Miriam Goderich, and Jane Dystel.

Publisher's Acknowledgments

We're proud of this book; please send us your comments through our Online Registration Form located at www.wiley.com

Some of the people who helped bring this book to market include the following:

Acquisitions, Editorial, and Media Development

Senior Project Editor: Tim Gallan

Senior Acquisitions Editor: Linda Ingroia

Copy Editor: Ben Nussbaum

Assistant Acquisitions Editor: Erin Connell

Recipe Tester: Emily Nolan

Nutritional Analyst: Patty Santelli

Editorial Manager: Pamela Mourouzis

Editorial Assistant: Carol Strickland

Illustrator: Liz Kurztman

Photography Art Director: Edwin Kuo

Photographer: David Bishop

Food Stylist: Brett Kurzweil

Prop Stylist: Randi Barritt

Production

Project Coordinator: Nancee Reeves

Layout and Graphics: Brian Drumm, Jacque Schneider, Erin Zeltner

Proofreaders: Angel Perez, Marianne Santy, TECHBOOKS Production Services

Indexer: TECHBOOKS Production Services

General and Administrative

Wiley Publishing, Inc.: John Kilcullen, CEO; Bill Barry, President and COO; John Ball, Executive VP, Operations & Administration; John Harris, Executive VP and CFO

Wiley Consumer Reference Group

Business: Kathleen Nebenhaus, Vice President and Publisher; Kevin Thornton, Acquisitions Manager

Cooking/Gardening: Jennifer Feldman, Associate Vice President and Publisher; Anne Ficklen, Executive Editor; Kristi Hart, Managing Editor

Education/Reference: Diane Graves Steele, Vice President and Publisher

Lifestyles: Kathleen Nebenhaus, Vice President and Publisher; Tracy Boggier, Managing Editor

Pets: Kathleen Nebenhaus, Vice President and Publisher; Tracy Boggier, Managing Editor

Travel: Michael Spring, Vice President and Publisher; Brice Gosnell, Publishing Director; Suzanne Jannetta, Editorial Director

Wiley Consumer Editorial Services: Kathleen Nebenhaus, Vice President and Publisher; Kristin A. Cocks, Editorial Director; Cindy Kitchel, Editorial Director

Wiley Consumer Production: Debbie Stailey, Production Director

Contents at a Glance

Cartoons at a Glance

By Rich Tennant

page 5

"I'm not sure what flavor you're tasting. I didn't use any spice rubs on the meat, however I dropped it several times on the way to the grill."

page 107

"It's a microwave slow cooker. It'll cook a stew all day in just 7 minutes."

page 63

"OK Cookie—your venison in lingonberry sauce is good, as are your eggplant soufflé and the risotto with foie gras. But whoever taught you how to make a croquembouche should be shot!"

page 159

"Do I like arugula? I love arugula!! Some of the best beaches in the world are there."

page 259

Cartoon Information:
Fax: 978-546-7747
E-Mail: richtennant@the5thwave.com
World Wide Web: www.the5thwave.com

Recipes at a Glance

Dips and Soups

Chicken

Beef, Pork, and Lamb

Fish and Seafood

Vegetarian

Pasta, Potatoes, and Rice

Baked Goods

Beverages

American

Southwestern and Tex-Mex

Mexican

Caribbean

South American

Japanese

Chinese

Indian

Southeast Asian

Mediterranean European and Middle Eastern

French

Table of Contents

Chapter 3: Fresh Spices, Aromatics, and Spicy Condiments 37

Chapter 4: Spicing Up Your Kitchen 51

Part II: Spicy Skills 63

Introduction

░ ░

*T*hough commonplace for centuries in the East, spices were the prized culinary treasures of royalty and the wealthy merchant class in the Western world until the nineteenth century. Fortunately for us, they are now widely available at a relatively low cost. Their scent today graces most kitchens worldwide. Spices give food depth, character, aroma, and above all, taste. Used in both savory and sweet dishes, spices offer you wide range of flavors to choose from and experiment with.

In this book, you discover that cooking with spices is easy and fun. *Cooking with Spices For Dummies* is divided into five parts that guide you through the world of spices so that you know how to make the most of the spices that are available to you. From historical tidbits to down-to-earth tips, you find out how to buy, prepare, combine, and cook with spices. You also discover some of the world's most-loved dishes and some exciting new recipes.

How to Use This Book

The world of spices is at your fingertips; you can discover it in this book. Embark on a culinary tour and discover the commodity that incited nations into wars.

This book takes a practical and modern approach to cooking so that you can create healthy and delicious meals without having special skills or spending a great deal of time in the kitchen. The featured recipes range from simple spice mixtures to sauces, soups, dips, main dishes, curries, chiles, grilled food, salads, vegetables, breads, sweets, and beverages. Recipes include healthier renditions of traditional favorites to delicious cultural specialties to sensational modern fare. All use spices in traditional or innovative combinations to create delectable dishes. And I even include a helpful rating for how spicy the dish is.

But before I jump into the recipes, I give you information on what spices are and how to use and combine them. You discover what equipment you need; how to buy, store, and prepare spices for cooking; and basic techniques to make spice blends, rubs, spiced oils, vinegars, and butters. With this knowledge, you'll be ready to cook and savor the flavors of spices from around the globe. Enjoy!

What I Assume about You

You don't need to have any prior cooking knowledge to use this book. The spices and recipes are fully explained, as are general cooking concepts that come up here and there. Just make sure that you have the right equipment and ingredients, and you'll be cooking with spices in no time. Even if you know a lot about cooking, you'll still find this book to be incredibly useful; not only for the recipes, but also for the spicy info and tips I've peppered throughout the book.

How This Book Is Organized

Cooking with Spices For Dummies is divided into five parts that guide you through every aspect of cooking with spices. It's filled with fascinating information, practical advice, and helpful cooking tips. The book takes you on a journey that spans the globe. Starting on the spice route, you discover what spices are and how they're used, what special equipment you might need, and how you, in your own kitchen, can take full advantage of spices. Then I present recipes that really spice up your cooking. Have fun and feel free to skip around. If you just want to look up the recipe for, say, Indian Chicken Curry, you can find it in the Index at the back of the book or in the Recipes at a Glance in the front of the book and get cooking.

The majority of the recipes are very easy to make, although a few are more challenging. To guide you, ballpark preparation and cooking times are given for every recipe. Additionally for each dish, you'll find a spice meter reading, from mild to hot and spicy, to let you know how spicy the dish really is.

Part 1: Taking the Spice Route

In this part, you discover what spices actually are and their place in history. You're introduced to individual spices, from the most widely used to the more exotic and unusual spices, in both fresh and dried forms. You find out their characteristics, how to buy and store them, and how to use up spices that are no longer fresh and potent. You also find out what tools you need (and what tools you don't need) to cook effectively and efficiently with spices.

Part II: Spicy Skills

This part gives you the treasured secrets of cooking with spices. I show you the basic techniques of cooking with spices — how to toast or dry roast spices and how to make spice blends, spice pastes, spiced oils, spiced vinegars, spiced butters, and seasoned flours. You also find out how to handle spices, avoid common spice-related mistakes, and fix a few cooking mistakes. You also discover what spices and ingredient combinations are key to many culture's cuisines. You then move on to menu planning and learn some kitchen strategies that make cooking easier and more enjoyable.

Part III: On the Starting Line

In this part, you find recipes for spice blends and rubs, marinades and sauces, salads, and light fare such as starters, soups, and snacks.

Part IV: From the Main Course to the Finish Line

This part presents spicy recipes for chicken, meat, seafood, vegetables, potatoes, grains, pasta, quick breads, sweets, and beverages.

Part V: The Part of Tens

Every *For Dummies* book ends with top-ten lists, and this one is no exception. I give you ten ways to present and garnish meals and ten Internet and mail-order sources for spices and unusual ingredients.

Icons Used in This Book

Look for these icons next to tidbits of useful information:

When you see this icon, expect to find interesting tidbits, lore, and information about a particular spice, recipe, or piece of equipment.

Here you find culinary tips and common-sense hints to make your cooking easier, more productive, and more enjoyable.

I use this icon when I want to give you an alternative recipe that can be made with a few simple changes to the main one.

I place this icon next to information that will help you prevent mistakes or when I want to warn you against doing things that may potentially cause a problem.

Part I
Taking the Spice Route

In this part . . .

I introduce you to individual spices, from the most widely used to the more exotic and unusual spices, in both fresh and dried forms. You find out their characteristics, how to buy and store them, and how to use up spices that are no longer fresh and potent. You also find out what tools you need (and what tools you don't need) to cook effectively and efficiently with spices.

Chapter 1

A Spicy Tale

In This Chapter

▶ Finding out what spices are

▶ Getting a bird's eye view of the history of the spices

▶ Discovering a few nonculinary uses of spices

Exotic, fragrant, inviting, alluring, delicate, sultry, delicious, flavorful — these are some of the words that you may associate with spices. Widespread travel and migration have exposed us to a variety of cultures and their respective cuisines. We've discovered the culinary secrets of how different people cook with once precious spices. Yet, these now commonplace ingredients have a spicy past. This chapter presents their story in brief.

Spicy Definitions

Sometimes you may wonder if a particular substance is an herb or a spice. It's not always an easy question to answer. Spices are seeds, fruit, berries, bark, roots, and Rhizomes (an underground stem that produces knobby roots) of plants. For example, cloves are buds; allspice and peppercorns are berries; chile peppers are fruit; cardamom and cumin are seeds; ginger and turmeric are Rhizomes; cinnamon is a bark. Sometimes a single plant provides both an herb and a spice. Take coriander, for example. The spice coriander is the seed of the plant that brings us the pungent leaves cilantro that are considered an herb. But there are a few tricks to help you distinguish between spices and herbs, both of which are generally found in the "spice" section of supermarkets.

Generally speaking, spices grow in the tropics and don't thrive in a home patio garden. Herbs, however, can be successfully grown at home in pots or in the ground. Thyme, oregano, and basil are herbs, whereas cinnamon, cloves, and vanilla are spices. There are some gray areas. Chiles, members of the *capsicum* family, are peppers that can be successfully grown at home or in the tropics and are considered a spice.

Cinnamon was burned as an incense along with sandalwood and myrrh in ancient religious ceremonies and rites.

Exploring the Use of Spices

Today, spices are taken for granted. Their relatively inexpensive price and widespread availability is a fact of modern life. We now see them as a source of pleasure, one that tantalizes our palates and enlivens our sense of smell. We use them liberally in food, perfume, extracts, alcohol, medicines, candles, and incense. Yet it wasn't so long ago that spices were such a valuable commodity in the West that only nobility and the very rich could afford them. Spices were a form of currency that were given as gifts to kings in the Middle East and in Europe and used as a form of payment for taxes and debt in England and Rome. The wealthy cooked with spices not only for taste, but also as a means to display their financial success. Spices were a symbol of honor and power.

Cloves were an ingredient in Greek, Roman, and Arabic love potions.

Today spices are mainly used for fragrance and taste. You'll find them in a range of products (perfumes, soaps, remedies, lotions, potpourri, scented oils, aromatherapy products, and candles, among others), but their primary use is in cooking and baking. Spices can be prime players in nearly every kind of dish — sauces, soups, stews, meatloaf, burgers, one-pot meals, dips, marinades, spice rubs and blends such as curry powder, barbecues, bread, desserts, and beverages. Sometimes only a single spice is featured, such as pepper in the classic French dish Steak au Poivre (Chapter 14). Most often, however, spices are combined to provide layers of flavor, like in dishes such as Beef and Bean Chili (Chapter 14) and Tandoori Chicken Cutlets (Chapter 13). From breakfast breads, such as Cinnamon Coffee Cake (Chapter 18) to the fancy dessert coffee New Orleans Café Brulot (Chapter 19), modern cooks and diners enjoy spices in a variety of dishes that are served throughout the day.

A Little Spicy History

Throughout the centuries, spices have played an important role in the economies of many nations. Most spices originated in the East — India, the Spice Islands (now known as the Moluccas, a part of Indonesia), and the

Malaysian archipelago. Spices made their way westward via land on camel caravans through what is now the Middle East. Routes also took spices through northern and eastern Africa. The first written chronicle to confirm that Middle Eastern merchants controlled the flow of spices is the Bible. In the Bible, it's said that King Solomon derived much of his wealth from the spice trade and through the gifts of spices that he received. The Queen of Sheba brought King Solomon presents, including spices, in an effort to prevent any threat to the trade routes that she ruled.

Middle Eastern traders maintained their monopoly for centuries. Throughout the region, spices were sold in large open-air bazaars. Tales of danger and death — that spices grew in snake-infested forests, for example — circulated to prevent customers and fortune seekers from heading to the East on their own.

Even today, the custom of selling spices in bulk in outdoor and indoor spice bazaars continues in India, Indonesia, Africa, and the Middle East.

During the Roman Empire, the Romans, aided by their powerful sailing fleet, fought Middle Eastern traders for control of the spice trade. The Romans were the next power to acquire dominance and maintained control of the spice trade until the fall of their empire. A limited amount of spices were grown in European monasteries after the fall of Rome and the Arabic world regained its former stature in the spice trade. Along came the crusades to the Middle Eastand the European interest in spices was revived. Caravans returned to Europe with silks, jewels, and spices.

In the thirteenth century, Marco Polo, the son of a jewel merchant, traveled east to China. His book detailing his adventures included accounts of the groves of spices that he saw. His chronicle caused others to set sail in search of the treasures in the East. Genoa and Venice gained control of the trade routes to the East and of the commodities of the East, including spices. It was during this century that spices were first used by the middle classes. Figure 1-1 shows the old spice route.

Spices weren't just for cooking. They were used in place of money for rent payments and governments began to tax them. As European powers parried for economic dominance, spices became a much sought-after commodity. An ounce of cardamom was a common laborer's annual wage; a sheep was valued at five ounces of mace.

Spices' nonculinary uses include perfumes, traditional medicines, and dyes. Ginger, for example, has been prescribed as a digestive aid, and cloves were used as a soothing agent for toothaches.

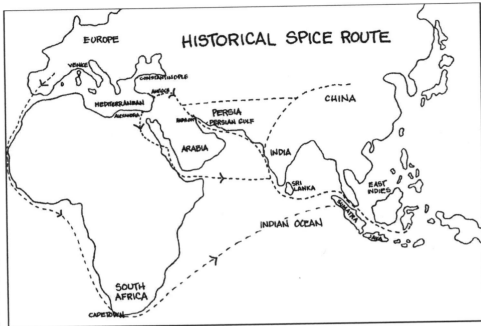

Figure 1-1:
The spice
route.

Voyages to the East were difficult. Pirates, hijackings, and tempestuous storms were all threats, but the prospect of huge profits was a strong motivator. Men risked their lives and their fortunes in search of spices. Spain sponsored Christopher Columbus's attempt to find a new route to the East Indies, but, as we all know, he landed in America, bringing home to Europe chiles, vanilla, and allspice. The Portuguese were the first to find a direct sailing route to the East, although it was considered a highly dangerous passage. Vasco de Gama, passing the unpredictably and stormy Cape of Good Hope, returned from his journey to the Spice Islands with a cargo of spices. By the early seventeenth century, the Portuguese had lost their role as leading spice merchants to the Dutch. The Dutch East Indies Company used Cape Town, South Africa, as a stopover point on the route. The British entered into a bitter and bloody conflict with the Dutch, and eventually succeeded in colonizing India and Sri Lanka, leaving the Dutch with only Java and Sumatra.

In the eighteenth century the United States entered the spice trade, using ports in Massachusetts and New York as the starting points for these perilous sea journeys. Today, the United States is the largest importer of spices in the world.

Presently, spices are grown outside their native areas; ginger thrives in Jamaica as well as in its native lands of Asia, for example. Until the twentieth century, spices were a catalyst of economic development. Today, formerly precious spices are grown by farmers in developing nations as extra cash crops, bringing only small profits that supplement the farmers' meager incomes. Yet, spices are no less valuable to the cooks who use them. To the trained culinary artist, the spices shown in Figure 1-2 are worth more than gold.

Figure 1-2:
Spices
galore!

Chapter 2

The Spice Rack: A Guide to Dried Spices

In This Chapter

▶ Individual dried spices and their uses

▶ Spices in condiments

Today's food is bursting with flavor — kitchens are filled with the fragrance of spices. An ever-increasing variety of spices are available to the home cook. In this chapter, I cover the most common spices, as well as some more exotic spices that you may have passed by. You get the facts about individual spices as well as commonly used spice blends and discover their culinary uses.

Many of the spices that are used in cooking and baking are dried. You may choose to buy them in their whole form or you may opt for the convenience of preground spices and blends.

If you'd like to get an idea of the taste of a particular spice, open the jar and smell its aroma. Or if you're dealing with a whole spice, rub a little between your fingers to release the oils and aroma.

Some spices need to be toasted in order to fully release their flavor. See Chapter 5 for instructions on how to prepare spices.

Searching the Spice Rack

A world of spices awaits you; all you need is to discover it. This section takes a look at some of the most commonly used spices.

Check out Appendix C for some general quantity guidelines when working with the spices listed in this chapter.

Allspice

Profile: Dark brown to reddish brown in color, allspice is grown in Jamaica. Referred to by Jamaicans as *pimento* or *Jamaican pepper,* it has a sweet aroma with undertones of cloves, cinnamon, and nutmeg. In fact, allspice is so named because it seems like a blend of these spices. In baking, ground cloves can be used as a replacement.

Forms: Whole berries or ground

Uses: Cooking and baking. In Jamaica, allspice is a key ingredient in jerk rubs and sauces. It is also used in Indonesia, Malaysia, and South Africa in curries. In Europe and North America, it is found in ground meat pies and Swedish meatballs. In its ground form, it is also used in sweetbreads, pies, cakes, and cookies.

Anise or aniseed

Profile: Indigenous to the eastern Mediterranean, anise is a small, light-colored seed that is oval in shape and slightly flat. It has a sweet licorice flavor and aroma. Fennel is a suitable replacement.

Forms: Whole seeds

Uses: Cooking, baking, and beverages. It is primarily found in savory breads as well as sweet pastries, cookies, and cakes, but it can also be a seasoning for carrots, seafood stews, or soups. Pernod and Ouzo are popular cordials that derive their flavor from anise.

Achiote (annato)

Profile: Known by two names, *achiote* and *annato,* this spice is native to the Caribbean and to the American continents. It is a reddish, small triangular seed with a negligible peppery flavor. Primarily used as a colorant, it imparts a reddish to yellow-orange tone to a variety of dishes, from chicken to rice. Turmeric and saffron are alternatives.

Form: Whole seeds or ground

Uses: Cooking. Achiote is commonly used in small amounts in Puerto Rican, Jamaican, and Latin American cookery as a natural food dye. The color is released by heating the spice in any fat, such as lard, butter, or oil. Achiote seeds can also be infused in hot water to release the spice's tint, such as in water for boiling rice.

Achiote gives cheddar cheese its yellow color.

Caraway

Profile: Grown in Europe, these light-brown, oval seeds feature a distinctive tapered point at both ends and a slight lengthwise indentation (see Figure 2-1). Their strong flavor is somewhat reminiscent of anise and dill.

Forms: Whole seeds, occasionally ground

Uses: Cooking and baking. Caraway is the principal spice in rye bread. It is also used to flavor mild Dutch cheeses such as Gouda or Edam. Caraway is popular in northern European and Slavic cookery and is found in goulashes, cabbage, coleslaw, soups, stews, and potato dishes.

Figure 2-1:
You
commonly
see
caraway
seeds in rye
bread.

Cardamom

Profile: Cardamom pods are oval in shape and contain the seeds that hold the spice's flavor (see Figure 2-2). Most often you will find pale green pods, the color they are in their natural state. Avoid white pods, which have been bleached, a process that diminishes both their color and flavor. Black cardamom pods are too harsh for general use.

Spicy coffees

In Arabic countries, strong coffee is often scented with cardamom by adding bruised pods to the pot. You can try this at home by adding a few pods to a coffeemaker pot, brewing, and straining out the seeds as you pour the coffee. You can also add a dash of ground cardamom to the coffee grounds before brewing in a drip or plunger-style pot. Cinnamon is a secret ingredient in Viennese coffee. Lightly sprinkle a bit of cinnamon on coffee grounds before brewing to obtain a unique flavor.

The flavor of green cardamom hints of citrus, coriander, and ginger. There really is no substitute for its subtle sweetness in cooking. In baking, however, you can substitute ground cinnamon.

Forms: Whole pods or ground seeds.

Uses: Cooking, baking, and beverages. Native to India, cardamom is featured in many Indian curry dishes, as well as in Indonesian, Malaysian, South African, and eastern Mediterranean cookery. It is also used to flavor puddings and baked goods. In Scandinavia, ground cardamom is the primary spice in many baked goods.

When using whole cardamom pods, remember to bruise the pods slightly with the flat side of a knife to help release the seeds and the flavor. See Chapter 5 for instructions on bruising.

Figure 2-2:
Cardamom pods need to be bruised before being used.

CARDAMOM PODS

Cayenne or ground red pepper

Profile: Made from ground dried cayenne chile peppers, this spice is sometimes marketed as ground red chile pepper. Reddish orange in color, it has a sharp, fiery bite and should be used sparingly.

Forms: Ground

Alternative forms: Tabasco sauce or liquid hot red pepper sauce, Chinese or Asian hot red chile oil

Uses: Cooking and baking. Cayenne is used in many hot and fiery cuisines around the globe, such as Mexican, Cajun, Indian, South American, and Caribbean cuisines. It is used in curries, stews, spice rubs, soups, marinades, sauces, and cheddar cheese dishes, as well as in baked goods such as corn bread and cheddar crackers. Some modern chefs put a pinch in sweet baked goods to add a subtle zip.

Add zing to your food by adding a pinch of cayenne to dips, cheese sauces, soups, or seasoned flour instead of ordinary black or white pepper.

Celery seed

Profile: The tiny, pale-brown seeds from the celery plant have a slightly bitter, distinctively celery-like aroma and flavor. Use sparingly because their flavor is quite pronounced.

Forms: Whole seeds, occasionally ground

Alternative forms: Celery salt and celery pepper

Uses: Cooking. The seeds can be sprinkled into coleslaw, tomato dishes, salads, salad dressings, pickles, and fish dishes. The spice is sometimes added to dry spice rubs.

Chile pepper powders

Profile: Relatively new to the scene, several spice manufacturers are marketing a range of dried ground chiles beyond the more familiar cayenne. Some of the varieties of chiles available are ground ancho, ground Anaheim or California, ground arbol, ground California cayenne, ground or flaked chipotle, ground habanero, ground jalapeno, and ground New Mexican, a chile pepper that's available in various heat levels.

Chile pepper powders can be found in some groceries and specialty shops, as well as through online merchants Most ground chile pepper powders are labeled mild, medium, or hot. The spice companies listed in Chapter 21 indicate the heat factor of their spices.

Homemade chili powder

Commercially prepared chili powder often contains salt and chemical additives to prevent clumping. The good news is that you can make your own and season to your own taste — mild to fiery hot. Combine 4 tablespoons of ground Anaheim or ancho, or mild to medium New Mexican chili peppers, or good quality paprika; 1½ to 2 tablespoons ground cumin; 2 teaspoons oregano that you've crumbed between your fingers; 2 teaspoons garlic powder; 1 to 3 teaspoons cayenne; and ½ teaspoon salt in a spice mill and grind to a smooth powder. Alternatively, put the preground ingredients in a bowl and stir to mix. The chili powder can be stored in a covered container for up to 6 months.

Dried Anaheim chile peppers are sometimes referred to as California, ancho, or red Colorado and are generally mild with a slight bite. New Mexican chiles can vary in heat from mild to hot, so read the label to make sure that the type you use for chili powder are mild to medium. If you're grinding your own chiles, remove the stem and seeds before grinding. If you use paprika, which is not as strong as the chiles and also lacks their characteristic tanginess, you will probably use the larger amount of cumin and cayenne.

Pure ground chiles are not to be confused with American or Southwestern chili powder, which is actually a mixture of spices.

Forms: Ground

Alternative forms: Whole dried chiles of many varieties

Uses: Cooking. These can be used in marinades, sauces, stews, chilis, soups, salad dressings, dips, or in seasoned flour, cornmeal, or breadcrumbs.

Chili powder

Profile: A reddish brown combination of spices made popular by Southwestern and Tex-Mex cooking, chili powder usually includes ground mild to medium hot California, also called Anaheim, or New Mexican chili pepper, paprika, cumin, garlic, cayenne or ground red pepper, and sometimes salt and anticaking agents.

Forms: Ground

Uses: Cooking. The most popular use of chili powder is in chili con carne and vegetarian chili dishes. It is also used in marinades and sauces and sprinkled on salads or dips such as guacamole.

In the United States and Canada, chili powder is a spice comprised of a combination of spices; however, in foreign lands and foreign cookbooks, what is referred to as chili or chili powder is actually cayenne or ground red pepper.

Cinnamon and cassia

Profile: Cinnamon, native to Sri Lanka, Burma, and India, is the bark of an evergreen tree of the laurel family. It's rolled into quills and broken into pieces (see Figure 2-3). Cinnamon has a pungent sweet aroma and flavor and is pale brown. Cassia, native to Burma and grown throughout Indonesia and the West Indies, also comes from a small evergreen tree of the laurel family and has a reddish brown color True cinnamon, also known as *Ceylon cinnamon,* is often difficult to find. In the United States, most of what is considered cinnamon is, in fact, cassia. If you do find true cinnamon, it is more expensive than cassia. True cinnamon is called *canela* in Mexico and can be found in Mexican or Latin American grocery stores.

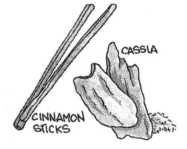

Figure 2-3:
Cinnamon sticks and cassia bark.

Forms: Whole sticks and ground

Alternate forms: Cinnamon sugar and liquid cinnamon essence or extract

Uses: Cooking, baking, and beverages. Cinnamon is used in a variety of dishes worldwide — curries, soups, spice rubs, pumpkin and winter squash, poached fruit, mulled and hot beverages, and, most notably, in baked goods. In Mexico, cinnamon is typically added to chocolate. Difficult to grind in a mortar and pestle or hand mill, it can be ground more easily in an electric spice mill.

Cloves

Profile: Cloves are the dried, unopened buds of a tree native to Indonesia (see Figure 2-4). Currently, East Africa is the largest producer of cloves. Cloves have a pleasantly warm and spicy bite and fragrance. The flavor is intense, so use sparingly.

Figure 2-4:
Cloves look like little dried buds.

Forms: Whole and ground

Uses: Cooking, baking, and beverages. Cloves are used to add flavor to a multitude of dishes throughout the world. Whole cloves are used in poaching liquids, hot beverages, curries, and, most commonly, to stud ham. Ground cloves are used in spice rubs and blends, as well as in a variety of sweet baked items such as pumpkin pie and spice cakes, or a pinch can be added to winter or summer squash soups. Cloves are very difficult to grind at home, so use pre-ground cloves in spice mixes or rubs.

Coriander

Profile: Coriander is the seed from the plant that produces the herb cilantro. Native to the Mediterranean, it is also grown in India, Indonesia, Malaysia, South and Central America, and South Africa, as well as throughout Europe. The buff-colored seeds resemble white peppercorns. Their flavor is warm, sweet, and rich, with citrusy undertones.

Because ground coriander loses its potency quickly, it's best to grind your own in a pepper mill designated for only that purpose.

Forms: Whole seeds and ground

Uses: Cooking. Coriander is used throughout the globe. It is a major component of curry powder, Thai and Southeast Asian saté marinades, Indonesian and Malaysian dishes, North and South African recipes, Mexican cooking, and Mediterranean and Middle Eastern cuisine. It is excellent when freshly ground and sprinkled over fish, chicken, or salads. It can be added to poaching liquids for seafood, chicken, or fruit. Coriander is often combined with cumin — its sweetness offsets the bitterness of cumin.

Toast whole coriander and cumin seeds before grinding or adding to recipes to bring out the full potential of the flavor. See Chapter 5 for instructions.

Crushed red pepper flakes

Profile: These are the dried seeds from chile peppers and pack quite a hot and fiery punch. Use them sparingly — about ¼ to ½ teaspoon is enough for most recipes. Most people know crushed red chile flakes as a condiment in their local pizza parlor, where they can choose to sprinkle the flakes on their slice.

Forms: Whole seeds

Uses: Cooking. In small doses, they're marvelous in Mediterranean, and South American foods, such as seafood stews, tomato-based pasta sauces, tomato sauces, chili, as well as spice rubs and blends. They are also used in India, the Middle East, and the African continent.

Crushed chile flakes are the star of this spicy condiment. Combine 1 tablespoon of crushed red chile flakes with 3 tablespoons of olive oil, ½ to 1 teaspoon of salt, and 2 cloves of pressed or finely minced fresh garlic. Use the mixture as a spicy condiment on burgers, fish, chicken, or lamb; toss it with green beans or collard greens; add a touch to fried onions; or top Mediterranean hummus or white bean dip with a teaspoonful. Refrigerate in a covered container for up to 4 weeks.

Cumin

Profile: Cumin, a skiff-shaped, white or black seed hails from Egypt and has been used throughout the Mediterranean for centuries. It has a strong aroma and flavor with a slightly bitter aftertaste. White seeds are the most commonly available.

Forms: Whole seeds and ground

Uses: Cooking. Cumin has traveled far and wide and is used in kitchens throughout South America, India, Europe, Indonesia and Malaysia, Africa, the Middle East, the Mediterranean, Mexico, and the American Southwest. It's a component of both chili powder and curry powder. It's terrific in a variety of dishes from those regions, such as regional and ethnic stews, soups, and legume dishes, as well as with vegetables such as eggplant and carrots and in avocado guacamole. It is sometimes added to cheeses, such as Danish havarti, as shown in Figure 2-5.

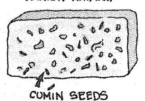

DANISH HAVARTI

CUMIN SEEDS

Figure 2-5:
A delicious
match.

Curry powder

Profile: Curry powder is a blend of several spices. There is no standard formula. Curry powder can include cumin, coriander, dried chiles, cardamom, cinnamon, cloves, fennel, peppercorns, mustard seeds, ginger, fenugreek, and turmeric. In Indian, Indonesian, and Malaysian cookery, the spices are often added to the recipe singly and not mixed beforehand.

One of the more popular and widely available forms of curry powder in America is the Madras style, the type that is used to season the food of southern India. Each area of India as well as Indonesia, Malaysia, East and South Africa, and the Caribbean create their own signature blends. Southeast Asian cooks use wet curry pastes instead of dried curry powder. The sources in Chapter 21 offer a wide array of curry powder blends from various cuisines such as Indian, Jamaican, and Balti, in various degrees of spiciness.

The color of the mixture can range from bright yellow, as in Caribbean curry powders, to deep red, such as some Indian styles. The heat meter of curry powder can also vary from mild to fiery hot.

Curry powder should not be used raw, but should be sautéed in a little vegetable oil, alone or added to already sautéed onions.

Forms: Ground

Uses: Cooking. Curry powder is used in curries, chicken or tuna salad, mayonnaise, spice mixes, legume dishes, and soups.

Curry powder is sometimes referred to as a *masala*. The word *masala, a term* used throughout India and southern Asia and Africa, means a mixture of spices.

Dill seed

Profile: Dill is the seed of the plant that gives us the feathery herb dill. Its flavor is reminiscent of its leafy counterpart. Although similar to caraway, it's much milder.

Forms: Whole seed

Uses: Cooking. Dill seed is used in spice rubs, pickles, potato salads, with root vegetables such as potatoes, parsnips and carrots, and with salmon marinades and cured preparations such as gravlax.

Fennel

Profile: Fennel, shown in Figure 2-6, is a seed from the licorice-flavored vegetable, (fennel bulb or fennel root,), which is popular in Mediterranean cooking. Pale green to beige in color, the seed of the fennel plant has a pungent anise-like flavor and aroma. It is an ingredient in Chinese five-spice powder and is also added to some curry powders. Anise is a substitute.

Forms: Whole seed, occasionally ground

Uses: Cooking and baking. Fennel seasons Italian sausages and is used in Mediterranean fish dishes, tomato sauces, and pickles. It is sometimes added to Mediterranean baked goods, both savory and sweet.

Toast fennel seeds to release their flavor before crushing or grinding them. See Chapter 5 for instructions.

Figure 2-6:
You need to toast fennel seeds before using them.

FENNEL SEEDS

Fenugreek seed

Profile: The leaves of the fenugreek plant are an herb and the angular, mustard-yellow seeds are a spice. They have a tangy flavor with the bitterness of burnt sugar. Buy the seeds and grind them yourself, as ground fenugreek loses its potency quickly.

Form: Whole, occasionally ground

Uses: Fenugreek is a seasoning used in both Middle Eastern and Indian cooking. It is added to some curry powder blends.

Filé powder

Profile: Filé powder, (pronounced FEE-lay or fih-LAY,) is made from the leaves of the sassafras tree, which are dried and ground. It has an earthy, woody taste and aroma. Its flavor is reminiscent of soft drinks like sarsaparilla beer and root beer.

Forms: Ground

Uses: Cooking. File powder is added at the end of cooking when making Cajun or Creole seafood, chicken, or sausage gumbos, and stews. Filé not only adds flavor, but it also helps thicken the dish.

Five-spice powder

Profile: Five-spice powder is a pungent, Chinese spice blend that is comprised of equal amounts of ground star anise, fennel or anise seeds, Szechuan or black peppercorns, cinnamon, and cloves or ginger.

Forms: Ground

Uses: Cooking. Five-spice powder is primarily used in Chinese cooking, particularly marinades, roasts, and stir-fries. It is also used in Pan-Asian cooking in the United States.

You can make your own five-spice powder by mixing 1 teaspoon of each of the ground spices listed above in a bowl. Store the mix in a container for up to three months. Ground star anise is sometimes hard to find, so grind your own in a spice grinder.

Garam masala

Profile: Garam masala is blend of warm and fragrant spices such as coriander seeds, peppercorns, cardamom, cinnamon, and cloves. It is used in the cuisine of northern India. Unlike southern Indian curry masalas, it contains no chiles or turmeric.

Forms: Ground

Uses: Cooking. Garam masala is generally sprinkled on a finished or cooked dish, although in some instances it is added to the early cooking stage as a flavoring agent.

Garlic powder, garlic flakes, and garlic salt

Profile: Garlic powder is the ground form of dried garlic. It has a similar flavor and aroma as fresh garlic but is milder. Garlic flakes are dehydrated chopped garlic. Garlic salt is garlic powder that has been seasoned with salt.

Forms: Ground and dehydrated

Alternative forms: Fresh garlic, bottled fresh chopped garlic

Uses: Cooking. Use it in spice blends, spice rubs, and some sauces. Although some people substitute dried for fresh garlic in cooking, dried garlic lacks the pungent character of its fresh counterpart. Fresh garlic is preferable for cooking.

Ground ginger

Profile: Ground ginger is the dried, powdered form of fresh ginger that is native to Asia. It has a slightly sweet and pungently spicy taste and aroma. The ground spice is tangier and a bit hotter than its fresh counterpart.

Forms: Ground

Alternative forms: Crystallized, candied, or preserved ginger, and fresh ginger

Galangal

Galangal is a spice used in Thai curry pastes and Southeast Asian cooking. It resembles ginger as both are Rhizomes and have a similar flavor, but galangal has a more peppery bite.

Because it's difficult to find outside of Asia, use ginger to replace galangal in Thai and other Southeast Asian recipes that call for it.

Uses: Baking and beverages. Ground ginger is perfect for baking and is a primary ingredient in such favorites as gingerbread, spiced cookies, ginger ale, pumpkin pie, and other sweet baked goods. It is also used in spice blends and spice rubs. Note that ground ginger is not interchangeable with its alternate forms.

Juniper berries

Profile: Juniper berries are small, reddish blue-black berries with a wrinkled surface that come from an evergreen tree. Their taste is bittersweet with the faint aroma of turpentine and of pine trees.

Forms: Whole

Uses: Cooking. Crush the berries slightly before using them to bring out the flavor. The berries are often paired with game, such as venison and rabbit, particularly when prepared as stews. They are also used to season pork, duck, and pates. Juniper berries are primarily used in Northern Europe, such as the Scandinavia countries and Germany.

Juniper berries are the aromatic flavoring of gin, the popular liquor.

Lemon grass and sereh

Profile: Lemon grass is native to Southeast Asia. When fresh, it has a flowery lemony aroma and taste. When dried, it loses much of its character, but dried can be used if fresh isn't available. It is available dried and chopped into strips or curls which look similar to dried lemon peel. Lemon grass is also available ground into a fine powder and in this form it is called sereh.

One fresh lemon grass stalk is equivalent to 1½ to 2 tablespoons dried strips. When you add dried strips, treat them as the recipe directs for fresh — they should be sautéed or infused in liquid

Sereh or dried ground lemon grass is strong and can be added to a recipe without sautéing. One teaspoon of sereh is equivalent to 1 stalk.

Forms: Dehydrated and ground

Alternative forms: Fresh lemon grass stalks and preserved, bottled lemon grass

Uses: Cooking. Used primarily in Thai, Vietnamese, Southeast Asian, and fusion cuisine, it is wonderful in marinades, sauces, soups, stews, and curries. Some chefs steep lemon grass in cream, milk, coconut milk, sugar syrup, and fruit juice, which is used for custards, puddings, ice creams, sorbet, or poaching liquid.

Mace

Profile: Mace is produced from the reddish-orange net-like coating of a nutmeg. Its flavor is similar to nutmeg, but is slightly more intense. Because it has a strong taste, use it sparingly.

Forms: Ground

Uses: Cooking and baking. Mace is primarily used in baked goods, cheesecakes, and puddings, but sometimes flavors bechamel or cream sauce, egg dishes, and sausages and pates. In Malaysian and South African cookery, it is added to stews and curries.

Mustard seed

Profile: Several varieties of mustard seed exist — white, yellow, brown, and black. Yellow and white, both native to the Mediterranean, come from the same plant and are fairly large. Their flavor is mildly spicy and sweet. A different plant brings us the brown variety, which is native to Asia and India. The brown seeds are hot and spicy with a slightly bitter taste. Black seeds, another type from India, are very sharp and pungent.

Forms: Whole, dried English mustard powder

Alternative forms: Prepared mustards such as Dijon, whole-grain; German; American; and flavored mustards such as tarragon, honey, or white wine; and mustard oil.

Uses: Cooking. Mustard seeds need to be dry roasted or sautéed in a little vegetable oil to bring out their flavor. The white and yellow seeds are used in pickling and prepared mustards. Prepared mustards and dried mustard powder are used in salad dressings and sauces as well. Dried mustard powder is often an ingredient in spice rubs. Brown seeds are primarily used as one of the seasonings in Indian cooking and can be a component of curry powder. Mustard seeds and mustard products are excellent with vegetables, paté, pork, ham, chicken, beef, and, of course, hot dogs.

Nutmeg

Profile: Nutmeg is the reddish-brown seed of the nutmeg tree, an evergreen of the Spice Islands. It's shown in Figure 2-7. The football-shaped seed is rather large, about the size of an apricot pit. Its lacy outer covering becomes the spice mace. Nutmeg has a pleasantly sweet aromatic flavor, with traces of mace and cinnamon. Use it sparingly as even a generous pinch can be detected in savory recipes.

Forms: Whole and ground

Uses: Cooking, baking, and beverages. For the tastiest result, freshly grate nutmeg. You can also use preground, but the flavor will be slightly diminished. Popular throughout the world, nutmeg is an excellent seasoning in savory recipes such as spinach dishes, ricotta cheese filling for lasagna, quiche, and egg fillings, as well as in cheese sauces. It is also used in many spice mixes, both savory and sweet. Nutmeg is a wonderful addition to many desserts such as custards, puddings, fruit pies, spice cakes, and muffins. It is also used in beverages such as mulled drinks and sprinkled on holiday eggnog as a final touch.

Figure 2-7:
Grate nutmeg in your favorite hot beverages.

NUTMEGS

Quatre épices

Nutmeg is an ingredient in quatre épices, the classic French spice combination used for charcuterie and to season patés, poultry, pork, and vegetables. Make your own quatre épices (which means *four spices*) by mixing ½ teaspoon ground white pepper, ¼ teaspoon ground nutmeg, ¼ teaspoon ground cinnamon, and a pinch of cloves.

Onion powder

Profile: Onion powder is the ground form of dehydrated onion. It has a similar flavor and aroma as the fresh, but is milder.

Forms: Ground

Alternative forms: Onion salt, onion flakes, and fresh onions

Uses: Cooking. Use in spice blends, spice rubs, and some sauces. Onion powder is not a substitute for onions or scallions in cooking. It lacks the texture and depth of flavor.

Paprika

Profile: Paprika is made from finely ground dried red peppers. There are two basic types, sweet and hot, depending on the type of peppers that are used. The sweet variety is most common. The label should indicate whether the paprika is hot or sweet. Those that list neither specification are often a blend of the two.

Paprika's pungent flavor ranges from mildly sweet to mildly hot with a slightly bitter aftertaste. Like the taste, the color can also vary from reddish orange to deep red. Hungarian paprika is the best quality available, but Spanish paprika is also excellent.

Forms: Ground

Uses: Cooking. The national spice of Hungary, paprika is used in goulashes, paprikash, chicken dishes, soups, and stews. Paprika is also popular in Spanish and Portuguese cooking. It is one of the ingredients in some commercial southwest American chili powders.

Use paprika to give food a bit of color by sprinkling a few pinches on pale or white food such as chicken, fish, potatoes, and cauliflower.

Peppercorns and pepper

Profile: Peppercorns are actually berries. For centuries, they have been prized by cooks for their spicy sharpness. There are three main varieties: black, white, and green. Pink peppercorns come from a different plant but mimic the shape and taste of the others. Sometimes they are sold in a colorful mixed peppercorn blend.

Black peppercorns have the most complex and spicy flavor and are the most widely used. There are several types of black peppercorns, each with its own distinctive characteristics. Bright and boldly flavored Tellicherry, richly spiced and balanced Malabar, and strong and hot Brazilian are a few of those available. The type is often listed on the label.

It is generally accepted that white peppercorns are not as spicy as some of the black peppercorns, although some prominent chefs disagree. What is true is that white pepper is hotter than its black counterpart. It is often used to season lightly colored food and white sauces where dark flecks of pepper aren't desired in the presentation. Green peppercorns, which are most often preserved in brine or vinegar, have the mildest flavor.

Forms: Whole, ground, and cracked

Uses: Cooking and baking. Pepper is used in most of the world's kitchens to flavor a variety of foods. Black and white pepper are used in savory breads, crackers, dips, soups, stews, meat, poultry, seafood, vegetables, and grains. A few fresh grinds atop salads and pasta are often the tasty final touch added right before serving or at the table. Green peppercorns are used mostly in creamy sauces that dress up steaks, chicken, duck, and fish. Pink peppercorns are generally combined with white and/or black peppercorns in a blend. Some chefs like to mix black and white peppercorns in a mill. Try it for a change of pace.

You can crush peppercorns coarsely with a mortar and pestle. Alternatively, wrap the peppercorns in a clean kitchen towel or place them in plastic bag and then crush them with a heavy skillet, such as a cast iron one, or with a rolling pin. Most people use pepper mills to grind pepper. They're discussed in more detail in Chapter 4.

Poppy seed

Profile: Poppy seeds are tiny bluish-gray seeds with a mildly nutty taste and slightly sweet aroma. Note that poppy seeds used for cooking have none of the effects of the opium poppy.

Forms: Whole

Uses: Cooking and baking. Often sprinkled on top of rolls and bread, poppy seeds are sometimes used as a filling in baked goods such as breads and pastries from northern and eastern Europe. Poppy seeds are also delicious when sprinkled over cooked noodles and added to *vinaigrettes* (oil- and vinegar-based salad dressings), as well as creamy salad dressings.

Saffron

Profile: Saffron is the most expensive spice in the world. The dried stigma of the crocus flower (see Figure 2-8), it must be harvested by hand. Because of the high cost of production, adulteration often occurs. Look for wiry threads that have a deep reddish-orange color. If there are light strands among them, the product may not be pure saffron. Note that ground saffron can also be a candidate for tampering.

Saffron is not used only for the yellow color it imparts to food. It has a warm aromatic flavor as well. A word of caution: Don't add more than a recipe calls for, as too much can give food a slightly medicinal taste.

Forms: Whole threads, occasionally ground

Uses: Cooking and baking. Saffron is used primarily in Mediterranean, Spanish, Indian, and Latin American cookery. It lends both color and flavor and is widely used in rice dishes such as Italian *risotto* and Spanish *paella*. It is also a component of *bouillabaisse,* the classic French seafood soup. Saffron is also used in baking, particularly in Sweden, to give bread and rolls a lovely yellow tint.

It takes nearly 5,000 crocuses to produce one ounce of saffron.

Figure 2-8:
Saffron
threads
come from
crocus
flowers.

CROCUS FLOWER

SAFFRON THREADS

Salt

Profile: Not typically classified as a spice, salt is the most universal of all seasonings. Although it has no aroma, salt has a rather strong taste that not only heightens natural flavors (including those of spices) but also harmoniously blends the flavors of various ingredients in a dish. Salt is covered in this book because it is almost always offered with pepper.

Salt for cooking comes in three basic types: coarse (or Kosher) salt, common or table salt, and sea salt. Kosher is often the choice of professional chefs for cooking. Common salt can include some anticaking agents to keep it flowing freely, and it is often iodized to provide additional iodine in the diet. Sea salt is produced in both medium and fine grades, and either can be used for cooking. Like Kosher salt, sea salt contains no additives or preservatives. Some chefs swear by sea salt and can taste the subtle differences in the flavor of sea salt from different regions. Sea salt from France is touted as the top, and that which is labeled *Fleur de Sel* is considered to be the best.

Finely ground common or table salt is the only type suitable for baking, and it is also perfect for general cooking.

Forms: Ground: Kosher or coarsely ground, medium, and fine

Uses: Cooking and baking. It is widely used as a flavoring agent as well as a preservative.

Sesame seed

Profile: The most frequently found form is the small-hulled white to beige seed whose pleasantly nutty and sweet flavor is strengthened when toasted. Toasting is recommended for cooking unless the food is to be deep fried. Unhusked seeds, generally black or brown in color, are also available.

Forms: Whole

Alternative forms: Chinese dark sesame seed oil, tahini

Uses: Cooking and baking. In its whole form, sesame seeds are primarily used in Western cultures in baking where they are scattered on rolls, bread, and pastries. The seeds are also used in Chinese cookery, such as chicken coated with sesame seeds, as well as in Korean and Japanese cuisine. In China, dark or toasted sesame oil is one of the principal flavorants. In the Middle East, tahini, a ground sesame seed paste, is used in sauces and in dips such as hummus.

Star anise

Profile: The rusty reddish-brown spice is shaped like a multi-pointed star or daisy (see Figure 2-9). It has an intensely strong licorice aroma, similar to anise.

Forms: Whole, occasionally ground

Uses: Cooking and baking. Primarily, star anise is used in Chinese and Vietnamese cooking. It is one of the dominant flavors in Chinese five-spice powder.

Figure 2-9:
Hard to believe that licorice comes from this spice.

Szechuan pepper

Profile: This dried whole berry is not related to peppercorns or chile peppers. It has a rusty red color and crinkly exterior. The flavor is pungent and spicy with a citrusy undertone, and it can be "peppery" hot. Use it sparingly.

Forms: Whole

Uses: Cooking. Szechuan pepper is generally used in Chinese stir-fried dishes. Direct heat (from the stove) accentuates its flavor. The spice is also one of the components of Chinese five-spice powder.

Turmeric

Profile: Turmeric, like ginger, is a Rhizome. Most commonly used in its dried form, it is a deep, rich, golden-yellow color with a slightly musky and bitter aftertaste.

Forms: Dried

Uses: Cooking. Turmeric is used to impart color to foods such as rice and is one of the spices in curry powder. It is also used in pickles, chutneys, and kedgeree. Although it is not a true substitute for costly saffron because it lacks saffron's gentle fragrance and subtle taste, turmeric is often used as a substitute because it is relatively inexpensive.

Turmeric will stain whatever it touches: your fingers, countertops, or clothing.

Using your bean

To use a vanilla bean, cut off a tiny piece at the tip of the pod. Slit the pod lengthwise with a sharp paring knife to reveal the tiny, flavorful seeds. Scrape out the seeds and use the seeds in a recipe.

Don't throw out the vanilla bean after scraping. Add it to a container of sugar and make your own vanilla-flavored sugar

Vanilla beans can also be put into a liquid whole. You can save the bean for another use by washing it, drying it, and then wrapping it in plastic wrap or foil.

Another option is to make your own vanilla extract by infusing brandy or vodka. See Chapter 5 for tips on infusing.

If you don't want to use the bean to flavor other foods, make sure that you keep whole or partially used beans tightly wrapped in plastic or stored separately in a jar so that the scent doesn't enter your other foodstuffs.

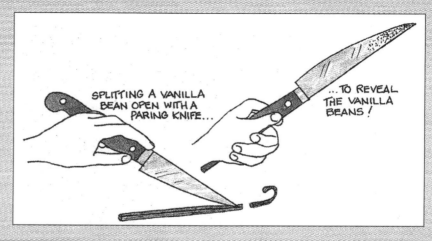

SPLITTING A VANILLA BEAN OPEN WITH A PARING KNIFE... ...TO REVEAL THE VANILLA BEANS!

Vanilla

Profile: Native to Mexico, the vanilla bean is the pod of a tropical orchid. The slender pod is cured and dried to bring out its delicately sweet and aromatic flavor. The pod is dark brown and wrinkled in appearance. Whole beans can be expensive, but their flavor is exquisite. Look for whole beans that are pliable.

Tahitian vanilla is the most prized and is the widest bean. Other varieties hail from Madagascar and Mexico. The alternative form, pure vanilla extract (see Figure 2-10), which is made by steeping the bean in alcohol, is more commonly used than the bean. Imitation flavored extracts, such as vanillin, contain no true vanilla, but are synthetic products.

Figure 2-10:
A vanilla bean and vanilla extract.

Forms: Whole

Alternative forms: Pure vanilla extract

Uses: Cooking, baking, and beverages. Vanilla is used worldwide in pastries, ice cream, puddings, desserts, confections, candies, sauces, and even in savory dishes such as lobster and sweet potatoes. You'll also find it in most recipes that contain chocolate. Vanilla is added to soft drinks, such as cream soda, and to cordials, such as Galiano and creme de cacao.

Chapter 3

Fresh Spices, Aromatics, and Spicy Condiments

* *

In This Chapter

▶ Making the most of garlic, ginger, and other fresh spices

▶ Discovering what condiments are spiced based

* *

*W*e're fortunate today that all spices aren't only found in dried or powdered forms. Food markets are loaded with bins of fresh garlic and ginger. Chiles, from the ubiquitous jalapeno and serranos to the more exotic bird's eye and Scotch bonnet, are available fresh. Whole and dried forms such as habanero, pasilla, and guajillo are also sold in produce departments of supermarkets. Lemon grass, too, is becoming more commonplace.

In this chapter, I cover fresh spices and flavoring agents, from preparation to usage to storage, and the condiments whose taste is derived from spices.

For some general suggestions on how much or how little of a spice to use when improvising recipes, check out Appendix C, which presents guidelines for the ingredients discussed in this chapter as well as Chapter 2.

Fresh Spices and Aromatics

Fresh spices impart a lovely fragrance and lively taste to foods. In this section, I go over everything you need to know about fresh garlic, ginger, lemon grass, and lime leaves; from buying, to preparation, to storage. Additionally, you'll find complete information on how to use fresh chiles as well as dried chiles, which are often sold alongside fresh produce. And what cook can do without aromatics such as onions, shallots, scallions, and leeks? These four ingredients enhance the flavor of any dish.

Is your garlic sprouting?

If a garlic clove has a small green sprout in the center, the garlic can taste bitter, but you can remove the sprout. Cut the clove in half lengthwise and take out the green bit. However, if most of the head of garlic has sprouted, toss it out or plant it in the garden and grow your own garlic chives. They produce lovely pale purple flowers.

Fresh garlic

Most of the world's cuisines rely on garlic for some of their flavor. Garlic, a relative to leeks, onions, and scallions, is characterized by a strong, somewhat pungent flavor and an appealing aroma. Garlic is typically sold in whole heads wrapped in a white to mauvish-white papery skin that holds the individual cloves together. Each clove is also covered in a thin skin. Choose heads that are firm to the touch. Shriveled or soft cloves indicate that the garlic is already going bad.

Like onions, garlic should be stored in a cool, dry place with plenty of air circulation. You can also keep garlic in a special garlic keeper. Whole heads should last for a month or two; separated cloves may go bad within a few days. Store chopped garlic and peeled cloves in a covered container in the refrigerator.

Separate only the cloves you will be using by pulling them gently from the head. In most cases, you'll also need to peel the garlic. Put the garlic on a flat surface, such as a cutting board, and firmly but gently tap the side of a knife against the clove. The skin should loosen. Be careful not to smash the clove or the garlic will release too many of its oils and it will burn more easily.

Because garlic cloves are small, it's easiest to chop or mince them with a paring knife, as shown in Figure 3-1. Try to make the pieces as uniform in size as possible. You can also use mini food processors for this task.

Fresh garlic cloves are available peeled and bottled, and chopped garlic is also available. Look in the refrigerator section of your supermarket. Buying garlic in either form is convenient, but note that you may want to add more garlic than the recipe calls for because the flavor of bottled garlic isn't quite as strong as that of fresh garlic.

When using fresh garlic, check the size of the cloves. Most recipes are written for plump cloves that come from the outer section of the head. If the head is particularly small or you're using the smaller cloves toward the center of the bulb, you might want to use extra.

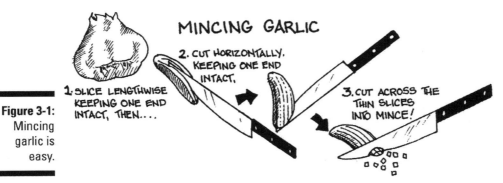

Figure 3-1: Mincing garlic is easy.

When recipes in this book call for garlic cloves, use medium-sized ones unless I specify otherwise.

Elephant garlic is a hybrid form grown mainly in California. The heads are quite large, but the taste is much milder.

½ teaspoon of chopped garlic = 1 plump clove of garlic that is minced.

Most often, garlic is added to vegetables that have already been softened, such as onions or leeks. When cooking garlic, make sure that you have an adequate amount of cooking oil or butter in the pan and stir frequently to prevent scorching. Burner heat should be medium-low to medium.

Get more life out of ginger

Fresh, unpeeled ginger should normally last about 3 weeks in your refrigerator. If you buy a large piece and you don't plan to use it all right away, you can store it. Unpeeled ginger can be wrapped tightly in plastic wrap and frozen for up to 4 months. Alternatively, you can preserve it in sherry or Madeira wine. Peel the ginger, slice it thinly, and place the slices in a clean jar or bottle. Pour in enough dry sherry to cover the ginger completely. Put the lid on the jar and refrigerate for up to 3 months. Remove the ginger and mince the slices as you need it. Although some of the sherry flavor will be absorbed by the ginger, it's still fine to use for most recipes. Use the sherry that you stored the ginger in for cooking when you want a gingery flavor in a dish.

Fresh ginger

The smell and taste of ginger hints of the exotic, but its use has spread throughout the world. Currently, most ginger comes from Jamaica, although China and India are also major producers. Often called a root, it is actually a Rhizome, an underground stalk that sends forth knobs. Some cookbooks refer to fresh ginger as ginger root.

You can easily break large pieces of ginger with your hands, so you can always purchase a section that's the size you need. Fresh ginger should have a spicy fragrance. Look for knobs that are firm to the touch with smooth skin. Thin skin is another indication of freshness. Wrinkled or withered skin is a sign that the ginger is past its prime. Older ginger has a stringier, woodier texture.

Sometimes, very fresh ginger or spring ginger has a slightly purple or pinkish tint on the tip of its knobs and extremely thin skin that doesn't need to be peeled. However, most ginger that's on the market has a buff-colored skin that does need to be removed; in most instances, ginger should be peeled before using. Occasionally a recipe calls for unpeeled, grated ginger, usually to make a marinade.

To peel ginger, use a paring knife or vegetable peeler. To mince ginger, slice it into thin, coin-sized rounds and then stack a few of the rounds and cut them into thin strips. Cut the strips crosswise into smaller pieces and mince. This procedure is illustrated in Figure 3-2.

When cooking or preparing sauces, fresh ginger is best; when baking or making spice mixtures, ground ginger is preferable.

MINCING PEELED GINGER

☆ TO PEEL GINGER, USE A PARING KNIFE OR A VEGETABLE PEELER.

1. TO MINCE THE PEELED GINGER, SLICE IT INTO THIN COIN SIZED ROUNDS,

2. STACK A FEW ROUNDS AND CUT INTO THIN STRIPS.

3. CUT STRIPS CROSSWISE INTO SMALLER PIECES AND MINCE!

Figure 3-2: Mincing ginger.

1-x-1-inch piece of fresh ginger = 1 tablespoon minced ginger

Chile peppers

Chile peppers are one the greatest of all exports from the American continent! They've traveled the world, lending their flavor to many of the world's best-loved dishes. Unlike most spices, they have little fragrance. But they have plenty of taste, which can vary from mild to fiery.

An abundant variety are available on the market, from the tiny, pungent Thai or bird's eye to the mild pasilla. Generally speaking, the smaller the chile, the more heat it has. Note however, that the heat quotient varies within each variety. Sometimes you'll buy a jalapeno or serrano that is very hot; another time you'll buy a seemingly identical pepper that turns out to be much milder. You might want to taste a tiny bit on your tongue to see if you need to adjust the amount that you add to a recipe. Use an amount that you feel comfortable with — regardless of whether it's less or more than a recipe calls for.

Getting the whole score on chiles

All peppers are rated according to their heat factor. This rating, which is measured in Scoville units, gives a good indication whether the chile is mild, medium, or hot. The Scoville points range from 0 for any color bell pepper to 300,000. Pasillas score 2,500 units and are considered mild; guajillo and ancho have 3,000 units and are considered mild to mediu; chipotle and jalapenos receive a tally of 10,000, indicating they are medium-hot, and the hottest of them all, the habanero or Scotch bonnet, receives a whopping 300,000 Scoville units. Sometimes you can find dried chiles labeled with Scoville units, but you may also see them marked as mild, medium, hot, or very hot. This type of marking is called the heat factor.

What's in a name?

Here's where chiles can cause a bit of confusion. Fresh Poblanos become anchos when they're dried; jalapenos when smoked and dried become chipotles. To make matters more confusing, different regions in Mexico refer to the same variety of chile by different names. This confusion has crossed the border to the United States and is furthered by food writers and chefs. Other countries also have their own pet names for chiles. Fortunately, because chiles are becoming increasingly popular, names are becoming more standardized. To make sure of how hot they are, remember to check the Scoville points or heat factor.

Figure 3-3 shows a variety of different chiles.

Buying fresh chiles

Look for fresh chile peppers that are firm to the touch and that have smooth, unwrinkled, and unblemished skin with no signs of molding from being stacked and misted in supermarkets.

The color of the chiles should be bright and vivid regardless of whether they are red, green, orange, or yellow. Note that the color is not a good indicator of the chile's heat. It's the size and variety that count. Generally, the smallest varieties are the hottest and the larger ones are milder.

Preparing fresh chiles

To prepare fresh chiles, cut off the stem, cut them lengthwise, and remove the seeds and ribs (the white membranes inside the chile). Much of the heat of a chile comes from its seeds, so removing all the seeds is generally advisable, but you can brave the heat and keep a *few* of the seeds if you want. Slice the chile pepper into thin strips and then cut the strips crosswise into fine pieces.

Because the oils and resins in the chile pepper emit heat, your fingers can become irritated and even feel a little burned when you handle chiles. Thorough washing doesn't always get rid of the chile oil that gets into your skin and nails. To protect yourself, you should wear thin latex or rubber gloves. Remember to keep your fingers away from your face — your lips and eyes in particular — and always wash your hands after handling chile peppers.

Chile contest

Topping the list of the most beloved chiles in the United States are green jalapenos, which are available fresh, canned, and bottled. Chipotles are really smoked jalapenos, which are available both dried and canned. Other popular varieties in America include the smaller red or green serranos, tiny red or green bird's eye or Thai chile peppers, and long, thin, red cayenne chile peppers.

Dried chile peppers

You'll find many dried chile peppers in the produce section of supermarkets. The most commonly available are pasilla, guajillo cascabel, habanero, Anaheim, ancho, chipotle (smoked jalapeno), and the small, thin Chinese or Szechuan pepper. Dried chile peppers are most often labeled with the Scoville units or a heat factor number.

You should handle dried chile peppers with the same caution you use when handling fresh chiles.

Reconstituting dried chiles

Dried chiles always need to be reconstituted by soaking them for 10 to 15 minutes in hot, but not boiling, water. After soaking, remove the stem and seeds and chop as you would fresh chile peppers. Dried Chinese chile peppers used in Szechuan cooking are not reconstituted but used whole and added to a stir-fry for flavor. You don't need to eat them!

Making dried chile puree

Reconstitute the chiles, remove the stem and seeds, and save a bit of the water the chiles soaked in. Put the chiles in a mini food processor or blender with a small amount of the soaking liquid and puree until smooth. This puree can be kept in the fridge in a covered container for a week or frozen in an airtight container for 6 to 8 months. Use it in small amounts (½ teaspoon to 1 tablespoon, depending on the quantity of the product you're making and your individual taste) in marinades, condiments, curry pastes, mayonnaise, or dips. You can also add some to ketchup for a burger topping or use it with foods where you want that chile taste. The hotness depends on the type of chiles that you pureed.

Dry roasting fresh and dried chiles

Roasting chiles heightens the flavor and adds a slightly smokier taste to sauces and dips. It's quick and easy to do; the only thing to watch out for is not to cook them too long or they'll become bitter.

Chile puree bonanza

You've made chile puree and perhaps you're wondering what to do with it. Why not make *harissa*, a spicy condiment from the North African countries of Morocco and Tunisia that is also a familiar accompaniment on tables in Mediterranean France. In a skillet, dry toast 2 teaspoons coriander seeds and 1 teaspoon cumin seeds and grind in a spice mill. Alternatively use 1½ teaspoons ground coriander and 1 teaspoon ground cumin. In a bowl or a mini food processor, combine 3 tablespoons of chile puree with the coriander, cumin, ½ teaspoon of salt, 2 to 3 cloves of pressed or finely minced garlic, and ¼ cup virgin olive oil. Put the mixture in a container and top it with a thin layer of additional olive oil. Cover and refrigerate for up to 2 weeks. Always cover leftovers with a bit more olive oil to prevent spoilage.

Harissa is traditionally used to spike Moroccan style lamb, chicken, vegetable stews called *tajines,* soups, and couscous. But this condiment is more versatile than that. Use it as a marinade or basting sauce for chicken, fish, shrimp, beef, lamb, pork, or ribs. You can add 1 tablespoon of fresh lemon, lime, or orange juice, if you wish, when using harissa as a marinade or basting sauce. Add a dollop to salad dressings for a chilled vegetable salad that features a combination of blanched veggies, such as green beans, broccoli, zucchini, or carrots. Spike mashed potatoes or mashed sweet potatoes by stirring in a small amount before serving. You can also garnish or add a small amount to dips and spreads such as tahini, hummus, baba ganoush, guacamole, and pureed white or black beans.

To dry roast fresh chiles, do the following:

1. **Heat a griddle or skillet over medium heat until hot.**

2. **Add whole chiles and cook, shaking them in the pan or turning the chiles until the skin is softened and lightly charred.**

   They do not need to be peeled before use.

3. **When the chiles are cool enough to handle, remove the stem and slit the chile. Take out the seeds with the tip of a paring knife.**

Here's how to dry roast chiles that have been dried:

1. **Heat a griddle or skillet over medium heat until hot.**

2. **Add whole chiles and cook, pressing them with a spatula or pancake turner until you can smell them.**

   This process should take only a few seconds.

3. **Flip the chiles over and cook them on the opposite side for a few seconds longer.**

4. **When the chiles are cool enough to touch, remove the stem and shake out the seeds.**

   Alternatively, slit the pods and take out the seeds with the tip of a paring knife.

If you've mistakenly eaten too much of a chile pepper, don't drink water. Try a dairy product like milk or yogurt. Or you can eat some cooked rice, which cools your taste buds. Eating bread or other starches also helps.

Fresh lemon grass and lime leaves

Lemon grass and lime leaves hail from Southeast Asia. Each has a distinctive citrusy perfume, but make no mistake, lemon zest is not a true substitute for lemon grass, nor is lime zest a substitute for lime leaves. Their flavor is more subtle and flowery. Both lemon grass and lime leaves can be found in Thai curries, marinades, and sauces. Either can lend their flavor to tea, broth, coconut milk, milk, or cream. Infuse or steep them in the hot liquid as directed in Chapter 5.

To use lemon grass stalks, one of which is shown in Figure 3-4, cut off the root end and grassy stalks as you would when you cut a scallion. Peel away a few layers of the tough outer leaves to reveal the softer inner core. The core can be finely chopped for curry pastes or coarsely sliced. If the lemon grass is being added to a liquid, you must bruise it gently by hitting it with the flat side of a knife, slightly cracking its stalk, so that its flavor is released.

Figure 3-4:
Look for lemon grass stalks that are firm and unblemished.

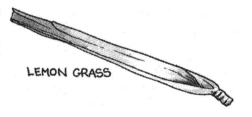

LEMON GRASS

Not technically a spice but an aromatic, lime leaves are the leaf of the makrud lime. They're also called Kaffir or Thai lime leaves. They are sold fresh, frozen, and dried. Fresh leaves have the best aroma and flavor. If you buy a packet and can't use them all right away, you can freeze the leaves in a self-sealing plastic bag. If using frozen or dried, you might want to double or triple the amount called for in a recipe. Their flavor won't be as strong as that of fresh lime leaves.

Onions, shallots, leeks, and scallions

Although not classified as spices, onions, shallots, leeks and scallions are aromatics and are used more than any other flavoring agents.

Look for onions and shallots that are firm to the touch and avoid any that are sprouting a green growth from the top. Store them in a cool, dry place where there is ample air circulation, perhaps in a small basket. There are many types of onions, each with its own characteristic flavor: yellow, white, Bermuda, Vidalia, Spanish, and Walla-Walla. For general cooking purposes, use the common yellow-skinned onions unless a recipe calls for another variety.

Chop or slice onions and mince shallots in evenly sized pieces so that they cook evenly.

Leeks or scallions should also be firm and the leaves a vivid green without signs of withering or yellowing. Rinse them well before slicing. Trim the root and most of the green leaves. Peel and discard any tough layers. Slice them evenly up to the beginning of the green. Scallions can be sliced into rounds; however, you might want to cut a leek in half lengthwise and then thinly slice it into half-moons.

Leeks are very gritty and you'll need to make sure no dirt remains. After slicing, put them in a colander or strainer and wash them well under running water. Drain the water completely and then pat them dry with a paper towel before sautéing them.

Spicy Condiments

Piquant, salty, savory, spicy — these words describe the characteristics of condiments. In this section, I cover condiments from the most common (mustard) to the more exotic (sambal oelek). Condiments are often added to a recipe during cooking but sometimes are served alongside to allow the diner to add an extra touch of flavor to a dish.

Prepared mustard

Prepared mustard isn't just for hot dogs and hamburgers. This spicy condiment is used in salad dressings and mayonnaise where it help the emulsification process. You can also find mustard lending flavor to marinades, sauces, cheese dishes, stews and soups. There are dozens of varieties available, each with its own characteristic taste. Whole-grain mustard has a crunchy texture whereas blended mustard is velvety smooth. What follows is a quick guide to some you might come across.

English

English mustard is hot! It has a distinctive bite and should be used sparingly. Made from yellow mustard seeds, it is sometimes given an extra boost of yellow color by the addition of turmeric.

Dijon

Made from brown mustard seeds, this classic French mustard is pale gold. It has a smooth texture and a sharp, somewhat salty flavor. White wine or ver-juice (the sour juice from unripe grapes) is added, along with salt and other spices or herbs such as tarragon. It is wonderful with steaks, chops, pork, ham, as well as with cheese or in cheese dishes. It's also delicious in creamy Dijon sauce served over boneless chicken breasts. It's the best choice for use in salad dressings, marinades, and mayonnaise.

Whole-grain

There are several varieties of whole-grain mustard on the market, ranging from mild to spicy in flavor. One of the best of this type is the French Meaux mustard, which is generally sold in crocks. To prepare Meaux, black or brown seeds are partially crushed then mixed with vinegar and spices. Meaux mustard is somewhat hot and spicy. It's delicious with cold meat, sausage, and cheese.

German

Yellowish-brown in color, German mustards are smooth and can range from moderately spicy to very spicy, but all have sharp bite. They are prepared from black mustard seeds, spices, and vinegar. They are an excellent complement to sausage, frankfurters, and cold meat.

American

Sugar, vinegar, and spices are combined with pale mustard seeds to prepare American-style mustard. Mildly flavored and bright yellow in color, this mustard is sweeter than other types. It can be used with cold meats, sausages, cheese, and on the all-American hot dog and burger.

Flavored mustards

Flavored mustards are just mustards to which other ingredients are added to alter or enhance the taste. Tarragon, honey, white wine, basil, champagne, garlic, red pepper, and tomatoes can be used. Generally, the texture of flavored mustard is smooth, and the mustard flavor can range from mild to moderately spicy. Many flavored mustards are imported from France, although honey mustard is an American favorite. They can be used in the same way and as a substitute for other mustard.

Worcestershire sauce

This popular spicy sauce was created in India by the English. A soy-based liquid, it has a vinegary, garlicky, and mildly spicy flavor. It is widely used to season sauces, gravies, and beverages.

Asian sesame oil

Sesame oil comes in two varieties: a mildly flavored, light-colored oil that's used for general cooking and the toasted Asian variety, which has a dark, rich color and a strong sesame aroma and taste. Asian sesame oil is used to accent Chinese dishes and other Asian dishes. A small amount is generally added for flavor to a sauce, marinade, or stir-fried dish.

It is not necessary to stir-fry with Asian sesame oil. Use peanut oil instead, because it has a high burn point and is less expensive. Add a dash of sesame oil for flavor at the *end* of cooking.

Fish sauce

Used throughout Southeast Asia, particularly in Thailand and Vietnam, fish sauce has an extremely pungent, almost overbearing aroma and a strongly fermented and salty taste. Called *nam pla* in Thailand and *nuoc mam* in Vietnam, there is no real substitute. Once opened, it should be refrigerated. Because most recipes that require its use don't call for salt, if you omit the fish sauce, make sure you season the dish with salt to taste.

Tabasco and jalapeno sauce

This fiery hot sauce made from tiny tabasco chile peppers and fermented with salt and vinegar hails from Louisiana. The name *tabasco* is the trademark of the McIlhenny family and only their product can bear it. Consequently, all other brands label their product as hot red pepper sauce or some close variation. A few dashes can add quite a fiery punch to any dish.

Sambal oelek in the Netherlands?

The search for spices in the fifteenth century was fierce. Whoever controlled the spice trade had power and wealth. This quest led to the discovery of America by Columbus who was actually looking for an alternate route to the East Indies. The Dutch were dominant in the spice trade, having successfully sailed the world in search of spices. They set up colonies in the Dutch East Indies, now part of Indonesia, and Malaysia. Cape Town, in South Africa, was the stopping point on the spice route and a Dutch colony for the Dutch East Indies Spice Company. The colonists and traders used many Malay and Indonesian cooks in their homes and settlements, and the early traders brought their new-found culinary tastes back home to the Netherlands way back in the fifteenth century! Spices and sambal oelek are a part of the Dutch table. In modern Amsterdam, you'll find many restaurants that feature Indonesian cooking and the traditional rijstaffel (rice table), a feast featuring up to 30 different dishes, all served with rice.

Jalapeno sauce, which is green in color, is also marketed by the McIlhenny company, as well as other manufacturers. Use it sparingly.

Asian or Chinese hot chile oil

This red-colored oil is eye-popping hot. A staple of the Chinese kitchen, it is made from vegetable oil and chile peppers. Once opened, its shelf life is about 6 to 8 months, but it will last much longer if refrigerated. Take caution with how much you use — a few drops go a long way!

Sambal oelek and ground chile paste

A condiment in Thailand, Indonesia, and the Netherlands, sambal oelek (or sambal ulek) is another product derived from chile peppers. It's sometimes labeled as ground chile paste. To manufacture it, red chiles are ground and bottled. Sambal oelek paste is extremely potent and hot and can be used in place of crushed red chile flakes or where ground hot chiles are called for. Always refrigerate it after opening. It is available in ethnic shops and some supermarkets. A similar condiment, Chinese chile paste, is more finely ground and often contains garlic.

Chapter 4

Spicing Up Your Kitchen

▶ Finding out which spices are absolutely essential and how to store them

▶ Discovering which basic and special kitchen tools you really need

*W*hen you begin to cook with spices for the first time, you might need a little guidance to start you off in the right direction. The suggestions in this chapter include not only what spices to buy, but also how to buy them and keep them at their best so the food you make has the fullest flavor. In this chapter, you'll also discover the special kitchen equipment you need to cook with spices and the kind of culinary gear you'll need on a day-to-day basis.

Buying Spices

Spices, which only a few years ago were relegated to a shelf or two in food stores, have recently grown in significance in American home cooking. Spices are increasingly available in a variety of stores — supermarkets, pharmacies and department stores, ethnic groceries, cookware shops, specialty shops, farmers markets, modern spice bazaars that are wholly devoted to the sale and blending of spices, and Web sites. Whatever spice seller you choose, buy spices in stores that have high merchandise turnover to ensure that the spices you buy haven't already lost some of their potency before you bring them home. Here are some additional spice-buying tips:

✔ Buy spices in small quantities, excluding those that you use frequently.

✔ Whole spices last a year or more.

✔ For longer shelf life, buy whole spices and grind them in small quantities yourself. Home-ground and store-bought ground spices can be stored for up to six months.

✔ Replenish old stock periodically.

✔ Save money by making your own spice blends or rubs.

The basic spice collection

When you browse through the spice section of your market, you'll find a varied assortment to choose from. Here's a list of what you need the most when you're stocking your shelves:

- Cayenne or ground red pepper
- Chili powder
- Cinnamon, ground
- Cloves, whole
- Coriander, whole
- Crushed red pepper flakes
- Cumin, whole or ground
- Curry powder, preferably labeled Madras-style
- Garlic powder
- Ginger, ground
- Mustard, dried English
- Paprika, Hungarian or Spanish
- Black peppercorns, whole
- White peppercorns, whole or ground
- Salt
- Turmeric
- Vanilla extract

See Chapter 7 for specific ethnic spice and herb combinations.

Your best bet: Whole or ground?

Whether using whole or ground spices is best depends on what you're making and how much time you have. Some days you might want to make your own curry pastes, curry powder, or spice blends and rubs from scratch. Other times, it may suit you to buy prepared mixes. A few spices are definitely more convenient if bought ground, such as cinnamon and cloves. Others, such as coriander, allspice, and cumin, can be ground easily in a spice mill. You can store home-ground spices for up to six months in a tightly sealed container. Their flavor is always fresher than their commercially ground counterparts. If you have the time, grind your whole spices only as you need them.

Get real pepper flavor! Ground pepper loses its distinctive taste quickly and easily. Peppercorns are best if they're purchased whole and freshly ground each time.

Storing Spices

Don't even think about hanging a spice rack above or next to the stove! Near the stove is by far the worst place to keep spices. Heat, residual heat, moisture, and light significantly shorten the life of spices and dried herbs. Both spices and herbs should be stored far from any heat source.

Keep dried spices in a cool, dark, and dry place in a well-sealed container. Spices often send forth a strong aroma, regardless of whether the jars are tightly closed. Consequently, spices shouldn't be stored near food that can absorb their flavor, such as chocolate or rice and other grains. It's best to store spices in a cabinet of their own or with canned goods.

Shelf life

Believe it or not, spices do have a limited shelf life. This is not only true for fresh spices such as ginger, garlic, and lemon grass, but for dried spices as well. Whole spices can last for a year or longer. Once opened, ground spices only last from four to six months before their flavor lessens. One exception is dried mustard, which lasts for over a year.

Preground spices gradually lose their potency. Within six months, their strength has diminished significantly. You don't have to toss them out at exactly six months, but you may need to add an extra pinch or two (to taste). Replace spices when you notice that the aroma has weakened or the color has faded. If you use weakened spices, your recipes won't have the flavor that is intended.

Replace any spices that you know are old or that have been lurking in the back of your cupboard for an unknown period of time.

Storage containers

Most spices come in their own bottles or cans. However, if you buy blends at a spice shop, make your own blends, or grind your own spices, you need to store these in a proper vessel. Spices should always be stored in airtight containers, preferably with minimal airspace.

Glass

Small glass bottles or jars with screw-on lids are the best choices for storing spices. Glass won't absorb any flavors or become discolored. Glass jars can be washed and used interchangeably. Try to use these if possible.

Plastic

Plastic containers with tight-sealing lids are acceptable. However, they soak up the aroma and take on colors, such as the yellow of turmeric or curry powder or the red of chili powder and cayenne. Even the dishwasher may not be able to remove these colors completely. If you choose to use plastic, make sure that you always store the same spice in the same container.

In a pinch you can store freshly ground or blended spices in a small resealable plastic bag. Let the spice settle at the bottom and roll the excess of the bag around the spice, release any air, and then seal the bag.

Storing fresh spices

Unlike dried spices, which should be kept in containers in a cool dry place, some fresh spices should be refrigerated. Lemon grass, lime leaves, ginger, and chile peppers all need refrigeration. Ginger can be loosely wrapped in paper towels; lemon grass and lime leaves can be placed in plastic bags. All can be kept in the vegetable crisper of your fridge and should last from two to three weeks.

Ginger wrapped in plastic can also be frozen. Simply slice of a frozen piece and thaw briefly before using. Lime leaves can be frozen in a resealable bag, but their flavor will diminish so that you'll need to use double the amount that's called for in a recipe. Whole heads of garlic should be stored in a cool, dry place with good air circulation, such as the place you keep onions or potatoes.

Small pottery garlic keepers, sold in some specialty shops, keep garlic fresher longer.

Storing fresh spice pastes and sauces

Whether homemade or commercially prepared, spice pastes, such as Thai curry pastes, jerk sauces, barbecue sauces, and ready-made mustard should always be stored in the refrigerator. Commercial products can be kept on the shelf, unopened, until the use-by or best-by date, but once they're opened and refrigerated, they should be used within six to eight weeks. Mustard is an exception; it can last in your refrigerator for a year after it's been opened.

Discard any product that has an "off" odor, is discolored, has a musty smell, or is moldy.

Using up older spices

Although ground spices should be tossed out and replaced after approximately six months, you might feel a pang of guilt throwing your spices away and think that you must use them somehow. Here are a few simple ideas for how you can use up those oldies but goodies that have been hiding in your cabinet.

- Add a pinch or two more than a recipe calls for, whether it's savory or baked goods. This is especially true of cayenne or ground red pepper, curry powder, and chili powder.

- Use older spices with other, fresher spices in a spice blend, rub, or marinade. The effect of the older spices won't be quite as strong as that of the younger spices.

- Combine ground cinnamon with sugar for cinnamon sugar. Add a bit of allspice or a pinch of grated nutmeg to the mix if you'd like.

- Add a pinch of ground cinnamon or nutmeg to French toast batter or pancake batter.

- Combine spices such as ground garlic, onion, curry, or cayenne to softened butter or margarine. Follow the instructions for spiced butters in Chapter 5.

- Use the spices in spiced oils, vinegar, or flour. Follow the instructions in Chapter 5.

- Use the spices in a poaching liquid for chicken or fish or for fresh or dried fruit. See Chapters 10 and 18.

- Use ground spices as a complementary or colorful garnish.

- Sprinkle paprika on potatoes, chicken, fish, or vegetables.

- Sprinkle chile pepper powder, cayenne, ground chili powder, or cumin on guacamole for Southwestern or Mexican dishes.

- Add a pinch of cinnamon, cardamom, allspice, or nutmeg to desserts such as fruit pies and cobblers or as an accent or garnish for whipped cream.

- Put a dash of ground cinnamon or cardamom in the coffee grounds when you brew coffee.

- Put cinnamon sticks in coffee or hot chocolate or simmer cider or red wine with a stick or two. See Chapter 19.

- Add whole cloves or whole allspice berries to hot drinks such as cider or wine along with cinnamon sticks and a piece of orange or lemon zest. See Chapter 19.

- Garnish eggnog with ground nutmeg or allspice.

Spicy Tools

There's nothing like the aroma and taste of freshly ground spices. Once you start using them, you'll probably get hooked. But in order to take advantage of whole spices that you grind yourself, you may need a few specialized items, especially if you prepare your own rubs and blends or toast and grind whole spices. You won't need much, just a few well-chosen accoutrements. Having the right tools in any kitchen makes it easier for you, the cook, to prepare delicious meals. Proper equipment helps you zip through tasks that otherwise could be arduous or require multiple steps. This section offers a look at some of the spice-related cooking gear that can make your time in the kitchen better spent and more enjoyable.

Pepper mills

Pepper mills come in all sizes, from miniature to the oversize grinders that are often used by waiters in fine restaurants. Figure 4-1 shows a common version. Choose mills that have adjustable settings so you can change how fine the grind is. The best mills have a sturdy grinding mechanism that lasts for years.

PEPPERMILL

Figure 4-1:
A common peppermill.

If you grind more than one type or color of pepper, you should designate a separate mill for each — one for black peppercorns, another for white, and another for mixed colors. That way the residue and flavors of one type don't mix with another.

Whole coriander can also be ground in a pepper mill, but you'll need to have a mill that's used only for that purpose. Coriander is wonderful on vegetables, chicken, pork, lamb, and seafood, as well as on fruit or vegetable salads.

Salt mills

Salt mills look similar to pepper mills but contain coarse salt that you can grind to a medium or fine powder.

Hand spice mill

Hand spice mills look similar to large pepper mills. One is shown in Figure 4-2. They have a crankshaft and an opening on top to hold the whole spices and a container below to catch the ground spices. They're easy to use and can be found anywhere quality cookware is sold. They can also be bought from specialty spice vendors.

Never wash a pepper, salt, or spice mill. Water makes the gears rust.

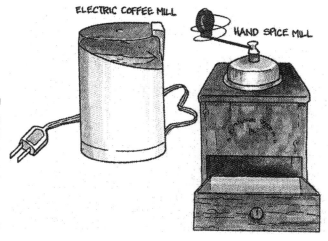

Figure 4-2:
A manual and an electric machine for grinding spices.

Electric mills

For speed and ease, you might want to choose an electric spice mill. An electric spice mill is just an electric coffee grinder that you use exclusively for spices. Search the shelves in the appliance section of a department or cookware store for a small, inexpensive coffee grinder with a well-fitting lid (see Figure 4-2). Use the grinder only for spices, never for coffee; otherwise, your coffee will take on the flavor of whatever spices you have recently ground.

Using an electric spice mill is easy. Fill the container partially with spices, no more than one-third full, and cover. Simply flip the machine on and let the appliance perform its magic. In less than a minute, you'll have freshly ground spices.

One caveat: Spice flavors do remain in the grinder after use, and because an electric grinder shouldn't be washed (to protect the motor and prevent rust), you can get rid of spice residue in the grinder by grinding dry bread crumbs, which should leave the grinder clean to use for other spices. You may need to repeat the process of grinding bread crumbs several times if you were working with a particularly intense spice. Of course, you can wipe the grinder bowl clean with a slightly damp cloth.

Some hand and electric mills allow you to adjust the grind. For most spices, choose the setting that grinds the finest. If you want to crack peppercorns, set it more coarsely and pulse.

Mortar and pestle

The simple-to-use mortar and pestle, which has been used for centuries to both grind spices and prepare spice pastes, is still used today. It's effective, but it takes more time than using a hand mill or electric mill. If you do use a mortar and pestle, make sure that the bowl is deep enough so the spices don't pop out. Grind a small amount of the spices (only about a tablespoon or two at a time) in a circular motion. Mortar and pestles made of ceramic or marble are preferable to wooden ones. Ceramic and marble don't absorb any aroma or flavors and can be easily washed.

Spices such as cinnamon sticks and star anise are difficult to grind at home. They cannot be easily ground with a mortar and pestle, but an electric spice mill makes grinding them easier.

Nutmeg graters

Nutmeg graters are petite, only a few inches in height and width with small holes for fine grating. Some have a little container on top with a lid so you can store a partially grated nutmeg (see Figure 4-3).

If you don't have a nutmeg grater, you can use a grater that's designed for grating hard cheeses such as Parmesan or Romano or the smallest holes on a four-sided grater.

Figure 4-3:
A nutmeg grater and a four-sided grater.

Graters

Four-sided graters are an essential tool in any kitchen. One is shown next to a nutmeg grater in Figure 4-3. With a variety of hole sizes to choose from, you can grate anything from vegetables to cheese to some flavorful additives. Fresh lemon, orange, and lime zest, peeled or unpeeled fresh ginger, and whole nutmeg can be grated on the finest side of the grater.

Garlic presses

Garlic presses are widely available, but they're not always suitable for preparing garlic for cooking. The press (shown in Figure 4-4) turns peeled whole cloves of garlic into fine threads, which is fine if you're adding the garlic to a marinade, uncooked sauce, or salad dressing. However, when cooking garlic, always mince it instead of pressing it. Garlic that has been pressed has released its oils and burns very easily. If burned, it imparts such an unpleasant flavor that burned garlic should be discarded, and you must start again with fresh garlic.

Figure 4-4:
When cooking garlic, mince it rather than press it.

GARLIC PRESS

Basic Kitchen Gear

With the vast array of cookware items available in department stores, specialty shops, and supermarkets, deciding what exactly is needed can be difficult for even an experienced cook. You can easily end up with several things you rarely use.

Buy the basics first, preferably basics of the best quality that you can afford. Fill in with unusual or specialty items as you go along. Here's a look at what you'll need to make the most of the recipes in this book.

Pots, pans, and bakeware

Pots and pans, the workhorses of any kitchen, should be well crafted and have a thick bottom that won't warp when heated. Aluminum, copper, and cast iron are excellent heat conductors and help spread the heat evenly. Using nonstick pans or not using them is your choice. You might prefer plain aluminum, stainless steel pots with an aluminum or copper core or bottom, or plain or enameled cast iron. Pots should have tight-fitting lids and handles that are securely attached. Make sure that the pots are easy for you to lift, both filled and unfilled. Consider before you buy it how heavy the pot will be when it's filled with food or liquid!

Other cooking gear you need

Cookware:

- 1½ quart saucepan with lid, for vegetables and reheating
- 3-quart saucepan with lid, for vegetables, rice, and reheating
- 5-quart Dutch oven with lid, for soups, stews, and boiling pasta
- 8-inch slope-sided nonstick skillet for toasting spices, making omelets, and general low-fat cooking
- 10- to 12-inch skillet, nonstick or plain finish with lid
- Baking sheet
- Broiling pan

- Roasting pan with rack
- 9-x-5-inch bread pan
- 8-x-8-inch square pan
- 2-quart shallow baking dish

Appliances:

- Food processor, mini processor, or hand blender for pureeing
- Microwave for quick cooking and reheating

Utensils:

- Cutting boards, one for vegetables and bread and one for meat, poultry, and seafood
- Vegetable peeler
- 3- to 4-inch paring knife
- 8-inch chef's knife
- Serrated slicing knife for bread and tomatoes
- 8- to 10-inch bamboo or metal skewers for kebabs
- Graduated mixing bowl set
- Graduated measuring spoon sets, preferably two or three
- Graduated dry measuring cups
- Liquid measuring cups in 1- and 4-cup sizes
- Can opener
- Corkscrew
- Medium-size, medium-mesh strainer or sieve for draining and sifting
- Colander for draining pasta and other foods
- Cooling rack
- 1½ to 2 inch basting or pastry brush

Pastry brushes can be expensive. Save money by buying a 1½ to 2-inch paint-brush at a hardware store.

Part II
Spicy Skills

The 5th Wave · By Rich Tennant

"It's a microwave slow cooker. It'll cook a stew all day in just 7 minutes."

In this part . . .

1 show you the basic techniques of cooking with spices, including how to toast or dry roast spices and how to make spice blends, spice pastes, spiced oils, spiced vinegars, spiced butters, and seasoned flours. You also find out how to handle spices, avoid common spice-related mistakes, and fix a few mistakes that you may have inadvertently made. You also discover what spices and ingredient combinations are key to many culture's cuisines. You then move on to menu planning and find out about some kitchen strategies that make cooking easier and more enjoyable.

Chapter 5

Spicy Know-How

. . . .

In This Chapter

▶ Toasting and sautéing spices

▶ Making spice blends, rubs, and pastes

▶ Making spiced oils, vinegars, and butters

▶ Making your own seasoned flour, cornmeal, and crumbs

. . . .

Before you begin to cook with spices, you'll need to learn a few techniques that will allow you to use spices to their fullest potential. In this chapter, you'll find out how to toast and grind spices, how to make your own spice blends, rubs, and pastes, as well as how to prepare spiced cooking oils, vinegar, and flour.

Spicy Techniques

Preparing spices for cooking is surprisingly straightforward. You don't need any special culinary skills and you don't have to worry about complicated or confusing processes. Most of the time, all you have to do is measure the proper amount of a spice and follow one of the simple procedures listed in this chapter.

Toasting or dry roasting

Toasting is an easy technique that brings out the aroma and flavor of certain spices, particularly cumin, coriander, mustard seeds, and fennel seeds. This process is often used in Indian cooking and is an essential step when preparing your own curry powders. Toasting is a common technique in many regional or ethnic dishes that use whole spices.

To toast spices, follow these steps and check out Figure 5-1:

1. **Place a heavy-bottomed skillet (preferably nonstick) over medium-low to medium heat and warm the skillet for about 1 minute.**

2. **Add the spices that you want to toast. Cook the spices, stirring occasionally, until their aroma opens fully and they become quite fragrant.**

   At this point, their color should begin to darken slightly. The whole process should only take a minute or two.

3. **Remove the pan from the heat and transfer the toasted spices to a bowl so that they don't continue to toast due to the residual heat in the skillet.**

   The spices are now ready to be ground in a spice grinder or with a mortar and pestle.

Figure 5-1:
Toasting spices in a heavy skillet.

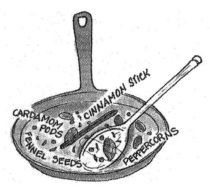

There's one exception to the basic toasting process — exotic and expensive saffron. Toast saffron by enclosing it in a piece of aluminum foil. Place the foil in the skillet and cook for 30 seconds to 1 minute per side. Remove the saffron from the packet and crumble before adding it to a dish.

If the spices burn, discard them and start over. Burnt spices have an unpleasant aftertaste.

Sautéing

Some spices are sautéed in a little butter or oil, most often along with onions, garlic, or ginger, before any other ingredients are added. These spices can be whole, such as cinnamon sticks, allspice berries, and whole cumin, cardamom, and cloves. Even some herbs can be sautéed whole, such as bay leaves and fresh rosemary. Ground spices and spice mixtures, such as curry powder or chili powder, are almost always sautéed for a minute or two before other ingredients or liquids are added.

To sauté spices, add the spice to the heated vegetable oil or butter or to the cooked onions, garlic, or ginger. The burner should be set to medium-low to medium. Stir frequently so the spice doesn't scorch. Take no chances here or you'll have to start again from scratch. If the phone rings, pull the pan off the heat! Normally after the spice is sautéed, meat, poultry, vegetables, or a liquid is added.

Uncooked curry powder has a raw taste. If you need to add additional curry powder to taste after a dish is nearly cooked, heat some vegetable oil or butter in a skillet. If you want, you can add some onion. Cook the onion, if desired, until it's translucent, about 5 minutes. Then add the additional curry powder and cook, stirring frequently, for 1 to 2 minutes. Follow this method when adding curry to mayonnaise for chicken or tuna salad — you'll taste the difference. Let the mixture cool before stirring it into salad dressing or mayonnaise.

Grating

Only a few spices are grated. These include fresh ginger, either peeled or unpeeled, and whole nutmeg. You can also purchase a nutmeg grater or a special ginger grater. Ginger and nutmeg can also be grated with the smallest holes on a four-sided grater.

Grinding

Grind spices in electric or hand-powered spice mills or with a mortar and pestle. Don't try to grind too large an amount at one time. In a mill, fill the upper container to a maximum of one-third full. In a mortar and pestle, grind only a few tablespoons at a time. Do not try to grind spices in a food processor. The container and blade are too large, so the food processor doesn't produce a fine-enough powder.

After grinding, you may want to sift the ground spices through a strainer or sieve to remove any remaining large pieces or to achieve a consistently fine texture.

For the best flavor, grind spices only a day or two ahead of when you plan to use them in a recipe.

Bruising or crushing

Some spices must be bruised or crushed slightly in order to release the flavor or to unlock their seeds. Lightly crush these spices by placing the flat side of a knife or the back of a spoon over the spice and tapping gently with your hand. The following spices should be bruised:

- **Cardamom pods** are always bruised before use in order to release their seeds. If a whole pod is called for in a recipe, bruise the pod before adding it to the recipe, as shown in Figure 5-2. If the cardamom is to be ground, bruise and remove the seeds and grind only the seeds.

- **Fresh lemon grass** is always crushed slightly to release its flavor before adding it to any dish. If the recipe asks you to chop fresh lemon grass instead of using a whole piece, you won't need to crush it before chopping because chopping will release the flavor.

- **Juniper berries** are slightly crushed before adding them to stews or pâtés to expose their flavor and aroma.

- **Garlic** is sometimes put through a press. This is, in essence, crushing the garlic. Use pressed garlic in recipes if the garlic will not be cooked, such as salad dressings, marinades, dips, and dipping sauces. Putting garlic through a press releases its oils and the garlic can burn more quickly if as a result. Garlic can also be minced, which releases less oil.

- **Peppercorns** are often crushed or cracked for use in dishes such as Steak au Poivre or to make peppery rubs and dips.

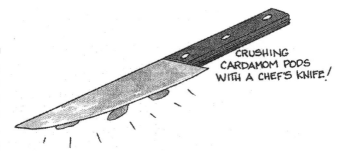

Figure 5-2:
It's easy to crush cardamom pods.

CRUSHING CARDAMOM PODS WITH A CHEF'S KNIFE!

Mincing and chopping

Only fresh spices are minced or chopped. These include garlic, ginger, lemon grass, and fresh chiles such as jalapeno, serrano, bird's eye, or Thai. Both garlic and ginger should be peeled first and minced finely. When using lemon grass, discard the tough outer leaves and mince the softer inner core. When preparing fresh chiles, cut off the stem, slit the chile in half, and remove the seeds and discard them. Then mince finely.

Some cooking gurus consider makrud, or kaffir lime leaves that are used in Thai cooking, a spice. Fresh ones can be left whole or thinly sliced before being added to a recipe.

Infusing or steeping

Spices that are gently heated in liquid over medium-low heat until the liquid is barely simmering are said to be *infused* or *steeped*. During this procedure, the flavor of the spice or combination of spices is transferred to the liquid. Water, broth, milk, cream, coconut milk, olive or vegetable oil, vinegar, or sugar syrup can be infused.

There's no hard and fast rule about how long to steep. Feel free to personalize infused liquids to your taste — you can experiment with the length of time you steep the spices within the suggested range. The longer a spice steeps, the more flavor it will release.

To infuse a spice's flavor into a liquid, follow these steps:

1. **Add the spice or spices to the liquid in a saucepan.**

2. **Heat over medium-low to medium heat until the liquid bubbles gently but doesn't boil.**

3. **Remove the pan from the heat and let the spice steep in the hot liquid for 10 to 30 minutes, depending what a recipe indicates or how strong a flavor you want.**

   Saffron only needs to steep for 5 minutes.

Sometimes the liquid is passed through a strainer and the whole spices are discarded, (as in beverages, soups, sauces, syrups, and dessert preparations.) The liquid is then used in recipes as directed. Other times the spice stays in the liquid while it is stored in a clean container for future use (as in vinegars or some marinades) and is strained just before use. As a general rule, powdered spices are usually strained immediately through a strainer that's lined with a paper coffee filter. Whole spices generally remain in the liquid and are strained right before use.

Poaching liquids, which are used for fruit, chicken, fish, and marinated vegetables, are infusions. The process used to make poaching liquids is slightly different than the one above, as poaching liquids don't steep off the heat but simmer gently for up to 30 minutes.

Infuse it

Infusion lends a particular taste or color to a liquid or food. Sometimes saffron is prepared for use by infusing it in a little hot water. The following list contains a few examples of infused liquids. Experiment a little bit and come up with your own combinations.

- Milk, cream, and coconut milk can be infused with a split vanilla bean, ginger, cinnamon, or lemon grass while making custard, pudding, ice cream, or custard pie.

- Milk, cream, and coconut milk can be infused with garlic, lemon grass, ginger, chiles, peppercorns, cardamom, coriander, mustard, or nutmeg when making a creamy sauce, soup, or Southeast Asian or Thai curry.

- Saffron, turmeric, and curry powder are added to water while cooking grains such as rice or barley so that liquid and spices are absorbed by the grains.

- Water or broth can be infused with peppercorns, ginger, garlic, chiles, cinnamon sticks, whole allspice, whole cloves, cardamom pods, and a host of other spices for soups, stews, curries, and savory poaching liquids.

- A combination of water or wine and sugar can be infused with cinnamon sticks, allspice berries, whole cloves, and cardamom pods to create a liquid for poaching fresh and dried fruit.

- Hot beverages such as wine, cider, coffee, and tea can be infused with spices, although the process is slightly different. See Chapter 19 for details.

Your Spicy Signature

Let the fun begin! The following sections show you how to add your own special touches to many recipes and foods.

Making spice blends and rubs

Spice blends are just a combination of dried spices that are used in cooking and baking, whereas rubs are a spice blend that's rubbed on meat, poultry, or fish before grilling or sautéing. You may find many prepared spice blends such as Cajun spice, barbecue spice, or pumpkin pie spice on supermarket shelves, but they are really quite easy to prepare at home. Chapter 9 has several recipes; you can follow them directly or, once you feel confident, alter them slightly or disregard them entirely as you make your own special mixtures. Generally, it's best to grind whole spices separately when preparing blends and rubs, and then combine them. If you're short of time, you can use preground spices. But every rule has its exception, and in this case, it's curry powder. To make a curry powder, the entire lot of whole spices should be toasted together and ground together in small amounts, and then the entire mixture should be stirred to blend.

To make spice rubs and blends, simply measure the spices that have been ground and combine them by stirring them together. You might want to sift the mixture through a sieve, but doing so isn't always necessary.

Use the rub by wetting the piece of food with a little olive oil or lemon juice and then coating the item evenly with the rub.

Making spice pastes

Spice pastes are merely spice blends that are made from fresh or "wet" ingredients such as fresh garlic, ginger, chiles or lemon grass. Occasionally the "wet" ingredients are combined with dried spices and with a bit of liquid, such as water, vinegar, citrus juice, or tomato paste or puree. They should be fairly thick and not too runny.

Spice pastes are used to flavor simmered one-pot meals, such as curries, as well as for marinades for meat, poultry, or seafood. Thai Curry Paste, (Chapter 9) and Jamaican Jerk Sauce and Chile Adobo Sauce, (Chapter 10) are examples of spice pastes.

Spice pastes can be made in a food processor or mini food processor fitted with a metal blade. Just pulse until you have a paste. Add a tiny bit of liquid to make the paste a bit smoother or easier to handle if you're using the paste as a marinade. You can also use a mortar and pestle. Using a mortar and pestle isn't quick, and it isn't easy, but the paste has a finer texture than if you use a food processor. You may want to combine the two methods by starting to chop the fresh spices with a food processor and finishing them with a mortar and pestle. Add liquid as necessary to the paste to create the right consistency and blend with a spoon.

To turn a dry spice rub into a paste, add a little olive oil to the spice mixture. You can also add a little fresh minced garlic or ginger; some chopped fresh parsley, basil, oregano, thyme, cilantro, or chives; or even freshly grated lemon, lime, or orange zest. The mixture can be rubbed onto fish or poultry that will be baked or grilled.

Making spiced oils

Some spiced oils, such as garlic, lemon, and chile oils are available on super-market shelves, but you can make your own easily (see Figure 5-3). Spiced oils can be drizzled on broiled, baked, grilled, or sautéed seafood, chicken, chops, or steak. They can even liven up cooked vegetables. You can sauté vegetables, seafood, and poultry in seasoned oils if you want to add extra flavor. Spiced oil can replace plain olive or vegetable oil in homemade vinaigrettes, which you can use as a marinade or a salad dressing. Spiced oils can also be tossed with pasta or noodles or used instead of butter in mashed potatoes.

SPICED OILS

Figure 5-3:
Spiced oils
have, you
guessed
it, spices
in them!

Spiced oils are an infusion. They're not difficult to make. Here's the basic method:

1. **In a saucepan, heat the oil with the spices over medium-low heat until the oil is hot and bubbles gently, about 10 minutes.**

   Remove from the heat. Do not let the oil burn, which you'll know if it begins to discolor or smoke or allows the spices to become dark.

2. **Let the mixture steep for 15 to 30 minutes.**

3. **Strain out any ground spices through a fine strainer or cloth-lined medium strainer.**

   Leave whole spices in the oil and strain before each use. If you use fresh spices, such as garlic or ginger, you'll need to strain it.

Following are a few suggestions for making your own spiced oils. I also give you the appropriate steeping time.

- ✔ **Curry oil:** Use 1 cup of olive oil and 2 teaspoons of curry powder. Steep for 30 minutes and strain.

- ✔ **Chili oil:** Use 1 cup of olive oil and 1 teaspoon of chili powder plus ½ teaspoon crushed red pepper flakes, ½ teaspoon cayenne, and 1 plump clove of garlic, minced. Steep for 30 minutes and strain.

- ✔ **Cumin, dill, or fennel seed oil:** Use one cup of olive oil and 2½ tablespoons of one of the seeds. Steep for 30 minutes. Strain before each use.

- ✔ **Ginger oil:** Use 1 cup of peanut oil and 1½ inch piece of fresh ginger, coarsely chopped. Steep for 15 to 20 minutes and strain.

- ✔ **Garlic oil:** Use 1 cup of olive or peanut oil and 6 cloves of garlic, lightly bruised. Steep for 30 minutes and strain.

- ✔ **Cinnamon oil:** Use 1 cup of peanut, safflower, hazelnut, or walnut oil and 2 cinnamon sticks, broken in half. Steep for 30 minutes. Strain before each use.

Store the oils in clean bottles that you've labeled and dated. Spiced oils that use fresh ingredients like garlic should not be kept for more than a few days because the infusion is a ripe place for bacterial to grow. For other oils, if you store them in a cool, dark place, the oils can keep for 2 weeks, or you can refrigerate them for about 1 month.

Bring refrigerated oils that have coagulated to room temperature before using or heat the bottle in warm water in the sink.

Make it a combo

Multi-spiced oils or vinegar offer a new range of flavors. Try mixing these combinations of spices with 1 cup of cooking or olive oil, or with 2 cups of wine or fruit-flavored vinegar. Add a piece of lemon or orange rind with the spices for a citrusy taste. Simmer and strain as directed for making spiced oils or add the spices to the vinegar and let the flavor ripen as directed for making spiced vinegars.

- ✔ 6 cardamom pods, a teaspoon of whole coriander, and a cinnamon stick

- ✔ 1-inch piece ginger, sliced, 1 clove garlic, sliced, and 1 to 2 shallots, halved

- ✔ 1 to 2 shallots, 1 to 2 stalks lemon grass, bruised, and 1 to 2 cloves garlic, sliced

Making spiced vinegars

Like oil, vinegar absorbs the flavor of whatever spices are added to it. Spiced vinegars are even easier to make than spiced oils. Spiced vinegars can be used wherever you normally use vinegar, such as in salad dressings, marinades, or sauces.

A variety of vinegars are suitable for spicing. Commonplace cider vinegar and red or white wine vinegars are perfect. For a less sharp taste and Asian flair, use rice wine vinegar. Sherry vinegar has a pleasantly robust flavor and also works well. Because of its exquisite sweetness, flavor, and fragrance, balsamic vinegar is not used to make spiced vinegar, although balsamic can be spiked with a little fresh garlic or ginger when you make a salad dressing.

When making spiced oil or vinegar, remember to label and date the bottles!

Although some people heat the vinegar and follow the process for making spiced oils, you don't have to do all that work. Here's an easy and effective method for making spiced vinegars: Simply put the spice or spices in a clean bottle. Add the vinegar. Cover and store in a cool, dark place without opening for 2 weeks so the flavor deepens. Occasionally shake the jar during this time. Strain the vinegar after the flavor has fully developed and pour the vinegar into a clean bottle.

Make sure that the vinegar completely covers the spices in the bottle. If it doesn't, add extra vinegar. This will prevent the spices from molding or going "off."

Here are some flavorful and delicious spiced vinegars that I recommend:

- ✔ **Chile vinegar:** Add 8 to 12 whole chile peppers, such as jalapeno, serrano, or bird's eye peppers to 2 cups of cider vinegar, white wine vinegar, or sherry vinegar.

- ✔ **Garlic vinegar:** Add 6 plump cloves of peeled garlic to 2 cups of white wine vinegar or sherry vinegar.

- ✔ **Ginger vinegar:** Peel and slice a 2-inch piece of fresh ginger. Add it to 2 cups of rice wine vinegar or white wine vinegar.

- ✔ **Dill seed, cumin seed, fennel seed, or celery seed vinegar:** Add 2½ tablespoons of one of the seeds to 2 cups of cider vinegar, white wine vinegar, or rice wine vinegar. This vinegar benefits from being heated briefly with the spices. Heat over medium heat until hot and allow the vinegar to cool before bottling and setting it aside to steep.

Spicy salads and marinades

If you've made spiced oils or vinegar, use them in this basic salad dressing. The dressing can also be used as a marinade for meat, poultry, or seafood. Use either flavored oil or vinegar, but not both. If you're using flavored oil, use half flavored oil (2 to 3 tablespoons) and half olive or vegetable oil along with a plain vinegar.

Basic Vinaigrette: In a bowl, combine ¼ teaspoon salt, ¼ teaspoon freshly ground black pepper, ¼ teaspoon Dijon mustard, and 2 tablespoons of vinegar. Whisk in 4 to 6 tablespoons of olive or vegetable oil. Taste for salt. This recipe can be doubled or tripled. You can also whizz the first four ingredients together in a blender. Remove the plastic knob in the center of the top of the blender and then, with the motor running, pour the olive oil through the hole in the top.

Making spiced butters

Flavored butters (also known as composed butters) are comprised of softened butter that is blended with spices, herbs, or lemon juice. Flavored butters are easy to make by hand or in a food processor. They can be spread on bread and rolls, used as an accent for cooked vegetables, or top grilled or sautéed meat, poultry, or seafood. Spiced butter can also be rubbed on raw poultry or fish before cooking and it makes a wonderful basting butter for roasted chicken or turkey. It can also be used in mashed potatoes, tossed with noodles or rice, or placed on top of polenta.

Here's the procedure for making spiced butter:

1. **Put softened butter in a bowl or in the bowl of a food processor that you've fitted with a metal blade.**

2. **Add the flavoring agents and stir with a fork, if using a bowl, or pulse in a food processor.**

   The butter and other ingredients should be blended evenly.

3. **Spread the butter along a piece of plastic wrap and roll to form a log approximately 1½ inches in diameter.**

4. **Twist the ends of the plastic wrap to seal.**

   The butter can be frozen for a month or two and pieces can be sliced off as you need it (see Figure 5-4). It can also be kept in the refrigerator for 3 to 4 days.

Figure 5-4:
Slicing
spiced
butter.

Here are a few suggestions for spiced butters. The quantities can be doubled or tripled.

- ✓ **Garlic butter:** Add 1 to 2 cloves of minced or pressed garlic to 4 table-spoons of softened butter. If you want, add 1 teaspoon of minced parsley or chopped chives. You can also add 1 teaspoon of dry sherry or fresh lemon juice.

- ✓ **Ginger butter:** Add 1 to 2 teaspoons of minced fresh ginger to 4 table-spoons of softened butter. You can also add 1 teaspoon of dry sherry.

- ✓ **Mustard butter:** Add 2 tablespoons of Dijon mustard, 1 teaspoon of honey, and 1 teaspoon of fresh lemon juice or dry sherry to 4 table-spoons of butter.

- ✓ **Cayenne-lemon butter:** Add 1 tablespoon of finely grated lemon zest, 1½ teaspoons of fresh lemon juice, and ⅛ to ¼ teaspoon of cayenne to 4 tablespoons of butter.

Making spiced flour, cornmeal, and crumbs

Spiced flours can replace plain flour when making batters or flouring poultry for food that is to be sautéed or deep-fried. Spiced flours, cornmeal, or crumbs can also be used as a crispy coating for steak, veal cutlets, chicken cutlets, fish fillets, shrimp, clams, calamari, and vegetables such as eggplant and zucchini.

To make spiced flour, cornmeal, and crumbs, simply combine all-purpose flour, cornmeal, or breadcrumbs with the spices in a bowl and stir to blend. The mixture can be stored in a covered container in the cupboard and is ready whenever you want to use it.

After you've dipped food into the spiced flour, cornmeal, or crumbs, you should discard the remaining mixture because it could become a breeding ground for bacteria.

Although sautéing and deep-frying are the most popular ways of cooking coated foods, some folks who are watching their weight or fat intake prefer to lightly spray a baking pan with olive or vegetable oil and bake cutlets, egg-plant, or fish fillets in an oven of 350 to 375 degrees, until the food is cooked through and the coating is lightly golden brown.

Here are a few suggestions to make your own spiced blends for coating:

- **Cayenne spiced:** Add 1 teaspoon of cayenne and ½ teaspoon of salt to 1 cup of all-purpose flour, cornmeal, or breadcrumbs.

- **Triple chile spiced:** Add ½ teaspoon Anaheim (marketed also as California) or Arbol ground chile pepper powder, either ¼ to ½ teaspoon ground chipotle or jalapeno chile powder, and a dash of ground haben-ero chile powder (or, if you're feeling less adventurous, a dash of cayenne) to 1 cup of all-purpose flour, cornmeal, or breadcrumbs.

- **Chili spiced:** Add 1 tablespoon chili powder, ½ teaspoon ground cumin, ¼ teaspoon garlic powder, and ½ teaspoon salt to 1 cup of all-purpose flour, cornmeal, or breadcrumbs.

- **Mustard-cumin spiced:** Add 1½ teaspoons dried mustard, ½ teaspoon ground coriander, ½ teaspoon salt, and 1 tablespoon chopped chives or parsley to 1 cup of all-purpose flour, cornmeal, or breadcrumbs.

- **Cumin-coriander spiced:** Add 1½ teaspoons ground cumin, 1½ teaspoons ground coriander, ½ teaspoon salt, and ¼ teaspoon freshly ground black or white pepper to 1 cup of all-purpose flour, cornmeal, or breadcrumbs.

- **Garlic, cayenne, and two pepper spiced:** Add 1 teaspoon cayenne, ½ teaspoon freshly ground black pepper, ¼ teaspoon ground white pepper, ½ teaspoon dried thyme leaves, ½ teaspoon salt, and ¼ teaspoon garlic powder to 1 cup all-purpose flour, cornmeal, or breadcrumbs.

- **Curried flour:** Add 2½ teaspoons curry powder, ½ teaspoon salt, and ¼ teaspoon garlic powder to 1 cup of all-purpose flour.

You can also add 2 to 3 tablespoons of fresh, finely grated Parmesan or Romano cheese to any seasoned coating mixture.

Go nuts! For added texture and taste, substitute sesame seeds or finely chopped nuts, such as peanuts, for some of the flour, breadcrumbs, or corn-meal. Press the seeds or nuts into the food to make sure they stick. Foods coated in sesame seeds or nuts should be sautéed over a slightly lower heat than you would normally use and watched carefully to ensure the coating doesn't burn. Medium heat should work well. Try to use peanut oil, which has a higher burn point than most other cooking oils.

Dredging

To *dredge* means simply to lightly coat food, most often poultry, fish, or meat, in seasoned flour, cornmeal, or breadcrumbs. Put the seasoned coating mixture in a shallow dish or pie plate. With a paper towel, pat dry the food to be dipped. Some cooks like to line the bowl with a large piece of waxed paper or parchment paper and put the seasoned coating mixture on top. You can turn the food, and/or tip and move the paper gently in order to evenly coat the food. Shake the food gently after dredging so any excess is removed. Dredging is shown in Figure 5-5.

The only catch is not to dredge too much in advance or the coating becomes soggy. Dredge immediately before you're ready to cook.

Some recipes ask you to dip the food into milk or a beaten egg before dredging the food in the dry ingredient. To keep your fingers from getting too messy, use two hands. Dip the food into the wet ingredient with one hand; then transfer the food to your other hand when you dip it into the dry ingredient.

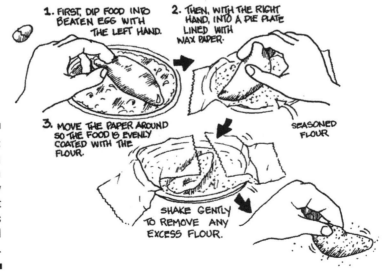

DREDGE YOUR FOOD!

1. FIRST, DIP FOOD INTO BEATEN EGG WITH THE LEFT HAND.

2. THEN, WITH THE RIGHT HAND, INTO A PIE PLATE LINED WITH WAX PAPER.

3. MOVE THE PAPER AROUND SO THE FOOD IS EVENLY COATED WITH THE FLOUR.

SEASONED FLOUR

SHAKE GENTLY TO REMOVE ANY EXCESS FLOUR.

Figure 5-5:
Dredging food is a simple way to coat it with spices and seasonings.

Chapter 6
Make No Mistakes

* * *

In This Chapter

▶ Learning the best way to handle hot spices

▶ Avoiding the most common faux pas

▶ Fixing your mistakes

* * *

*I*n this chapter, you'll discover the safety tips for handling hot spices, such as chiles, as well as how to protect your countertops and clothes when handling spices that stain, such as turmeric. Additionally, you'll find a few tricks to fix common culinary mistakes, such as adding too much salt or over-spicing a recipe. All is not lost: You won't need to order pizza! These simple suggestions can save a recipe if something has gone wrong.

Handling Spices

You don't need to watch out for much when working with spices but there are a few spices and spice blends that require some extra attention or special care.

- **Fresh chiles:** The resins in chiles can burn your skin. Make sure you keep your fingers away from your face, especially your eyes, nose, and lips. Wash your hands well after touching chiles or their seeds. If you're sensitive to the heat of fresh chiles or you're preparing several of them, consider wearing latex or rubber gloves to protect your hands.

- **Cayenne or ground red pepper, chile pepper powders, chili powder, cumin, curry powder, curry paste, crushed red pepper flakes, jerk sauce, jerk rub, Cajun rub, Caribbean rub:** These spices pack a hefty heat punch and you should use caution when handling them. All contain chiles and can be quite hot. If they've spilled onto your hands, wash your hands well and keep your fingers away from your face.

✔ **Turmeric, saffron, annato (achiote), and curry powder:** These spices
will stain hands, countertops, and fabrics a yellow or reddish yellow
color. If they spill, wipe them up immediately. If the area is stained, rub
the spot gently with a kitchen or bathroom cleanser. If fabric becomes
stained, treat it as soon as possible with a stain remover and wash it.
What about your hands and fingernails? Wash them as soon as possible
to ensure that you don't transfer the stain to something else. Any residual color on your skin should fade quickly.

Spicy Damage Control: What to Do When You've . . .

Everyone slips up now and then. Measuring incorrectly and adding too much
of something or too little of something else is easy. But all is not lost! You can
learn a few tricks to help you hide these blunders. The dish won't be perfect,
but if the error isn't too big, you'll still be able to eat (and hopefully enjoy)
the food.

Used too much salt

Using too much salt is one of the most common mistakes cooks make, but it
doesn't always end in disaster. You do have a few options. How you save the
day depends on the kind of dish you're making.

✔ If a soup, stew, or curry is too salty, you can add a quartered raw potato
and simmer the dish longer. The potato should absorb some of the salt.
Remove the potato with a slotted spoon and discard it. Alternatively,
you can add a little sugar, starting with ¼ teaspoon and adding more
until the dish is more palatable.

✔ You can try doubling the recipe and omitting salt in the second batch.
Combine the batches and adjust the seasonings to taste.

✔ If you've salted a dish that uses soy sauce or Thai fish sauce, you're
probably out of luck because these ingredients have a very high amount
of sodium, but even here you can try by doubling the batch and using
less of the salty item.

✔ Put overly salted cooked vegetables, such as green beans, carrots, peas,
and zucchini; plain cooked legumes; or plain rice or barley in a strainer
or a colander and rinse with water. The flavors you have added will
probably be rinsed away too. Reheat, taste, and adjust the seasoning.
You might top the dish with a little spiced butter or spiced oil.

✔ If the shaker spews out too much salt onto raw meat, poultry, or fish, rinse with water and pat dry with a paper towel. Season again as directed and cook.

✔ If you've oversalted cakes or breads, sorry, there's no hope of correcting the boo-boo. The only thing you can do is toss the cake or bread out! The same goes for too much or too little spice. Unfortunately, baked goods can't be fixed.

Used too little spice

You've tasted the dish and it's not quite spicy enough for you. Recipes aren't set in stone. If you want a bit more chili powder or cinnamon, go ahead and add a small amount when you're preparing the dish. But it's not always a question of adding more of one spice. Salt can be the answer, as it causes a chemical reaction the effect of which is to blend flavors. Many times a pinch or two of salt will heighten the flavors and bring them together. Simple additions of salt are fine when you're making a sauce, a dip, paté or vegetables, but some dishes require a different approach.

✔ **Simmered dishes:** Tasting any long-cooking dish, such as sauces, soups, stews, chilis, and curries, as it cooks is important. Determine through tasting whether you need extra spices. You may need to add more if the spices you used are getting older or have been exposed to heat and light, making the flavor and color deteriorate. Add a bit of extra spice and simmer a while longer to let the spices meld into the ingredients. A pinch or two of salt added towards the end of the cooking time helps marry the flavors.

✔ **Grilled, roasted, baked, or sautéed meat, poultry, or fish:** Spike any of these dishes with spiced butters or spiced oils that have a complementary taste. Sometimes the dish only needs a quick dash of salt. A little freshly ground pepper or ground coriander can also help.

Curry is a special case. If you're short on curry flavor, don't add extra curry into the dish until you've prepared it. Sauté the curry for a minute or two in a little butter or vegetable oil so that the flavor releases and the curry loses its raw taste. You can then add it to the dish.

Used too much spice

This generally happens if you've drastically changed the proportions of spices or measured incorrectly. The best thing for you to do is to double the batch and omit the spices from the second batch. Combine both batches, taste, and adjust the seasonings.

Made it too hot

Even the best cooks occasionally make dishes that are unpleasantly hot and spicy enough to burn the tongue. If you find yourself in this position, it may be because some of the ingredients you used were hotter than you bargained for, you had too free a hand and measured carelessly, or simply because the recipe itself is too spicy for your taste.

Some fresh chiles, even chiles of the same type, can be hotter than others. Check how hot the chile is by tasting a tiny piece of it. Removing the seeds and ribs does remove some of the heat, if needed. Chile pepper and curry powders can vary somewhat from manufacturer to manufacturer in their degree of heat. If you find that a dish is too hot, here are a few suggestions:

- ✔ Sweet cuts the heat! A little sugar, either white or brown, can lessen the effect of heat in a sauce, dip, or in a long-simmering dish.

- ✔ Extra liquid or a chopped or canned tomato or two can also be added to a long-cooking recipe in order to cut down on the heat, provided that you allow the dish to continue to simmer for at least fifteen to twenty minutes. The acid in the tomato provides some balance to counterbalance the heat.

- ✔ Double the batch and omit the hot spice or fresh chile. Combine the two batches and then adjust the seasonings.

Burned the spices

Sorry, but there's no chance of saving what you've made if you've burned your spices. Your only option is to throw away the burned spices and any ingredients cooked with them. Start fresh from scratch. However, when you grill meats that have been prepared with a spice rub, a bit of charring is just fine.

Burned garlic makes the food it's added to taste unpleasant. Fresh garlic needs to be stirred frequently when cooking. Make certain that the burner temperature of your stove is not too high.

Salt saving tips

Canned broth or bouillon cubes are salty. If you use them in a recipe, omit the salt called for. Taste for salt at the end of the cooking time and adjust by adding salt in ¼ teaspoon increments.

Add salt towards the end of the cooking time to dishes such as soups, stews, and sauces that simmer for a long time. Because the liquid reduces in long-simmering dishes, the salt can become more concentrated.

Chapter 7

Spicy Combos: A Guide to the Use of Spices and Complementary Ingredients

• •

In This Chapter

▶ Discovering which spices go together

▶ Exploring combinations for spices, flavoring agents, and ingredients from around the world

▶ Putting recipes together

• •

*I*f you've read the preceding chapters in this book, you know all about the most common spices and how to buy, store, and prepare them. But there's one bit of information that can help you use spices to their full potential that's still missing — how spices are combined. Here's where you can begin to put everything together. What makes Mexican, Thai, Indian, or Chinese food taste the way it does? Is it only the individual spices or is it the way that the spices are combined with each other and with other flavoring agents, such as soy sauce and lime juice?

Culinary traditions abound in each area of the world, preserved through practice from generation to generation. Using the spices and ingredients most available to them, every cultural group prepares food differently. The unique flavor combinations ultimately distinguish one cuisine from another. Understanding the principles of how to combine spices and flavors and knowing which basic ingredients are used in a certain cuisine are keys to learning how to cook with confidence and ease. This knowledge can help you shop at the market, follow a recipe, or improvise and create a dish on your own. And as an added bonus, knowing how to create flavorful combinations definitely makes menu planning easier.

Throughout the world, cooks take fresh seafood, meat, poultry, vegetables, and fruit and transform them into delicious meals. What may vary from place to place is the importance of a particular food item — such as rice, potatoes, mangoes, or even the carrot. Certain ingredients become prominent components of a specific cuisine — for example, pasta in Italy or beans in Mexico are a part of those countries' culinary signature.

North and South America and the Caribbean

Nowhere has the influence of foreign cultures had a greater effect on cooking styles than in the "New World." Exploration, trade, colonization, and wars have historically acted as catalysts that affect culture, including cookery, and by consequence they have transformed the culinary customs of regions. During the last 300 years, cooking in the Americas has undergone a number of changes. Early colonial influences of Spanish, French, British, and Portuguese cuisine, as well as traditional African cookery and Native American ingredients, can be tasted from the top of North America to the tip of South America and throughout the Caribbean (see Figure 7-1). But the cultural exchange has not been a one-way street. The Americas shared its wealth. It blessed the "Old World" with its native products — tomatoes, potatoes, corn, chiles, peanuts, vanilla, and chocolate.

Immigration and cross-cultural influences have shaped a range of new tastes and sparked the use of new ingredients, spices, and flavors. The America's culinary traditions continue to merge with those of more recent immigrants — from Italy and Greece; the Middle East; European countries such as Hungary, Germany, Scandinavia, and Russia; Asian nations including India, China, Japan, Thailand, and Vietnam; and African nations from Morocco to South Africa. Lively and flavorful, the cooking of the Americas is progressive — always ready to adopt, adapt, and innovate, all in the name of taste.

Mexico

Mexico brings us chile peppers galore, but they're not the only characteristic ingredients in this cuisine that is typically, but not always, fiery.

Spices: Arbol, ancho, cascabel, poblano, jalapeno, habanero, and serrano chile peppers; and garlic, cumin, cinnamon, cloves, cayenne, black pepper, sesame seeds, and vanilla

Herbs and other flavoring agents: Sherry, lime juice, lemon juice, vinegar, sour orange juice, tomato-based adobo sauce, fresh cilantro, and oregano

Ingredients: Tomatoes, jicama, avocados, butternut, olives, oranges, tortillas, rice, corn, cornmeal, chorizo, turkey, black beans, pinto beans, sour oranges, almonds, and chocolate

Figure 7-1:
The
Americas.

Tex-Mex and Southwestern

Beef chili and tacos are standard examples of Tex-Mex cookery (based on the combination of Texas and Mexican flavors). Southwestern fare (food primarily from Arizona and New Mexico) is characterized by the liberal use of spices and chiles and the use of more traditional Mexican fare such as Chiles Rellenos and salsas. Not content to rest with these staples, Southwestern chefs today are creating new and tasty combinations using these ingredients:

Spices: Cayenne, jalapeno, serrano, poblano, New Mexican, and guajillo chile peppers; and black pepper, garlic, chili powder, and cumin

Herbs and other flavoring agents: Oregano, cilantro, and lime juice

Ingredients: Tortillas, sour cream, cheddar or Monterey Jack cheese, kidney beans, and pinto beans

Make it sour

The sour oranges that are used in Mexican cooking can be difficult to find in the United States. The most well-known varieties of bitter oranges are Bergamot and Seville, which are used to make fine marmalades and flavored liqueurs such as curacao, Grand Marnier, and Triple Sec. Although sour oranges may look similar to Valencia and other common oranges, their flavor is distinctly tart, and they're not good for eating out of hand.

Some Mexican recipes call for sour orange juice. You can make a mock version of sour orange juice by combining equal amounts of fresh orange and lemon juice. For a quick side dish, pour the juice over jicama, cucumber, or avocado and garnish with cayenne or any ground chile pepper powder, cilantro, and chopped tomatoes. For a tart, but more traditional, salad dressing, combine equal amounts of sour orange juice and olive oil, add a pressed clove of garlic, and throw in a dash of cumin, cayenne, black pepper, and salt.

Cajun and creole

Cajun and creole cookery hail from Louisiana. Cajun cooking, noted for its rustic country style, reflects both French and Southern influences and relies on pork fat and *roux* (a long-cooked blend of fat and flour) for flavor. Highly seasoned, Cajun cooking uses more spices such as mustard, cayenne, white and black pepper, and chiles than creole cooking does. Echoing the flavors of France, Spain, and Africa, creole cooking is regarded as more sophisticated than Cajun cooking. It often features butter and cream instead of pork fat. In general, creole cooking uses more tomatoes. Both Cajun and creole dishes feature the trademark combination of bell peppers, onions or scallions, and celery. Filé powder is used by Cajun and creole cooks alike.

Spices: Cayenne, white pepper, black pepper, garlic, chile peppers, celery seed, and filé powder

Herbs and Other Flavorings: Thyme, sage, parsley, and Tabasco or other types of liquid red hot pepper sauce

Ingredients: Bell pepper, onions, scallions, celery, tomatoes, red beans, rice, cornmeal, Andouille sausage, crayfish, shrimp, and redfish

Andouille sausage is the hot and spicy smoked sausage that's used in Cajun cooking. Mexican chorizo sausage is an acceptable substitute.

South America

Modern South American or Latin cooking, whether from Chile or Brazil, prides itself on the use of fresh local ingredients. The cuisines have been influenced by the area's colonial past — namely under Spain and Portugal — and Africans brought from West Africa as slaves. The West African influence is particularly strong in Brazilian cooking.

Spices: Garlic, cumin, chile peppers, cloves, cinnamon, black pepper, and achiote (annato)

Herbs and other flavoring agents: Oregano, cilantro, vinegar, and palm oil

Ingredients: Rice, potatoes, sweet potatoes, corn, black beans, olives, tomatoes, bell peppers, almonds, pistachio nuts, raisins, plantains, bananas, coconut, coconut milk, and shrimp

Caribbean

Cookery in the Caribbean reflects that area's own native culture as well as various nations whose presence influenced the area — Spain, France, African nations, and even Asian nations, due to the importation of workers from the East. Caribbean food is characterized by freshness, taking full advantage of the regions succulent fruit, wonderful produce, and abundant seafood as well as by the use of, what else, spices!

Spices: Garlic, ginger, curry powder, allspice, cloves, chile peppers, Scotch bonnet peppers, white and black pepper, cayenne, nutmeg, mace, coriander, and annato (achiote)

Herbs and Other Flavoring Agents: mint, cilantro, thyme, lime juice, rum

Ingredients: rice, yams, tomatoes, bell peppers, scallions, coconut, coconut milk, papaya, mango, guava, bananas, plantains, avocado, tomato, kidney beans, black beans, shrimp, fish, goat, lamb

Scotch bonnet peppers look like miniature bell peppers and come in a range of colors, from yellow to orange to red. They are fiery hot, so use them sparingly. Take extra caution when handling them. They are also called habaneros.

The Mediterranean

The olive tree, which is native to the Mediterranean, can be considered the symbol of Mediterranean cookery. From Spain in the western Mediterranean to Syria in the Middle East (see Figure 7-2), the products of the olive tree — olive oil and olives — are primary ingredients in the area's cuisine, and their flavor is unmistakable. Because the Middle East was a trading center for spices that made their way to Europe from the Asian continent, spices have scented the dishes of the region for centuries. Fresh ingredients, particularly produce and seafood, abound, and they are most often enhanced by olive oil, fresh herbs, citrus, and spices. Mediterranean cooking is also influenced by the importation of indigenous American ingredients, most notably tomatoes and chiles.

Figure 7-2:
The
Mediter-
ranean.

Southern France and Italy

Dishes from the sunny Mediterranean are generally characterized by the liberal use of olive oil, garlic, and fresh herbs. Spices are also a major contributor to this flavorful cuisine.

Spices: Garlic, coriander, cumin, crushed red chile flakes, paprika, fennel seed, and nutmeg

Herbs and other flavoring agents: Mint, basil, parsley, oregano, rosemary, bay leaf, wine, lemons, oranges, and balsamic vinegar

Ingredients: Olive oil, olives, tomatoes, roasted peppers, eggplant, zucchini, pine nuts, almonds, hazelnuts, chickpeas, white beans, lentils, pasta, polenta, ricotta, mozzarella, Parmesan, Romano, and goat cheese

Liquid gold

Olive oil lends its distinct flavor to most Mediterranean dishes. In the United States, you can find domestic olive oil, as well as imports from Italy, France, Spain, and Greece. Olive oil's flavor can vary from very fruity to slightly fruity, depending on the region it comes from and on the grade of olive oil, which indicates the acidity of the oil. The best olive oils are cold-pressed, a process that keeps the acidity level low. Extra-virgin olive oil has an acidity level of 1 percent; virgin olive oil has an acidity level between 1 and 3 percent.

Extra-virgin olive oil has a more intense taste and can vary from a deep gold to a greenish-gold color. Use extra-virgin olive oil mainly for sauces and salad dressings. Virgin olive oil, which is less expensive but is also of excellent quality, is a paler greenish-gold or yellow gold than extra virgin and has a milder taste. Use virgin olive oil for general cooking.

Olive oil has a higher burn point than other cooking oils, except peanut oil, making it good for sautéing. Olive oil should not be used for baking, unless specifically called for (such as in a recipe for pizza dough.) Store olive oil in a cool, dry place for up to 6 months.

If the heat and humidity and high where you live, you might consider refrigerating your olive oil so it doesn't become rancid and have a peculiar taste. Refrigeration makes the oil coagulate and turn cloudy, so you'll need to let it come to room temperature before pouring.

Greece

Trademarks of Greek cooking include fresh lemon juice, olive oil, garlic, oregano, and, cinnamon. In southern France and Italy, tomatoes are often paired with olive oil and garlic and fresh herbs such as basil and parsley to create a lovely sauce. In Greece, tomato-based sauces are comprised of tomatoes, garlic, olive oil, oregano and. the spice cinnamon. The use of cinnamon gives the sauce a distinctively Greek flair.

Spices: Garlic, cinnamon, nutmeg, and black pepper

Herbs and other flavoring agents: Parsley, oregano, dill, lemon, and honey

Ingredients: Olive oil, olives, eggplant, pine nuts, feta cheese, and lamb

Spain

Olive oil and garlic are the primary players in this Mediterranean cuisine, most often accented by tomatoes, bell peppers, onions, and both black olives and pimento-stuffed green olives. Spanish cookery is also known as *Catalan* cookery.

Spices: Garlic, paprika, white pepper, black pepper, saffron, fennel seeds

Herbs and other flavoring agents: Oregano, bay leaf, parsley, sherry, sherry wine vinegar, and orange juice and orange zest

Ingredients: Rice, cod, chickpeas, tomatoes, bell peppers, onions, almonds, and seafood

Chickpeas, a staple in Mediterranean countries, are also known as garbanzo beans.

Portugal

Like Spanish cooking, Portuguese cooking relies on the combination of olive oil and garlic. Food is often accented by chile peppers. Portuguese cooks sometimes favor the use of cream.

Spices: Garlic, paprika, chile peppers, cayenne, nutmeg, and black pepper

Herbs and other flavoring agents: Parsley, lemons, and port wine

Ingredients: Olive oil, chorizo, bell peppers, tomatoes, cream

Middle East

Middle Eastern countries, such as Syria and Lebanon, were once the cross-roads of the trade route that connected the spice lands to the east with Europe. Garlic, parsley, and mint are the predominate flavors. As in Greece, tomatoes are often flavored with cinnamon.

Spices: Garlic, cumin, cinnamon, cloves, sesame seeds, black pepper, crushed red chile flakes, and chile peppers

Herbs and other flavorings: Parsley, mint, basil, dill, lemon, and honey

Ingredients: Tahini, olive oil, yogurt, bulgar wheat, pine nuts, almonds, barley, lamb, chickpeas, eggplant, tomatoes, and pita bread

Northern Europe

Russia, Germany, Sweden, Poland, Hungary, and The British Isles are far from the Spice Islands (see Figure 7-3). The cuisines of these countries do take advantage of spices, although not to the same degree as the cuisines of those countries that are closer to the spice route. Savory fare is mildly spiced; baked goods and warm beverages are also lightly seasoned.

Figure 7-3:
Northern
Europe.

Spices: Caraway seeds, dill seeds, nutmeg, cardamom, cinnamon, ginger, paprika, white pepper, black pepper, juniper berries, celery seed

Herbs and other flavorings: Parsley, marjoram, chervil, dill, vinegar, prepared mustard

Ingredients: Cream, butter, sour cream, cabbage, potatoes, strongly flavored cheeses such as cheddar and blue, beets, kielbasa, sausage, sauerkraut, beer

Fresh chervil is a delicate herb with a hint of anise flavor. It is not always available in produce departments and green grocers, but you can grow your own. Because dried chervil has very little flavor, use its relative, fresh parsley, as a substitute.

Africa

Although many people don't immediately associate the African continent with spices, Africa's cooking has been affected by the influences of trade, colonization, and immigration that have brought spices to other lands. Although African cooks make use of popular local ingredients, the culinary flavors and traditions of the Mediterranean, India, Malaysia, and Indonesia have left their impact on the cooking of this continent. From the northern coastal African countries of Morocco and Tunisia, to the West African coast, to the tip of

South Africa's Cape, you'll find highly spiced, rustic fare that's scented with garlic, ginger, chiles, and spice blends (see Figure 7-4). Uniquely African dishes can range from fiery hot to fragrantly spiced.

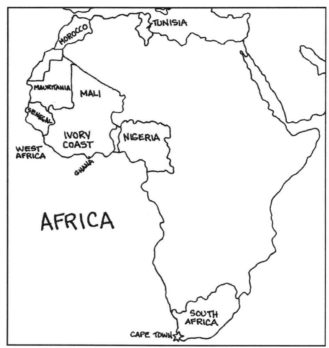

Figure 7-4: Key locales for great African cuisine.

North Africa: Morocco and Tunisia:

The cuisines of Morocco and Tunisia, two of the northernmost countries in Africa, present a mélange of African and Mediterranean influences. Their cooking is highly aromatic and flavorful and liberally seasoned with spices that are often associated with both the Middle East and with other Mediterranean countries.

Spices: Garlic, ginger, cumin, coriander, cardamom, cinnamon, cloves, crushed red chile flakes, chile peppers, cayenne, turmeric, sesame seeds, and saffron

Herbs and other flavoring agents: Mint, cilantro, parsley, honey, orange zest, lemon, and harissa

Ingredients: Dried fruits such as raisins and apricots, almonds, lentils, chickpeas, couscous, tomatoes, carrots, and lamb

Hot as harissa

Made from chile peppers and spices, harissa is a fiery-hot condiment used to accent Moroccan and Tunisian dishes. It's available, canned or jarred, in ethnic and specialty stores. You can also make your own — see Chapter 5.

West Africa

Cookery from West African countries, such as Ghana, Mali, and the Ivory Coast, is characterized by the use of garlic and the liberal use of chile peppers. Peanuts, coconut, and tomato are often combined in sauces that are spiked with chiles. The region's culinary traditions and its ingredients, such as yams, black-eyed beans, and bitter greens, moved across the Atlantic with slaves to the Americas.

Spices: Allspice, garlic, chile peppers, crushed red pepper flakes, ginger, black pepper

Herbs and other flavorings: Peanut oil, palm oil, cilantro, parsley

Ingredients: Tomatoes, okra, eggplant, peanuts, collards, corn, pumpkin, dried beans, coconut milk, coconut, yams, rice, mango, papaya, banana

South Africa

This nation's varied foods reflect the diversity of its people. Cape Town itself was a post on the East Indies spice route, and the Indonesian and Malaysian use of spices has been preserved through Cape Town's Cape Malay community. The Cape Malays are descendants of Malaysians brought by spice traders to the Cape of Good Hope in the seventeenth and eighteenth centuries. The country's large Indian population has also been a significant culinary influence.

Spices: Garlic, ginger, allspice, cinnamon, cloves, cardamom, coriander, curry powder, curry pastes, cumin, mace, nutmeg, turmeric, fennel seed, garam masala, white pepper, black pepper, chile peppers, and crushed red chile flakes

Herbs and other flavoring agents: Bay leaf, cilantro, parsley, mint, vinegar, lemon juice, and tangerine zest

Ingredients: Hominy, white cornmeal, corn, butternut, tomatoes, Swiss chard, coconut, coconut milk, mangoes, papayas, avocados, granadillas (passion fruit), queen pineapples, lamb, boerewors sausage, prawns, rock lobsters

Unsweetened coconut milk is found in Asian and Caribbean groceries and in the special-foods section of most supermarkets.

Asia

Without a doubt, Asia, shown in Figure 7-5, is the land of spices. It is to this region that early traders traveled in search of these precious commodities. It is here that you find the Spice Islands, including Java and the Malaysian archipelago, as well as Indonesia, Thailand, India, China, and Japan. The continent's cooking, though quite varied, is highlighted by spices — from fresh ginger and lemon grass to cinnamon, turmeric, fennel seed, cloves, coriander, and cumin. In each country, and within regions of each country, the combination of spices and other seasonings vary. Thai cooks add fish sauce and curry paste to their dishes; Chinese and Japanese cooks rely heavily on soy sauce, ginger, and garlic for flavor; Indians create a seemingly unending array of spice blends that are known as *masalas*. No matter what combination of flavors is used, Asian cooks accent their country's native bounty with spices.

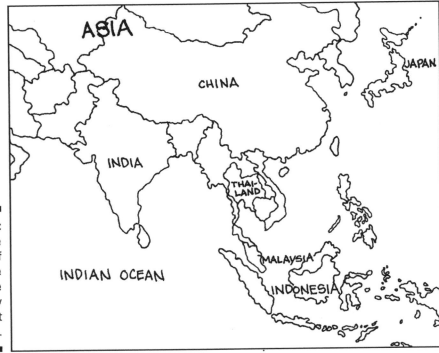

Figure 7-5:
The countries of Asia have given the world many great cuisines.

India

Indian cookery, whether from the north or south, is characterized by the liberal use of spices. Not all the dishes are fiery, but all are generously spiced. Dishes can contain up to fourteen different spices that create an elaborate layering of flavor and fragrance. Most Indian cooks have mastered the art of spicing and create their own *masalas* (spice mixes) and don't rely on commercial blends or curry powder.

Spices: Garlic, ginger, garam masala, cinnamon, allspice, cloves, coriander, cumin, curry powder, turmeric, saffron, fenugreek, fennel seed, black peppercorns, mustard seeds, cayenne, chile peppers

Herbs and other flavoring agents: Bay leaf, cilantro, mint, lemon, tamarind

Ingredients: Basmati rice, lentils, split peas, kidney beans, yogurt, coconut milk, coconut, tomato, onion, mango, cucumber

Thailand

Thai cooking is fragrantly scented with aromatic spices and herbs. It is often hot and spicy due to the liberal use of chile peppers, chile pastes, and curry pastes.

Spices: Lemon grass, ginger, chile peppers, chile paste, red or green curry paste, galangal

Herbs and other flavoring agents: Makrud lime leaves or Kaffir lime leaves, fish sauce (nam pla), soy sauce, holy or Thai basil, basil, mint, cilantro, and vinegar

Ingredients: Peanuts, peanut butter, coconut milk, rice, scallions, cucumber, carrots, and green beans

Indonesia and Malaysia

The deliciously complex cuisine of what were once considered the Spice Islands is always fragrantly spiced and is sometimes hot. It's characterized by the layering of flavors from native spices and flavoring agents.

Spices: Ginger, garlic, chile peppers, cardamom, cloves, curry powder, curry pastes, cinnamon, cumin, turmeric, mace, nutmeg, white pepper, black pepper, crushed red chile flakes

Herbs and other flavoring agents: Bay leaf, mint, cilantro, soy sauce, kecap manis, sambal ulek (chile paste), vinegar, and lemon and lime juice

Ingredients: Rice, coconut, coconut milk, papaya, banana, pineapple, mango, peanuts, peanut butter, brown sugar

Kecap manis is Indonesia's sweetened soy sauce and is only found in specialty groceries. To make a mock version, add 1 tablespoon of brown sugar to ½ cup of soy sauce.

China

Chinese cookery varies from province to province. The most popular styles in the United States are the fiery Szechuan, spicy Hunan, and mild Cantonese. Garlic, ginger, and soy sauce are used throughout the land. (See *Chinese Cooking For Dummies* for more information on the ins and outs of Chinese cookery, including the details on regional differences.)

Spices: Garlic, ginger, five-spice powder, dried chile peppers, crushed red pepper flakes, sesame seeds, star anise, and Szechuan pepper

Herbs and other flavoring agents: Orange zest, soy sauce, Chinese or toasted sesame oil, hot chile oil, sherry, bean pastes, oyster sauce, hoisin sauce, Chinese chile paste

Ingredients: Rice, rice noodles, cellophane noodles, bean sprouts, snow peas, dried cloud or wood ear mushrooms, oyster mushrooms, bok choy (Chinese cabbage), scallions, water chestnuts, and tofu

Japan

Japanese cooking offers simple blends of ingredients that produce a complex flavor. Often elegantly presented, Japanese food can feature intricately carved vegetables, such as radishes, cucumbers, and carrots, as a garnish.

Spices: Ginger, garlic, wasabi, and sesame

Other flavoring agents: Dashi (fish broth), pickled ginger, soy sauce, sherry, mirin and sake rice wines, vinegar, ponzu, and sesame oil

Ingredients: Rice, udon noodles, cellophane noodles, soba noodles, nori (dried seaweed, used most often in the United States for wrapping sushi), kombi (another type of seaweed), dried fish, daikon, radishes, carrots, scallions, Japanese eggplant, dried and fresh mushrooms, tofu, and miso

Regional Recipe Guide

Due to the transference of cultural influences from one region to another, similar flavors are found in more than one nation. For example, ginger and curry are found in the Caribbean as well as in India, South Africa, and Southeast Asia. Some recipes may be featured under the heading of more than one area and highlight the blending of culture influences caused by the travels of our ancestors. For example, Tomato Salsa (from Mexico) is eaten in various countries, although each region might have a slight variation and call it by another name, such as tomato sambal or tomato chutney. A salsa that started in Mexico can be used as a side dish to Indian as well as Indonesian dishes. The basic recipe in the book (Chapter 10) can be used as a salsa, a sambal, or a chutney!

Feel free to use regional side dishes, such as Spicy Green Beans (Chapter 16) or Curried Barley Pilaf (Chapter 17) with plain main courses. There are recipes in the book that don't have a specific country of origin. Some are cross-cultural or multinational; some just simple and straightforward, such as Grilled Lime-Cumin Chicken Cutlets (Chapter 13) or Fragrantly Spiced Maple Spareribs (Chapter 14).

The Americas

- ✔ **United States:** Southern Barbecue Rub (Chapter 9), Cajun Spice Rub (Chapter 9), Tangy Tomato Barbecue Sauce (Chapter 10), Zesty Cheddar Spread (Chapter 12), Down-Home Barbecued Chicken (Chapter 13), Beef or Pork Stew with Juniper and Chile Powder (Chapter 14), Cinnamon Coffee Cake (Chapter 18), Old-Fashioned Gingerbread (Chapter 18), and New Orleans Café Brulot (Chapter 19)

- ✔ **Southwestern and Tex-Mex:** South of the Border Marinade (Chapter 10), Tomato Salsa (Chapter 11), Black Bean Dip (Chapter 12), Southwestern Flank Steak (Chapter 14), Beef and Bean Chili (Chapter 14), Tex-Mex Meatloaf (Chapter 14), Vegetable Bean Chili (Chapter 16), and Cumin-Chile Corn Muffins (Chapter 18)

- ✔ **Mexico:** Chile Adobo Sauce (Chapter 10), Tomato Salsa (Chapter 11), Papaya, Mango, or Pineapple Salsa (Chapter 11), Mexican Tomato Soup (Chapter 12), Beef or Pork Adobo (Chapter 14), Fish Veracruz (Chapter 15), and Mexican Hot Chocolate (Chapter 19)

- ✔ **Caribbean:** Caribbean Spice Rub (Chapter 9), Jamaican Spice Rub (Chapter 9), Jamaican Jerk Sauce (Chapter 10), Mojo Sauce (Chapter 10), Papaya, Mango, and Pineapple Salsa (Chapter 11), Jerk Chicken (Chapter 13), Grilled Lime-Cumin Chicken Cutlets (Chapter 13), Shrimp Curry (Chapter 15)

- **South America:** Gingered Roast Chicken (Chapter 13), Brazilian Picadillo (Chapter 14), Hot and Spicy Roasted Ribs (Chapter 14), and Roasted Potatoes with Garlic and Cumin (Chapter 17)

Asia

- **Japan:** Teriyaki Sauce (Chapter 10), Yakitori (Chapter 13), and Tuna or Salmon Teriyaki (Chapter 15)

- **China:** Chinese Marinade (Chapter 10), Chinese-Spiced Baked Chicken (Chapter 13), Garlicky Broccoli Stir-Fry (Chapter 16), and Cold Spiced Noodles with Sesame Oil and Vegetables (Chapter 17)

- **India:** Indian Curry Powder (Chapter 9), Tomato Raita (Chapter 11), Indian Spiced Lentil Soup (Chapter 12), Indian Chicken Curry (Chapter 13), Tandoori Chicken Cutlets (Chapter 13), Indian Rogan Josh (Chapter 14), Masala Fish (Chapter 15), Shrimp Curry (Chapter 15), Spicy Green Beans (Chapter 16), and Greens with Mustard Seeds, Onions, and Tomatoes (Chapter 16)

- **Southeast Asia (Thailand, Indonesia, and Malaysia):** Thai Red or Green Curry Paste (Chapter 9), Southeast Asian Peanut Sauce (Chapter 10), Pickled Cucumber and Carrot Salad (Chapter 11), Mango, and Pineapple Salsa (Chapter 11), Spiced Carrot and Pineapple Sambal (Chapter 11), Southeast Asian Green Bean Sambal (Chapter 11), Indonesian Gado Gado (Chapter 11), Thai Chicken Curry (Chapter 13), Southeast Asian Chicken Saté (Chapter 13), Grilled Lime-Cumin Chicken Cutlets (Chapter 13), Indonesian Beef Saté (Chapter 14), Spice Islands Lamb Stew (Chapter 14), Southeast Asian Fried Flounder or Sole (Chapter 15), and Indonesian Peanut Noodles with Vegetables (Chapter 17)

Mediterranean

- **Mediterranean Europe and the Middle East:** Mediterranean Spiced Black Olives (Chapter 12), Hummus (Chapter 12), Tangy Yogurt Dip (Chapter 12), Roasted Eggplant Paté (Chapter 12), Mediterranean Spiced Chicken with Olives (Chapter 13), Spiced Roasted Vegetables (Chapter 16)

- **France:** Steak au Poivre (Chapter 14), Fragrantly Spiced Spinach (Chapter 16), Spiced Lemony Lentils (Chapter 16), Braised Cumin-Coriander Carrots (Chapter 16), Spiced Couscous with Currants (Chapter 17)

- **Italy:** Spiced Pepperonata (Chapter 12), Roasted Eggplant Paté (Chapter 12), Pasta Puttanesca (Chapter 17), Roasted Potatoes with Garlic and Cumin (Chapter 17), and Nut Biscotti with Anise (Chapter 18)

Northern Europe

- Hungarian Veal Goulash with Mushrooms (Chapter 14), Braised Red Cabbage with Caraway, Apples, and Bacon (Chapter 16), and Caraway, Cheese, and Bacon Beer Bread (Chapter 18)

Africa

- **West Africa:** Shrimp in West African Peanut Sauce (Chapter 15)

- **South Africa:** Pickled Cucumber and Carrot Salad (Chapter 11), Spiced Carrot and Pineapple Sambal (Chapter 11), Cape Malay Bobotie (Chapter 14), Curried Lamb Kebabs (Chapter 14), and Spiced Rice with Almonds (Chapter 17)

- **North Africa, Morocco and Tunisia:** Moroccan Spice Mix (Chapter 9), Mediterranean Spiced Black Olives (Chapter 12), Roasted Moroccan Monkfish (Chapter 15), Spiced Lemony Lentils (Chapter 16), and Spiced Couscous with Currants (Chapter 17)

Multi-National and General

- Peppery Marinade (Chapter 10), Spiced Sherry Orange Marinade (Chapter 10), Plum Salsa (Chapter 11), Savory Spiced Poaching Liquid (Chapter 10), Spiced Fruit Salad (Chapter 11), Curried Nuts (Chapter 12), Sunset Butternut Soup (Chapter 12), Gingered Roast Chicken (Chapter 13), Grilled Lime-Cumin Chicken Cutlets (Chapter 13), Coriander-Spiced Burgers (Chapter 14), Spicy Roast Pork (Chapter 14), Fragrantly Spiced Maple Spareribs (Chapter 14), Spicy Crab Cakes with Cilantro Sauce (Chapter 15), Gingered Zucchini or Summer Squash (Chapter 16), Mashed Vanilla-Scented Sweet Potatoes (Chapter 17), Curried Barley Pilaf (Chapter 17), Spiced Chocolate Loaf (Chapter 18), Spiced Apple Cake (Chapter 18), Spiced Poached Fruit (Chapter 18), Chocolate Cinnamon Sauce (Chapter 18), Vanilla Sauce (Chapter 18), Mulled Red Wine (Chapter 19), Hot Spiced Apple Cider (Chapter 19), Spiced Ice Tea (Chapter 19), and Bloody Mary Mix (Chapter 19)

Chapter 8

Spicy Game Plans

*B*efore you start cooking, there are a few things you can do to make your experience more enjoyable. You need to devise a menu, plan your shopping list, and think about how you will actually prepare the recipes.

Planning a Menu

Whether you're going to prepare an informal or an elegant meal for family or friends, you need to create a menu that not only suits everyone's taste but also accommodates your budget, your time constraints, and your desire to spend more (or less) time with guests. Menu planning is quite easy. Here are a few tips to help you through the process:

✔ Keep the menu simple.

✔ Feature one dish as a centerpiece and serve other dishes that are complementary.

✔ Pay attention to cultural origins and combinations and plan the menu around a central theme.

✔ Serve a simple side dish with a more complicated main dish or a plain entree with more adventurous side dishes.

✔ Serve a variety of food — a protein, a starch, and vegetables — so that the meal is nutritionally balanced.

✔ Pick foods as if you're picking colors off an artist's palate. Serve a variety of colors so that the meal is visually appealing. Stay away from a combination like chicken, rice, and cauliflower. It may taste good, but all the items are white.

> ✔ Make sure that the flavors are well-balanced, with complementary, yet contrasting, tastes and textures.
>
> ✔ Consider the practical aspects of food preparation — the time it will take you to make different dishes. Look for dishes that can be made ahead or are quick last-minute dishes.

Be your own guinea pig. If you want to make a new recipe, give the recipe a trial run with family, roommates, or close friends before serving it to guests.

Menu Sampler

There are numerous combinations of dishes that will form a meal, but to get you started, here are a few suggestions for regional and international menus, complete with main and complementary side dishes. To help you explore other possibilities, refer to the Regional Recipe Guide in Chapter 7 for a comprehensive listing of the recipes in this book by geographical area.

American: Down-Home Barbecued Chicken (Chapter 13); corn on the cob; Pickled Cucumber and Carrot Salad (Chapter 11);Old-Fashioned Gingerbread (Chapter 18)

Tex-Mex: Tortilla chips and Tomato Salsa (Chapter 11); Beef and Bean Chili (Chapter 14); Cumin-Chile Corn Muffins (Chapter 18)

Cajun: Grilled steak, chicken, or fish rubbed with Cajun Spice Rub (Chapter 9); french fries; salad or cole slaw; bread pudding served with Vanilla Sauce (Chapter 18)

Southwestern: Southwestern Flank Steak (Chapter 14); Roasted Potatoes with Garlic and Cumin (Chapter 17); salad with avocados; ice cream with Chocolate Cinnamon Sauce (Chapter 18)

Mexico: Beef Adobo (Chapter 14) or Shrimp in Chile Adobo Sauce (Chapter 15); tortillas or rice; Spiced Chocolate Loaf (Chapter 18) or Mexican Hot Chocolate (Chapter 19)

Brazil: Brazilian Picadillo (Chapter 14); rice; Spiced Fruit Salad (Chapter 11)

Chile: Gingered Roast Chicken (Chapter 13) or Hot and Spicy Roasted Ribs (Chapter 14); corn on the cob; salad; Mashed Vanilla-Scented Sweet Potatoes (Chapter 17)

Jamaica: Jerk Chicken (Chapter 13); rice or Curried Barley Pilaf (Chapter 17); any fruit salsa from Chapter 11; Gingered Tomato Salad (Chapter 11)

Caribbean: Shrimp Curry (Chapter 15); rice; Mango, Papaya, or Pineapple Salsa or Tomato Salsa (Chapter 11)

India: Tandoori Chicken Cutlets (Chapter 13); Spiced Rice with Almonds (Chapter 17); Greens with Mustard Seeds, Onions, and Tomatoes (Chapter 16) or Indian Rogan Josh (Chapter 14); rice; Tomato Raita (Chapter 11); chutney.

China: Cold Spiced Noodles with Sesame Oil and Vegetables (Chapter 17)

Japan: Yakitori (Chapter 13) or Tuna or Salmon Teriyaki (Chapter 15); rice; Garlicky Broccoli Stir-Fry (Chapter 16)

Southeast Asia: Southeast Asian Chicken Saté (Chapter 13) or Indonesian Beef Saté (Chapter 14); rice; Southeast Asian Peanut Sauce (Chapter 10); Pickled Cucumber and Carrot Salad (Chapter 11)

Indonesia: Indonesian Gado Gado (Chapter 11); Grilled Lime-Cumin Chicken Cutlets (Chapter 13) or Southeast Asian Fried Flounder or Sole (Chapter 15); any salsa from Chapter 11; any sambal from Chapter 11; rice

Malaysia: Spice Islands Lamb Stew (Chapter 14); rice; Plum Salsa (Chapter 11) or chutney

Thailand: Thai Chicken Curry (Chapter 13); rice; Southeast Asian Green Bean Sambal (Chapter 11) or Spicy Green Beans (Chapter 16)

Mediterranean: Hummus (Chapter 12) with pita bread; Mediterranean-Spiced Chicken with Olives (Chapter 13); roasted or mashed potatoes; Braised Cumin-Coriander Carrots (Chapter 16)

Italy: Pasta Puttanesca (Chapter 17); green salad with salad dressing made with garlic-spiced oil or vinegar (Chapter 5); cappuccino or espresso; Nut Biscotti with Anise (Chapter 18)

France: Steak au Poivre (Chapter 14); french fries; Fragrantly Spiced Spinach (Chapter 16); Spiced Poached Fruit (Chapter 18)

Hungary: Hungarian Veal Goulash with Mushrooms (Chapter 14); noodles; cooked beets or string beans

Germany: Sausage or pork chops; mashed or baked potatoes; Braised Red Cabbage with Caraway, Apples, and Bacon (Chapter 16)

North Africa: Sunset Butternut Soup (Chapter 12); Roasted Moroccan Monkfish (Chapter 15); Spiced Couscous with Currants (Chapter 17); Gingered Zucchini or Summer Squash (Chapter 16)

South Africa: Curried Lamb Kebabs (Chapter 14) or Cape Malay Bobotie (Chapter 14); Spiced Rice with Almonds (Chapter 17); Spiced Carrot and Pineapple Sambal (Chapter 11)

West Africa: Shrimp in West African Peanut Sauce (Chapter 15); rice; cooked spinach; chopped or sliced tomatoes and avocados

Beat the Heat

Perhaps you'd like to make a hot and spicy meal. Maybe you're thinking of Cajun or creole dishes, spiced barbecued or jerked foods, Caribbean, curries, Tex-Mex chilis, Indian, Thai, Indonesian or Malaysian foods. You'll need to make sure that your menu includes side dishes or condiments that cool the taste buds. Recipes that feature chiles or one of their by-products need accompaniments that balance and offset the heat.

Raw chopped cucumber, tomato, avocado, papaya and mango or grated carrot salads are wonderfully refreshing and offset the heat of spicy foods. Yogurt-based raita and fruit chutneys are popular with Indian dishes. Grated carrot and chopped cucumber salads with a vinegary dressing and mango and papaya salads or *sambals* (similar to salsas) are commonly served throughout Southeast Asia, Indonesia, Malaysia, and South Africa. Avocado, tomato, papaya, and mango salads and salsas are found in the Caribbean, Mexico, South America, and in the United States.

Simply prepared grains are also fabulous heat-beating dishes. Rice is often served alongside fiery and spicy foods. Cooks in Szechuan China, Southeast Asia, Indonesia, India, Malaysia, South Africa, Mexico, South America, and the Caribbean use rice to offset heat. In Morocco, couscous is the grain of choice. Barley, rice, and flatbreads such as pita are popular in the Middle East.

Basmati, used extensively in India and the Middle East, is a long-grain rice with a mildly nutty flavor and aroma. Basmati and its subtler American cousin, Texmati rice, are available in most supermarkets.

Cooking Strategies

After you've planned your menu, the next step is to make a shopping list. Check what staples you have on hand. (You may not need to buy, say, nutmeg or canned tomatoes.) Write your list in categories — spices, condiments, produce, meat, and so on so that you don't have to backtrack when going down supermarket aisles.

Organize yourself before you start cooking. Begin preparing the meal by working on the recipe that will take you the longest. Read the recipe through, making note of any kitchen equipment and tools you'll need. Take the appropriate utensils out of the cupboard and set them aside so that you don't have to search for them when you're actually cooking.

Next, grind any spices that you'll need and measure them and set them aside. Prepare all the vegetables that you'll need. That means peeling carrots, chopping onions, and the like. Then move onto meat, poultry, or seafood. When you have everything assembled (both the right equipment and the right ingredients), familiarize yourself with the recipe once again. Then get cooking!

Never measure spices, spicy condiments, or herbs over a pot or mixing bowl. You may end up with too much in your dish. Measure them and set them aside in a small dish or on a piece of plastic wrap or waxed paper. Add the spices to the dish at the time called for in the recipe.

Part III
On the Starting Line

The 5th Wave By Rich Tennant

"I'm not sure what flavor you're tasting. I didn't use any spice rubs on the meat, however I dropped it several times on the way to the grill."

In this part . . .

1 present recipes for spice blends and rubs, marinades and sauces, salads, and light fare such as starters, soups, and snacks. Many of the rubs, marinades, and sauces are used in recipes that come later in the book.

Chapter 9

Basic Rubs and Spice Mixes

In This Chapter

▶ Making rubs for meat, poultry, and fish
▶ Applying rubs

Spice *rubs* and *blends* are mixtures of spices that are used to flavor food. Making your own spice rubs and blends is easy, and the results are fresher and tastier than anything you can buy in a store. Spice *pastes,* such as the Thai Red or Green Curry Paste in this chapter, are a blend of spices to which fresh ingredients, such as garlic or ginger, or a little liquid is added.

Use the rubs to season sautéed meat, poultry, and fish as well as for barbecues and roasts. The rubs will form a tasty crust on the outside and flavor the food. You can rub the spice mixture onto the food or place the rub in a shallow bowl and dip the food directly in the rub. Alternatively, you can brush the item with a little olive oil, vegetable oil, or lemon juice before coating it with the spice rub. You can turn a rub into a paste by adding a little olive oil, vegetable oil, lemon juice, or water to the rub. No matter which method you use, apply the rub in an even layer and remember to wash your hands. You can put the rub on the food up to 24 hours before you intend to cook it. Discard any leftover rub that has come into contact with raw meat, poultry, or fish.

Spice blends, such as curry powder, curry paste, and pumpkin pie spice mix, should be used as ingredients as directed in the recipes in later chapters

The recipes in this section are sure to please. Of course, you can use the rubs and blends for your own enjoyment, but they also make an unusual and tasty gift. All of the recipes in this section can be doubled, tripled, or quadrupled as you wish.

Cajun Spice Rub

American in origin, this hot and spicy mix is superb for steak, fish, pork, or chicken.

Yield: *About ¼ cup*

Preparation time: *10 minutes*

Spice meter: *Hot and spicy*

2 teaspoons paprika

2 teaspoons freshly ground black pepper

2 teaspoons white pepper

2 teaspoons salt

1½ teaspoons dry English mustard

1½ teaspoons garlic powder

1 teaspoon onion powder

½ teaspoon dried thyme leaves

½ teaspoon dried oregano

½ to ¾ teaspoon cayenne, or to taste

¼ teaspoon ground sage (optional)

Combine all the ingredients in a bowl. Stir to mix evenly. Store in a covered container for up to 6 months.

Remember: *Dry English mustard is a hot and spicy powder. It's often added to recipes along with other spices. Mixed with a little water, it can be turned into a potent condiment and used like prepared English Mustard or other prepared mustard.*

Cook's Fact: *Cajun food, made world famous by Chef Paul Prudhomme, hails from New Orleans, Louisiana. Characterized by the use of spice and herb blends, this country-style cookery features such dishes as jambalaya, gumbo, and the Cajun classics, blackened steak, chicken, and fish.*

Per serving: Calories 23 (From Fat 6); Fat 1g (Saturated 0g); Cholesterol 0mg; Sodium 1164mg; Carbohydrate 4g (Dietary Fiber 1g); Protein 1g. (Sage not included.)

Caribbean Spice Rub

Hot and sweet, this zesty Caribbean rub gets its heat from curry powder and cayenne. Its sweetness comes from a touch of sugar and some spices, such as ginger, cinnamon, and nutmeg, that are often found in desserts. Jamaica's signature spice, allspice, is also included. Use this delicious rub for broiled, grilled, roasted, or sautéed chicken, pork, lamb, or fish.

Yield: *About ½ cup*

Preparation time: *10 minutes*

Spice meter: *Hot and spicy*

2 tablespoons homemade or good-quality curry powder

1 tablespoon paprika

1 tablespoon ground allspice

1 tablespoon salt

1 tablespoon freshly ground black pepper

1 tablespoon ground ginger

1 tablespoon ground cumin

1 tablespoon sugar

2 to 3 teaspoons cayenne

1½ teaspoons ground cinnamon

1 teaspoon freshly grated or ground nutmeg

Combine all the ingredients in a bowl. Stir to mix evenly. Store in a covered container for up to 6 months.

Cook's Fact: *Flavorfully spiced dishes and curried foods are popular throughout the West Indies.*

Per serving: *Calories 27 (From Fat 7); Fat 1g (Saturated 0g); Cholesterol 0mg; Sodium 876mg; Carbohydrate 6g (Dietary Fiber 2g); Protein 1g.*

Pumpkin Pie Spice Mix

Pumpkin pie mix is an American invention. It's available commercially, but you can make your own. The mix can be used in baked goods, such as pumpkin pie, pumpkin bread, apple pies, streusel topping for fruit crumbles, breakfast muffins, spice cakes, and cookies. It can also be used in savory dishes, such as mashed or glazed sweet potatoes, cubed or mashed butternut squash, or butternut squash soup.

Yield: *About ⅓ cup*

Preparation time: *5 minutes*

Spice meter: *Mildly to moderately spiced*

2 tablespoons ground cinnamon	*1 tablespoon ground ginger*
1 tablespoon plus 1 teaspoon freshly grated or ground nutmeg	*1½ teaspoons ground allspice or ground cloves or a combination of both*

Combine all the ingredients in a bowl. Stir to mix evenly. Store in a covered container for up to 6 months.

Tip: *Make this recipe before the holidays so that you have it on hand for Thanksgiving.*

Per serving: *Calories 22 (From Fat 8); Fat 1g (Saturated 1g); Cholesterol 0mg; Sodium 2mg; Carbohydrate 4g (Dietary Fiber 2g); Protein 0g.*

Basic Indian Curry Powder

You can use this basic curry *masala*, the Indian word for a spice mixture, instead of adding individual dried spices to most Indian and Caribbean curries. You can also use it whenever a recipe calls for curry powder.

Yield: *About ½ cup*

Preparation time: *15 minutes*

Spice meter: *Hot and spicy*

4 tablespoons whole coriander

2 tablespoons cumin seeds

1½ teaspoons black peppercorns

1 teaspoon fenugreek seeds

1 teaspoon fennel seeds

1 teaspoon black mustard seeds

4 to 8 dried, small, thin, red chile peppers, broken in small pieces or 1 to 2½ teaspoons crushed red chile flakes

½ cinnamon stick, broken in half

1½ to 2 tablespoons turmeric

1 teaspoon ground ginger

1 Combine the chile peppers or chile flakes, cinnamon, coriander, cumin, peppercorns, fenugreek seeds, fennel seeds, mustard seeds, chile peppers, and cinnamon stick in a medium-sized skillet, preferably a nonstick one. Place the skillet over medium-low heat and cook, stirring only once or twice, until the spices become quite fragrant and the spices darken slightly, about 3 to 4 minutes.

2 Place the toasted spices in a spice mill and grind into a fine powder, in batches if necessary.

3 Transfer the spice mixture into a bowl. Add the turmeric and ginger and stir to blend evenly. Store in a covered container for up to 6 months.

Cook's Fact: *There are many types of masalas or curry powders: northern and southern Indian, Indonesian, Malaysian, Caribbean, East African, and South African. The composition of masalas varies from region to region; each area has its own distinctive flavor combination.*

Per serving: *Calories 25 (From Fat 10); Fat 1g (Saturated 0g); Cholesterol 0mg; Sodium 5mg; Carbohydrate 4g (Dietary Fiber 2g); Protein 1g.*

Malaysian Curry Masala

Curry blends from Malaysia, Indonesia, and South Africa's southwestern Cape are more fragrant than hot. You can make this one hotter or milder by altering the amount of dried red chile that you use. Use it in dishes from these regions, such as curries, marinades, or soups, or try it whenever curry powder is listed as an ingredient.

Yield: *About ½ cup*

Preparation time: *15 minutes*

Spice meter: *Hot and spicy*

4 tablespoons whole coriander

2 tablespoons cumin seeds

2½ teaspoons black peppercorns

6 whole cloves

6 to 8 cardamom pods, bruised

2 to 6 dried, small, thin, red chile peppers, broken in small pieces or ½ to 2 teaspoons crushed red chile flakes

½ cinnamon stick, broken in half 2½ teaspoons turmeric

2 teaspoons ground ginger (optional)

1 Combine the chile peppers or chile flakes, cinnamon, coriander, cumin, peppercorns, mustard seeds, and cloves in a medium skillet, preferably a nonstick one. Place over medium-low heat and cook, stirring only once or twice, until the spices become quite fragrant and the spices darken slightly, about 3 to 4 minutes.

2 Put the toasted spices in a spice mill. Remove the seeds from the cardamom pods and add them to the spices in thespice mill. Grind into a fine powder, in batches if necessary.

3 Transfer the spice mixture into a bowl. Add the turmeric and ginger and stir to blend evenly. Store in a covered container for up to 6 months.

Tip: *If you're out of whole cloves, you can use ¼ teaspoon ground cloves. Add the ground cloves in Step 3 with the turmeric and ginger.*

Per serving: *Calories 22 (From Fat 9); Fat 1g (Saturated 0g); Cholesterol 0mg; Sodium 5mg; Carbohydrate 4g (Dietary Fiber 2g); Protein 1g.*

Jamaican Spice Rub

Use this blend as a rub on chicken, boneless chicken breasts, pork roast, pork tenderloin, pork chops, lamb chops, leg of lamb, or steak. Broil, grill, sauté, or pan-fry the poultry or meat to desired doneness. Similar in fragrance and composition to Ethiopian berbere (pronounced barry-baray), this rub can also be added to fish and poultry dishes and stews and soups.

Yield: *About ⅓ cup*

Preparation time: *10 minutes*

Spice meter: *Hot and spicy*

1 teaspoon salt	*1 teaspoon white pepper*
2 teaspoons sugar	*2 teaspoons dried thyme leaves*
1 teaspoon ground allspice	*2 teaspoons ground cumin*
½ teaspoon freshly grated or ground nutmeg	*2 teaspoons ground coriander*
¼ teaspoon ground cinnamon	*1½ teaspoons ground ginger*
1 to 1½ teaspoons cayenne	*1½ teaspoons garlic powder*
1 teaspoon freshly ground black pepper	*¼ teaspoon mace (optional)*

Combine all the ingredients in a bowl. Stir to mix evenly. Store in a covered container for up to 6 months.

Tip: *Keep this rub on hand and you'll be prepared to make quick and easy Jamaican-style chicken or pork.*

Per serving: Calories 26 (From Fat 6); Fat 1g (Saturated 0g); Cholesterol 0mg; Sodium 468mg; Carbohydrate 5g (Dietary Fiber 2g); Protein 1g.

Moroccan Spice Mix

Use this fragrant mixture as a rub for chicken, beef, lamb, or firm white fish, such as monkfish. You can also add a teaspoon to a tablespoon to lamb, chicken, or vegetarian stew. You can also use it to spice hamburgers, meatballs, and meatloaf.

Yield: *About ⅓ cup*

Preparation time: *10 minutes*

Spice meter: *Moderately spiced*

1 tablespoon ground cinnamon	*1 teaspoon ground ginger*
1 tablespoon dried thyme leaves	*1 teaspoon ground coriander*
2 teaspoons freshly grated or ground nutmeg	*½ to ¾ teaspoon cayenne*
2 teaspoons freshly ground black pepper	*¼ teaspoon ground cloves*
2 teaspoons ground cardamom	*½ teaspoon ground mace (optional)*

Combine all the ingredients in a bowl. Stir to mix evenly. Store in a covered container for up to 6 months.

Cook's Fact: *In Moroccan marketplaces, spice vendors sell spices in large bins. Each vendor also makes his own signature blend of spices, and no two blends are exactly alike.*

Per serving: *Calories 20 (From Fat 6); Fat 1g (Saturated 0g); Cholesterol 0mg; Sodium 2mg; Carbohydrate 4g (Dietary Fiber 2g); Protein 0g.*

Southern Barbecue Rub

Use this American favorite as a rub on pork, ribs, brisket, steak, or chicken. It's a perfect combination of hot, spicy, and sweet!

Yield: *About ¾ cup*

Preparation time: *10 minutes*

Spice meter: *Hot and spicy*

⅓ cup paprika

3 tablespoons brown sugar

3 tablespoons chili powder

2 tablespoons cracked black pepper

1 tablespoon cayenne

2 teaspoons dry English mustard

1½ teaspoons salt (optional)

Combine all the ingredients. Stir to mix evenly. Store in a covered container for up to 3 months.

Variation: *If you want, use a combination of cracked black and white pepper or crack any mixed peppercorn blend.*

Per serving: *Calories 35 (From Fat 9); Fat 1g (Saturated 0g); Cholesterol 0mg; Sodium 22mg; Carbohydrate 7g (Dietary Fiber 2g); Protein 1g.*

Thai Red or Green Curry Paste

The color of the paste depends on the color of the chiles that you use. Use red chiles for a red paste, green for a green paste. Store extra paste in the refrigerator in a covered container for up to 2 weeks. You can also freeze it for 1 month. It is used in Thai curries, such as the Thai Chicken Curry (Chapter 13), and in other Thai dishes.

Yield: *About ⅓ cup, enough for 1 to 2 curry dishes*

Preparation time: *15 minutes*

Spice meter: *Hot and spicy*

2 small to medium shallots, sliced, or 3 tablespoons finely minced scallions, the white part only

5 to 6 green or red bird's eye chiles, stems removed

4 cloves garlic, thinly sliced

¼-inch piece fresh ginger, thinly sliced (optional)

2 to 3 stalks fresh lemon grass (the inner core), thinly sliced, or 1 tablespoon dried lemon grass

¼ cup warm water

Combine all the ingredients in a food processor fitted with a metal blade. Puree into a paste, adding a little more water if necessary. After you've processed the paste in the food processor, you can pound it with a mortar and pestle if you'd like a smoother finished product. Store the paste in an airtight container in the refrigerator for up to 2 weeks or freeze for up to 1 month.

Tip: *In a pinch, you may substitute serrano chiles if you can't find bird's eye chiles, sometimes referred to as Thai chiles.*

Per serving: Calories 29 (From Fat 1); Fat 0g (Saturated 0g); Cholesterol 0mg; Sodium 4mg; Carbohydrate 7g (Dietary Fiber 1g); Protein 1g.

Chapter 10

Marinades and Sauces

A marinade is a seasoned liquid. Food placed into a marinade absorbs the taste of the marinade. Marinades boost the flavor of poultry, meat, and seafood. If you've never used a marinade, you'll be pleasantly surprised how doing so can enhance the taste and improve the texture of food. The acidic ingredients, such as lemon juice, buttermilk, vinegar, and wine, that are used in marinades tenderize meat and make it more succulent. Because marinades break protein, more delicate foods such as seafood and skinless poultry are best without a long marinating time — at most 1 hour, but 30 minutes or less is more like it. Meat and poultry with skin can stand up to marinades and benefit from longer marinating times: a minimum of 1 to 2 hours, and as long as 24 hours.

It's very important to discard already used marinades and not to serve them alongside cooked food; otherwise, the bacteria from the raw food can be transferred. It you want to have a little extra to serve alongside, take a bit out and keep it aside before you put the raw ingredients in the marinade.

Sauces can be used as condiments served alongside food to complement the flavor. Some sauces can also be used as marinades or as bastes, which are marinades that are brushed on towards the end of the cooking time. Basting helps to keep the food moist and more tender, but you need to take care that you don't baste too often or the outside might not be as crispy as you want. If you baste grilled food too early in the cooking process, the baste can burn.

Saucing and Marinating Tips

You can get the most out of your sauces and marinades by following a few simple guidelines:

- Marinate food in a non-reactive dish, such as one made from glass, stainless steel, or plastic, to ensure that the acid in the marinade doesn't cause a reaction with the container.

- Cover the container and marinate the food in the refrigerator, not at room temperature.

- Marinate skinless poultry for 15 minutes to 1 hour or as directed in a recipe. Most recipes call for 30 minutes.

- Marinate fish filets and shellfish for 15 to 60 minutes or as directed in the recipe. Most recipes call for 30 minutes.

- Marinate whole meat and poultry with the skin on for up to 24 hours. The minimum marinating time is approximately 1 hour, but flavor intensifies the longer the marinating time. Thick steaks and roasts may benefit if you poke the meat with a kitchen fork to make a few holes, but don't overdo it. Cubed meat can marinated for 2 to 3 hours.

- Turn the food over occasionally so that it marinates evenly on both sides. If you marinate a short time, one or two turns will be enough, but if you marinate for a long time, turn every few hours.

- Make sauces ahead and keep them in covered containers in the refrigerator. Don't freeze marinades or sauces.

- Never reuse marinades that have had raw meat, poultry, or seafood in them. Discard the marinade immediately to prevent contamination. The only exception is if the food has been baked in the marinade, in which case you can use any marinade as a sauce.

- Set aside some of the marinades and basting sauces to use as condiments if you want a little extra on the side, or make a double batch.

Teriyaki Sauce

This classic Japanese marinade can be used for steaks, pork chops, pork tenderloin, and chicken cutlets, as well as for tuna or salmon steaks. It will keep for 2 to 4 weeks in the refrigerator. The recipe can be halved or doubled. See the recipes for Yakitori (Chapter 13) and Tuna or Salmon Teriyaki (Chapter 15).

Yield: *About 1 cup*

Preparation time: *10 minutes*

Cooking time: *5 minutes*

Spice meter: *Mildly spiced*

⅔ cup soy sauce

⅓ cup mirin or dry sherry

2 tablespoons sake or water

3 tablespoons sugar or honey

2 plump cloves garlic, pressed or minced

1-inch piece fresh ginger, minced

2 teaspoons Chinese sesame oil (optional)

1 Combine all the ingredients in a saucepan over medium-low heat. Simmer, stirring once or twice, until the sugar is dissolved, about 3 to 5 minutes. Do not boil.

2 Cool completely before using as a marinade. Store the sauce in a covered container in the refrigerator until you're ready to use it.

3 To use, pour the marinade over the meat, poultry, or seafood and turn the food to coat it. Marinate in the refrigerator for a minimum of 20 minutes or up to 1 hour, turning occasionally. Broil or grill the food until it's cooked as you prefer.

Tip: *Sake is Japanese rice wine. Mirin is sweetened Japanese rice wine. Both are sold in Asian markets. Sake is also sold in wine and spirit shops.*

Tip: *You can substitute ginger liqueur for the sake or water in the recipe, but then omit the ginger that this recipe calls for.*

Per serving: *Calories 19 (From Fat 0); Fat 0g (Saturated 0g); Cholesterol 0mg; Sodium 689mg; Carbohydrate 4g (Dietary Fiber 0g); Protein 1g.*

Peppery Marinade

This simple marinade is good for filets of mild fish, such as flounder, trout, or weakfish, as well as for chicken cutlets or shrimp.

Yield: *1 cup*

Preparation time: *10 minutes*

Spice meter: *Mildly to moderately spiced*

1 cup buttermilk or plain yogurt
¾ teaspoon cracked black peppercorns
¾ teaspoon cracked white peppercorns

¼ teaspoon cayenne
¼ teaspoon dried thyme leaves
Pinch of salt

1 Combine all the ingredients in a small bowl. Stir to blend evenly.

2 To use, pour the marinade over the chicken or seafood and turn the item to coat it. Marinate in the refrigerator, turning occasionally, for a minimum of 40 minutes or overnight. Broil, grill, or bake fish or chicken; broil, grill, or sauté shrimp.

Variation: *Instead of black and white peppercorns, use 1½ teaspoons cracked mixed peppercorns. Cracked peppercorns are just that — peppercorns that have been cracked, but not ground.*

Per serving: *Calories 7 (From Fat 1); Fat 0g (Saturated 0g); Cholesterol 1mg; Sodium 25mg; Carbohydrate 1g (Dietary Fiber 0g); Protein 1g.*

Mojo Sauce

This versatile, garlicky sauce is a staple of Cuban cuisine. When cooking the garlic, keep the heat very low so that the garlic doesn't burn. The garlic takes a bit of time to cook, but giving the garlic time makes it sweeter. You can halve or double the recipe.

Yield: *About 1½ cups*

Preparation time: *10 minutes*

Cooking time: *15 minutes, plus cooling time*

Spice meter: *Moderately spiced*

½ cup virgin or extra virgin olive oil
8 to 10 plump cloves garlic, minced
1 teaspoon ground cumin
⅛ teaspoon paprika
½ cup fresh orange juice

½ cup fresh lime juice
⅓ cup chopped fresh parsley
1 teaspoon salt
¾ teaspoon freshly ground black pepper

1 Heat the olive oil in a skillet over medium-low heat. Add the garlic and cook, stirring occasionally, until the garlic becomes slightly golden. This process may take 10 or more minutes. Do not allow the garlic to burn or you'll have to discard it and start over.

2 Add the cumin and paprika and cook, stirring often, until the cumin becomes fragrant, about 1 minute longer. Add the orange juice, lime juice, parsley, salt, and pepper. Transfer the sauce to a bowl or jar and cool. Serve at room temperature. Before using, stir or whisk the sauce to blend it because the juice and oil can separate while the sauce stands.

Tip: Store leftovers in the refrigerator in a tightly sealed jar for up to 2 weeks. The oil will solidify, so bring any leftovers to room temperature or heat gently before using.

Per serving: Calories 46 (From Fat 41); Fat 5g (Saturated 1g); Cholesterol 0mg; Sodium 98mg; Carbohydrate 1g (Dietary Fiber 0g); Protein 0g.

Mojo magic

If you aren't already under mojo's spell, here are a several ways to try mojo. One of them is sure to win you over.

Mojo marinade: Use Mojo Sauce as a marinade for pork tenderloin, boneless pork roasts, pork or lamb chops, chicken pieces, or shrimp or scallop kebabs. Marinate meat and poultry for 3 to 24 hours, shrimp or scallops for 30 minutes to 3 hours. Remove the meat, poultry, or seafood from the marinade and pat it dry. Grill, broil, or roast the food. You can also marinate olives in mojo for a week or two in the refrigerator to enhance their flavor.

Mojo veggies: Mojo Sauce is also good with veggies. Toss a small amount with cooked broccoli, green beans, spinach, Swiss chard, greens, or boiled potatoes or toss grilled vegetables, such as eggplant or zucchini, in the mojo sauce. You can also marinate eggplant or zucchini, for an hour or two, that you plan to grill in the Mojo Sauce, but pat them dry partially before cooking so that they're not too wet. Top the grilled veggies with extra mojo.

Mojo sandwiches: Drizzle Mojo Sauce on sandwich rolls, Cuban bread, or lightly toasted Italian or French bread. Top with your favorite roasted meat, in particular pork (a traditional Cuban sandwich), or with cold cuts and cheese. Finish off the sandwich with a combo of tomatoes, lettuce, thinly sliced raw onions, and sliced pickled jalapenos or with roasted bell peppers and sliced pitted olives. Drizzle a little extra Mojo Sauce on top.

Mojo spread: Mix equal parts (such as 2 tablespoons each) of Mojo Sauce with mayonnaise and spread the mixture on rolls or bread. Mix 2 parts sour cream and 1 part Mojo Sauce (such as 2 tablespoons and 1 tablespoon) to create a topping for baked potatoes.

Quick mojo stir-fry: Sauté deveined, peeled shrimp or boneless chicken breasts cut into very thin strips in a little olive oil until nearly cooked, about 3 minutes. Add some Mojo Sauce and simmer for 2 minutes or until the shrimp or chicken is cooked through.

Chinese Marinade

This sweet, delicious marinade and baste can be used on chicken, pork, ribs, lamb, and beef.

Yield: *About 1½ cups*

Preparation time: *10 minutes*

Spice meter: *Moderately spiced to hot and spicy*

¾ cup hoisin sauce

⅓ cup rice wine vinegar or white wine vinegar

⅓ cup honey

1 teaspoon Chinese sesame oil

2 scallions, white part only, sliced

2 plump cloves garlic, minced

½-inch piece fresh ginger, minced

1 teaspoon crushed Szechuan peppercorns or ½ teaspoon crushed red pepper flakes

1 In a bowl, combine the hoisin sauce, rice wine vinegar, honey, and sesame oil and stir. Add the scallions, garlic, ginger, and Szechuan peppercorns and stir. Cover and refrigerate for up to 2 weeks or use immediately.

2 To use, pour the marinade over the meat or poultry and turn the item to coat it. Marinate the food in the refrigerator for a minimum of 30 minutes or up to 24 hours. Grill, broil, or roast the food, basting occasionally with the Chinese Marinade, until the food is cooked as you prefer.

Per serving: Calories 34 (From Fat 4); Fat 0g (Saturated 0g); Cholesterol 0mg; Sodium 130mg; Carbohydrate 8g (Dietary Fiber 0g); Protein 0g.

Savory Spiced Poaching Liquid

This flavorful broth can be used when poaching boneless chicken cutlets, fish filets, shrimp, or scallops.

Yield: *About 1 quart*

Preparation time: *10 minutes*

Cooking time: *15 to 30 minutes*

Spice meter: *Mildly to moderately spiced*

3⅔ cups chicken, vegetable, or fish broth or water

⅓ cup dry sherry or dry white wine

1 onion, quartered

1 carrot, cut into chunks

1 bay leaf

¾ inch piece fresh ginger, sliced into chunks

2 plump cloves garlic, sliced lengthwise into thirds

1½ tablespoons whole coriander

1 teaspoon black or white peppercorns

4 cardamom pods, bruised (optional)

2 whole cloves

1 to 2 jalapenos or serranos, halved, or ½ to 1 teaspoon cayenne (optional)

1 Combine all the ingredients in a large pot. Over medium heat, bring the liquid to a boil. Cover and reduce the heat to medium-low. Simmer for 30 minutes to allow the flavor to develop. Use immediately or cool and use later.

2 In a pot that's large enough to hold the food you'll be cooking, bring the liquid to a gently bubbling simmer over medium-low to medium heat. Add the food to be cooked. Allow the liquid to return to a gently bubbling simmer, but do not let it boil. Poach the food in the liquid until it is cooked through.

Tip: You can make this poaching liquid a day or two ahead of when you'd like to use it. Simply strain out the solids, using a sieve, and refrigerate the liquid in a covered container. Reheat to a simmer before using.

Per serving: Calories 13 (From Fat 1); Fat 0g (Saturated 0g); Cholesterol 0mg; Sodium 131mg; Carbohydrate 3g (Dietary Fiber 0g); Protein 0g.

South of the Border Marinade

This marinade inspired by Mexican cuisine is wonderful for most cuts of pork, beef, and chicken, such as chops, roasts, cutlets, or filets. It's also good with seafood such as shrimp, scallops, or white fish filets.

Yield: *About 1 cup*

Preparation time: *10 to 15 minutes*

Spice meter: *Moderately spiced to hot and spicy*

⅓ cup fresh lemon juice

⅓ cup fresh orange juice

⅓ cup olive oil

2 tablespoons minced fresh cilantro

3 scallions, white part only, sliced

2 plump cloves garlic, minced

1 tablespoon fresh minced oregano, minced or 1½ teaspoons dried

½ bay leaf, crumbled

1¼ teaspoons ground cumin

¼ teaspoon ground cinnamon

¼ teaspoon ground coriander

½ teaspoon cayenne or 1 to 2 fresh, sliced jalapenos or serranos

½ teaspoon freshly ground black pepper

½ teaspoon salt

1 Combine all the ingredients in a bowl. Stir to mix evenly.

2 To use, pour the marinade over the meat, poultry, or seafood and turn the food to coat it. Marinate in the refrigerator for a minimum of 2 hours or overnight. Grill, broil, or roast the food, basting occasionally, until it's cooked as you prefer.

Tip: *To get the most juice out of citrus fruit, leave the fruit at room temperature. Hold the fruit under the palm of your hand and roll it on the counter to help release the juice. Then cut it in half and squeeze.*

Per serving: Calories 46 (From Fat 41); Fat 5g (Saturated 1g); Cholesterol 0mg; Sodium 74mg; Carbohydrate 1g (Dietary Fiber 0g); Protein 0g.

Jamaican Jerk Sauce

Traditionally, this pungent, spicy sauce is made with Scotch bonnet peppers, known to be the hottest on the planet. You may substitute a much larger quantity of other hot chiles, such as bird's eyes, serranos, or jalapenos.

Most commonly, jerk sauce is used as a marinade for chicken and pork, but you can try it with kebabs, lamb, or ribs. The marinade can be made several days ahead and refrigerated until you're ready to use it. See the recipe for Jerk Chicken (Chapter 13).

Yield: *About 1⅓ cups*

Preparation time: *15 to 20 minutes*

Spice meter: *Hot and spicy*

2 teaspoons ground allspice

2 teaspoons dry English mustard

1 teaspoon salt

1 teaspoon freshly ground black pepper

½ teaspoon freshly grated or ground nutmeg

¼ teaspoon ground mace or additional ground allspice

¼ teaspoon ground cinnamon or ground cloves

1 tablespoon minced fresh thyme or 1½ teaspoons dried

1 tablespoon dark brown sugar, or more to taste

1 Scotch bonnet chile, seeded, or 12 to 18 serranos or jalapenos

5 plump cloves garlic, minced

10 to 12 plump scallions, white part only, coarsely chopped

½ cup orange or lime juice

⅓ cup white wine vinegar or cider vinegar

2 tablespoons vegetable oil

1 In a food processor fitted with a metal blade, combine the allspice, mustard, salt, black pepper, nutmeg, mace, cinnamon, thyme, and sugar and pulse to blend. Add the chile, garlic, and scallions and pulse to blend. Add the orange or lime juice and vinegar and pulse. Add the vegetable oil and pulse to combine. The mixture should be a thick paste. You can add additional juice if you want to thin it.

2 To use as a marinade, pour the sauce over the food and turn to coat. Marinate in the refrigerator for a minimum of 2 hours or overnight. Grill, broil, or roast the food, basting occasionally, until it's cooked as you prefer.

Per serving: *Calories 24 (From Fat 13); Fat 1g (Saturated 0g); Cholesterol 0mg; Sodium 112mg; Carbohydrate 3g (Dietary Fiber 0g); Protein 0g.*

Chile Adobo Sauce

Popular in the American Southwest and Mexico, this piquant, deep-red sauce is wonderful for marinating beef, pork, chicken, and shrimp. The Beef or Pork Adobo (Chapter 14) and the Shrimp Adobo (Chapter 15) both can be made with this sauce.

Yield: *About 1 ¾ cups*

Preparation time: *10 to 15 minutes*

Spice meter: *Hot and spicy*

8 to 10 dried guajillo or ancho chiles or a combination

2 tablespoons vegetable oil

4 plump cloves garlic, minced

½ teaspoon cumin seeds or ½ teaspoon ground cumin

¼ teaspoon ground cinnamon

¼ teaspoon freshly ground black pepper

2 tablespoons fresh chopped oregano or 2 teaspoons dried oregano

1 cup tomato puree or crushed canned tomatoes

⅓ cup water

¼ cup cider or white wine vinegar

1½ teaspoons salt

1 Cover the chiles with hot water until they're softened slightly, about 10 minutes. Remove the chiles from the water and then cut off their stems.

2 In a small skillet over medium-low heat, heat the vegetable oil. Add the garlic and cook, stirring occasionally, for 2 minutes. Add the cumin, cinnamon, black pepper, and oregano and cook, stirring constantly, for 1 minute. Add the tomato puree and simmer for 5 minutes. Remove the skillet from the heat and set aside.

3 In a food processor fitted with a metal blade, combine the chiles (with their seeds), water, and vinegar. Pulse until a thick puree forms. Add the garlic-tomato mixture and salt. Pulse until the mixture is blended. Let the sauce cool before using.

4 To use as a marinade, pour the chile adobo sauce over meat or poultry and marinate for 2 hours or overnight. It can also be used as a marinade for shellfish or fish; marinate for 15 to 60 minutes. Use the sauce as directed in the recipes for Adobo in Chapters 14 and 15, or do the following. Sauté meat or poultry and then simmer it in the sauce, or you may grill or roast the food, basting occasionally with the sauce. Bake fish to desired doneness, basting with the sauce, or if using shrimp, simmer the sauce and add the raw shellfish, such as shrimp or scallops, and cook the shellfish until done.

Cook's Fact: *There are two types of adobo sauce. The one featured in this recipe hails from Mexico. The other adobo sauce, which is from the Philippines, is a vinegary marinade featuring chiles and herbs.*

Per serving: *Calories 20 (From Fat 16); Fat 2g (Saturated 0g); Cholesterol 0mg; Sodium 94mg; Carbohydrate 1g (Dietary Fiber 0g); Protein 0g.*

Southeast Asian Peanut Sauce

This popular and versatile sauce appears in many versions throughout Southeast Asia. It can be used as a condiment for saté (an Indonesian dish of meat, fish, or poultry cubes served on skewers), grilled or sautéed meat, poached chicken breasts, rice, vegetables, and vegetable salads. Serve the sauce at room temperature. See the recipes for Indonesian Gado Gado (Chapter 11), Southeast Asian Chicken Saté (Chapter 13), Indonesian Beef Sate (Chapter 14), and Indonesian Peanut Noodles with Vegetables (Chapter 17), for some possible ways to use this sauce. It can be kept in a covered container in the refrigerator for 1 week.

Yield: *About 1¾ cups*

Preparation time: *10 to 15 minutes*

Cooking time: *5 minutes*

Spice meter: *Moderately spiced to hot and spicy*

¾ cup natural or creamy peanut butter, preferably unsweetened

1⅓ cups unsweetened coconut milk (about one can), chicken broth, or water

2 tablespoons rice wine vinegar or white wine vinegar

1 tablespoon brown sugar

1 tablespoon light soy sauce

2 plump cloves garlic, minced

¾ inch piece fresh ginger, minced

½ teaspoon cayenne, or 1 to 2 tablespoons sambal oelek or Chinese chile paste to taste

1 In a saucepan over medium heat, combine all the ingredients. Stir to mix evenly.

2 Bring the mixture to a boil and cook, stirring occasionally, for 3 minutes. Remove the sauce from the heat. Let the sauce cool to room temperature before using.

Cook's Fact: *Thai peanut sauce is normally made with coconut milk; the Indonesian version is often made with broth instead.*

Per serving: *Calories 64 (From Fat 51); Fat 6g (Saturated 3g); Cholesterol 0mg; Sodium 40mg; Carbohydrate 2g (Dietary Fiber 1g); Protein 2g.*

Tangy Tomato Barbecue Sauce

An all-American classic, this all-purpose sauce can be used anytime you would use its commercial cousin. The recipe can be halved or doubled. Refrigerate any sauce that you're not using right away. See the recipe for Down-Home Barbecued Chicken in Chapter 13 for one suggested use of this sauce.

Yield: *About 3 cups*

Preparation time: *10 minutes*

Cooking time: *5 minutes*

Spice meter: *Moderately spiced*

2 cups ketchup

¾ cups cider or white wine vinegar

¼ cup water or strong coffee

2 tablespoons Worcestershire sauce

1½ tablespoons chile powder

½ to 1 teaspoon cayenne or any ground chile pepper powder

2 plump garlic cloves, pressed or minced

½ small onion, grated, with its juice

Tabasco sauce to taste

1 In a small saucepan over low heat, combine the ketchup, vinegar, coffee, Worcestershire sauce, chile powder, cayenne, garlic, and onion. Stir to mix evenly. Simmer for 5 minutes. Allow to cool before using. Add tabasco to taste. Store in a covered container in the refrigerator for 2 to 3 weeks.

2 To use, baste or brush meat or poultry with barbecue sauce before and during grilling or broiling. Serve extra sauce on the side.

Variation: *Make an uncooked barbecue sauce by omitting the fresh onion and adding a heaping ¼ teaspoon of onion powder. Stir all the ingredients together in a bowl. When refrigerated in a covered container, this sauce will last 4 to 6 weeks.*

Per serving: *Calories 13 (From Fat 1); Fat 0g (Saturated 0g); Cholesterol 0mg; Sodium 131mg; Carbohydrate 3g (Dietary Fiber 0g); Protein 0g.*

Spiced Sherry Orange Marinade

This versatile marinade or basting sauce can be used for pork, chicken, boneless duck breasts, beef, tuna, or salmon.

Yield: *About 1 cup*

Preparation time: *10 minutes*

Spice meter: *Moderately spiced*

¼ cup orange or tangerine juice

¼ cup sherry

¼ cup soy sauce

2 tablespoons peanut or vegetable oil (optional)

2 tablespoons honey

1 tablespoon grated fresh orange or tangerine zest

1 shallot, minced

¾-inch piece fresh ginger, minced

3 to 4 whole cloves

3 to 4 cardamom pods, bruised with the side of knife

½ teaspoon ground coriander

¼ to ½ teaspoon cayenne (optional)

1 Combine all the ingredients in a small bowl. Stir to mix evenly.

2 To use, pour the marinade over meat, poultry, or seafood and turn the item to coat it. Marinate in the refrigerator, turning occasionally, for a minimum of 20 minutes or up to 24 hours. Broil or grill the food, basting occasionally, or sauté the food in a little butter or peanut oil until it's cooked as you prefer.

Variation: *Instead of using sherry, try sake, the Japanese rice wine, or dry white wine. For a nonalcoholic baste, substitute chicken broth or apple juice. Do not use cooking sherry, which is very salty.*

Per serving: *Calories 16 (From Fat 0); Fat 0g (Saturated 0g); Cholesterol 0mg; Sodium 258mg; Carbohydrate 3g (Dietary Fiber 0g); Protein 0g. (Optional oil and cayenne not included.)*

Chapter 11

Salsas and Salads

* *

In This Chapter

▶ Making salsas

▶ Making vegetable and fruit salads

* *

Salads don't just have to be the standby combo of lettuce and tomato with a bit of cucumber. Vegetable and fruit salads are traditional fare throughout much of the world, particularly in Thailand, Indonesia, Malaysia, South Africa, India, Mexico, the Caribbean islands, the American Southwest, and states such as Florida where the Caribbean influence is strong. Whether these salads are called a salsa in the United States, Mexico, and the Caribbean, or a sambal in Southeast Asia and Africa, spiced salads are a unique and scrumptious way to enhance an otherwise ordinary meal.

Most Americans are familiar with salsas as a dip for chips and a topping for burgers, but salsas are quite versatile. Salsas can be served as a marvelous side dish and as a condiment for a variety of recipes throughout this book. There are two basic types of salsas — one is made with raw vegetables or fruit, whereas the other kind is cooked briefly. Raw salsas can be stored in the refrigerator for up to two days before their fresh taste diminishes; cooked salsas, such as the Plum Salsa in this chapter, can last a week or two. Neither can be frozen.

Sambals can be made with wide range of fresh produce and spices. The combinations are endless. Some sambals are ingredients in Indonesian and Southeast Asian recipes; others can be used as a condiment in the way you would use chutney or ketchup. Their usefulness doesn't end here. Many sambals are served as salads or side dishes and they can be used as an accompaniment to rice dishes, curries, and grilled foods.

Most of the time, you'll use raw ingredients in salsas and salads, and the taste of the finished product will depend on the quality of the produce you use. To insure that your food has the best flavor and texture, buy the freshest produce.

It should have no signs of decay, such as soft spots or blemishes. If tomatoes or fruit aren't ripe, hold off making the dish until they're at their prime. Sometimes fruit isn't as ripe, and therefore sweet, as you'd like it to be. Taste a piece before you add it to a recipe and add a bit of sugar if you want additional sweetness.

Some salads can be prepared ahead and refrigerated. They only need a few last-minute touches before serving, such as dressing or garnishes. If you're serving a crowd, the recipes can be doubled.

Tomato Salsa

Originally a product of Mexico, salsa has become one of the United States' favorite condiments. Served most often as a condiment alongside everything from chips to burgers to grilled food, it's always a winner. Make it hotter by adding another chile or two.

Yield: *About 2½ cups*

Preparation time: *15 to 20 minutes, plus 30 minutes standing time*

Spice meter: *Moderately spiced to hot and spicy*

4 to 5 medium tomatoes, chopped, about 2 cups

1 small red or yellow onion, chopped, about ½ cup, or ½ cup minced scallions, white part only

1 plump clove garlic, minced

2 tablespoons fresh lime or lemon juice

2 to 4 jalapenos or serranos, seeded and minced, or to your taste, or ¼ to ½ teaspoon cayenne

½ teaspoon salt, or to taste

⅛ teaspoon freshly ground black pepper

Pinch to ⅛ teaspoon ground cumin

¼ cup minced fresh cilantro or flat-leaf parsley

Combine all the ingredients in a medium-sized bowl. Stir to mix. Cover and let stand at least 30 minutes before using.

Variation: *Add ⅓ cup canned, rinsed, and drained black beans; or ½ cup diced, peeled cucumber; or ½ cup diced avocado.*

Per tablespoon: *Calories 4 (From Fat 1); Fat 0g (Saturated 0g); Cholesterol 0mg; Sodium 31mg; Carbohydrate 1g (Dietary Fiber 0g); Protein 0g.*

Papaya, Mango, or Pineapple Salsa

This multipurpose salsa can be made with a variety of fruit. If the fruit is slightly underripe or not particularly sweet, add a small amount of sugar to taste, using the finest-grained sugar you can find.

An excellent match with grilled, roasted, or sautéed chicken, pork, or seafood, you can also serve the salsa with Southeast Asian, Caribbean, or Mexican dishes.

Yield: *6 servings*

Preparation time: *15 to 20 minutes*

Spice meter: *Moderately spiced to hot and spicy*

1½ cups peeled and diced papaya, mango, or pineapple	*¼ teaspoon ground coriander*
3 scallions, white part only, minced	*¼ teaspoon white pepper*
1 tablespoon fresh lemon or lime juice	*¼ teaspoon salt*
1-inch piece fresh ginger, minced	*¼ to ½ teaspoon crushed red chile flakes, to taste, or 1 jalapeno, seeded and minced*
1 plump clove garlic, minced	*2 to 3 tablespoons minced fresh cilantro or mint (optional)*
¼ teaspoon ground cumin	

1 In a medium-sized bowl, combine all the ingredients except the cilantro or mint. Stir to mix evenly.

2 Cover and refrigerate until serving. Right before serving, stir in the mint or cilantro.

Tip: *To get 1½ cups of diced fruit, you'll need 2 medium-sized papayas, 3 mangoes, or 1 large pineapple.*

Variation: *For fresh chutney, use papaya or mango and combine the fruit with the remaining ingredients in the bowl of a food processor. Pulse until a chunky puree forms. Serve with Indian or Caribbean curries. Refrigerate in a covered container for up to 1 week.*

Variation: *For fruity pico de gallo, combine 1 cup of pineapple with ⅓ cup diced red bell pepper, ⅓ cup peeled diced cucumber, 1 medium diced tomato, and all the other ingredients listed in the recipe.*

Per tablespoon: Calories 18 (From Fat 0); Fat 0g (Saturated 0g); Cholesterol 0mg; Sodium 100mg; Carbohydrate 4g (Dietary Fiber 1g); Protein 0g.

Plum Salsa

This versatile salsa is slightly tart and spicy. It requires a short cooking time, but it still tastes fresh. The salsa's so delicious and versatile, you might want to double the recipe. (It's easy: Just multiply the quantities in the ingredient list by 2.) It's a splendid complement to grilled, roasted, or sautéed pork, lamb, chicken or other poultry, and seafood. Although this salsa isn't a traditional accompaniment for Indian-style lamb and chicken curries, feel free to try it in Indian dishes. But that's not all. It makes an unusual dip with toasted pita wedges, focaccia, or tortilla chips — or try a dollop atop cheese and crackers. Plum salsa is also tasty on sandwiches.

In this recipe, use plums that are almost ripe — they won't be completely hard, but will be slightly firm when you press on the skin. If the plums are very sweet and ripe, feel free to add fresh lemon or lime juice to taste, about 1 tablespoon total, in Step 5. Leftovers can be refrigerated in a covered container for 1 to 2 weeks.

Yield: *About 1 cup*

Preparation time: *10 minutes*

Cooking time: *15 minutes*

Spice meter: *Moderately spiced*

1¼ pounds almost ripe plums

1 cup water

3 plump cloves garlic

1-inch piece ginger, peeled, divided into two ½-inch pieces

6 cardamom pods, bruised (optional)

1 teaspoon ground coriander

3 to 4 tablespoons honey, or to taste

½ to 1 teaspoon crushed red chile flakes

¼ teaspoon ground cumin

¼ teaspoon ground allspice

⅛ teaspoon garam masala (optional)

½ cup chopped cilantro

¾ teaspoon salt, or to taste

1 With a small knife, chop the plums coarsley by slicing the flesh off around the pits. You don't need to remove all the fruit from the pit. Do not discard the pit. Cut the fruit sections in half.

2 Put the plums and their pits into a medium-sized stainless or enamel-lined saucepan. Add the water, 1 clove of the garlic, ½ piece of ginger sliced into three coin-size pieces, the cardamom pods, and ½ teaspoon of coriander. Place over medium heat and bring to a boil.

3 Reduce the heat to medium-low and simmer for 5 minutes. Add the honey and simmer for 10 minutes longer.

4 Place a colander over a large bowl and drain the plums, reserving the juice if you want (see the sidebar "Plum bonus"). Pick out the pits, garlic, ginger pieces, and cardamom pods. Gently mash the plums with a wooden spoon. The texture should be slightly chunky.

5 Transfer the plums to a bowl. Add the remaining ½ teaspoon coriander, ½ teaspoon chile flakes, cumin, allspice, garam masala, and salt. Stir to combine. Taste and, if you want, add the remaining ½ teaspoon chile flakes or additional salt.

6 Cover the salsa. Let the flavors combine for 30 minutes, either at room temperature or in the refrigerator. Serve at room temperature or chilled.

Tip: *Make a spice bouquet garni, which is a little packet containing whole spices. The bouquet garni makes removing whole spices easier. It's a good technique to use for poaching and flavoring liquids or beverages. Wrap the whole spices in a piece of cheesecloth, tie it to secure, and then add the bouquet garni to the liquid. In this recipe, wrap the whole garlic clove, ginger, and cardamom pods and add as directed in Step 1.*

Variation: *Make nectarine and plum salsa by using ½ pound of nectarines and ¾ pound of plums. Alternatively, forego the plums entirely and make a version entirely of nectarines.*

Per tablespoon: *Calories 32 (From Fat 2); Fat 0g (Saturated 0g); Cholesterol 0mg; Sodium 110mg; Carbohydrate 8g (Dietary Fiber 1g); Protein 0g.*

Plum bonus

The reserved liquid from the Plum Salsa is a lovely shade of red, and it's also delicious. It would be a shame to throw it away. There should be about 1 cup of reserved liquid, and you've got a lot of options for how to use it. Here are a couple:

Spiced plum dessert sauce: Use the liquid alongside desserts as you would a sauce. You'll have your own ideas, but here are a few suggestions: Serve with vanilla or chocolate ice cream or frozen yogurt; cheesecake; rich chocolate cake or torte; plain, lemon, or ginger poundcake; lemon or chocolate souffle; or lemon or lime curd pie.

Spiced plum cocktail: Use the leftover liquid to make a refreshing drink. You should be able to make four 8-ounce servings. Refrigerate the reserved liquid from the Plum Salsa. Mix the chilled juice with 1 cup of pineapple or orange juice and stir well. To make one serving, combine ½ cup of the pineapple-plum juice in a glass and add ½ cup club soda or lemon-lime soda. Stir well. Spike with a shot of rum or vodka, if you want. Garnish with a thin slice of orange or lemon.

You can make a glass pitcherful of the drink (which highlights the color) by adding the mixed pineapple-plum juice with 2 cups of club soda and some rum or vodka. Make sure to stir the mixture each time before you pour. Garnish a pitcher with thinly sliced oranges and/or lemons.

Spiced Fruit Salad

This makes a superb side salad, and it's wonderfully refreshing as dessert. You can see a picture of it in the color section of this book. As an option, you can use vanilla sugar to add a special, subtle flavor; see Chapter 2 for how to make vanilla sugar.

Yield: *6 servings*

Preparation time: *30 minutes, plus 1 hour chilling time*

Spice meter: *Mildly spiced*

1 large or 2 small grapefruits, peeled and sectioned

2 oranges, peeled and sectioned

1 medium mango or papaya, diced, or 2 peaches or nectarines, diced

1 medium pineapple pared, cored, and diced

1 Granny Smith apple, cored, and diced

½ pint berries, such as blueberries, blackberries, or strawberries

1 banana, sliced (optional)

2 to 4 tablespoons sugar or vanilla sugar, depending on the ripeness of the fruit

1 to 2 tablespoons fresh lime or lemon juice

1½ tablespoons water

¾-inch piece fresh ginger, grated

¼ teaspoon ground allspice or cinnamon

¼ teaspoon ground cardamom

2 tablespoons fresh chopped mint

Freshly ground coriander (optional)

1 In a large bowl, combine the grapefruit, oranges, mango, pineapple, apple, and berries. Sprinkle the fruit with two tablespoons of the sugar and set aside.

2 In a small bowl, combine the lime juice, water, ginger, allspice, and cardamom. Add the banana to the mixed fruit now. Pour the spiced lime juice mixture over the fruit and stir to blend evenly. Taste and add additional sugar if you want it sweeter.

3 Cover and chill for at least 1 hour. Before serving, add the mint and stir to mix evenly.Grind fresh coriander on top of each serving, if you like.

Warning: *Sliced bananas (like avocados) can turn brown quickly once they're exposed to air, but if they're tossed with a squeeze of lime or lemon juice, they won't discolor. In this recipe, the bananas are added right before the mixed fruit is tossed with the lime juice mixture.*

Tip: *Use any combination of ripe fruit you like. Alter the selection of fruit depending on what's in season.*

Per serving: *Calories 146 (From Fat 7); Fat 1g (Saturated 0g); Cholesterol 0mg; Sodium 4mg; Carbohydrate 37g (Dietary Fiber 5g); Protein 1g.*

Southeast Asian Green Bean Sambal

This salad is a wonderful accompaniment to any grilled meat, poultry, or seafood. It can also be served alongside curries, satés, and other dishes from Southeast Asia or India.

Yield: *4 to 6 servings*

Preparation time: *10 to 15 minutes*

Cooking time: *5 minutes*

Spice meter: *Moderately hot and spicy*

¾ pound green beans, sliced in 1 to 1½ inch pieces

1½ tablespoons fresh lemon juice or white wine vinegar

2 teaspoons soy sauce

2 plump cloves garlic, minced

¼-inch piece ginger fresh, peeled and grated or finely minced

1 teaspoon ground coriander

½ teaspoon ground cumin

½ teaspoon crushed red pepper flakes, or 1 teaspoon sambal oelek, or ¼ teaspoon cayenne

½ teaspoon sugar

2 tablespoons vegetable oil

2 to 3 scallions, white and green parts, thinly sliced

1 ripe medium tomato, diced, or 2 plum tomatoes, diced

2 tablespoons chopped fresh mint or cilantro

1 Have a medium-sized bowl of ice water ready. In a large saucepan over high heat, cook the green beans in plenty of lightly salted boiling water until they're tender but crisp, about 4 to 5 minutes. Drain the beans in a colander and immediately plunge them into the ice water to stop the cooking. When they're cool, transfer the beans to a medium-sized bowl and set aside.

2 Combine the lemon juice, soy sauce, garlic, ginger, coriander, cumin, crushed red pepper flakes, and sugar in a medium-sized bowl. Beat the mixture gently with a fork while drizzling in the vegetable oil.

3 Add the green beans, scallions, tomato, and mint to the bowl. Toss to mix evenly.

Tip: *The salt in the cooking water causes a chemical reaction that sets the color so that that green vegetables don't turn olive-green after cooking. Any green vegetables, such as green beans or broccoli, remain bright green. Add a pinch of salt to the ice water as well for extra insurance.*

Per serving: *Calories 110 (From Fat 66); Fat 7g (Saturated 1g); Cholesterol 0mg; Sodium 376mg; Carbohydrate 11g (Dietary Fiber 4g); Protein 2g.*

Spiced Carrot and Pineapple Sambal

This salad, called a *sambal* throughout Southeast Asia, Indonesia, Malaysia, and South Africa, can be made up to several hours ahead and chilled.

Yield: *4 to 6 servings*

Preparation time: *25 to 30 minutes*

Spice meter: *Mildly to moderately spiced*

¼ cup fresh orange juice

1 tablespoon fresh lemon juice

1 tablespoon sugar

½ teaspoon salt

¼ teaspoon ground coriander

Pinch of ground cumin

Pinch of ground cinnamon or freshly grated or ground nutmeg

5 medium carrots, grated, about 2 cups

¾ cup finely chopped fresh or canned pineapple

2 tablespoons chopped fresh cilantro, mint, or parsley

1 In a medium bowl, combine the orange juice, lemon juice, sugar, salt, coriander, cumin, and cinnamon and stir to mix.

2 Add the carrots and stir to mix. Cover and refrigerate. Before serving, stir in the cilantro.

Variation: Omit the pineapple and add ⅓ cup raisins or currants after you add the carrots.

Per serving: Calories 59 (From Fat 3); Fat 0g (Saturated 0g); Cholesterol 0mg; Sodium 311mg; Carbohydrate 14g (Dietary Fiber 2g); Protein 1g.

Pickled Cucumber and Carrot Salad

This refreshing salad can be made several hours ahead. It's great with grilled food, curries, satés, and even burgers!

Yield: *6 servings*

Preparation time: *10 minutes, plus 1 hour chilling time*

Spice meter: *Moderately spiced to hot and spicy*

⅓ cup white wine vinegar or rice wine vinegar

3 tablespoons water

2 tablespoons sugar

½ teaspoon salt

⅛ teaspoon ground cumin

⅛ teaspoon white pepper

½ to 1 jalapeno or serrano, seeded and minced (optional)

1 English cucumber, seeded, peeled, and diced

1 medium carrot, coarsely grated

1 tablespoons fresh parsley, cilantro, or mint

In a medium bowl, combine the vinegar, water, sugar, salt, cumin, pepper, and jalapeno and stir to mix. Add the cucumber and carrot and stir to mix. Cover and refrigerate for 1 hour. Before serving, add the parsley and stir.

Tip: *If you're using fresh mint, chop it immediately before adding; otherwise, the mint can turn black.*

Per serving: *Calories 32 (From Fat 1); Fat 0g (Saturated 0g); Cholesterol 0mg; Sodium 203mg; Carbohydrate 8g (Dietary Fiber 1g); Protein 0g.*

Gingered Tomato Salad

Tomatoes aren't often paired with ginger, but the combination is delicious. Use whichever is ripest, either round plum tomatoes or Italian plum tomatoes, in this unusual salad. In winter, when tomatoes are out of season, you can buy imported vine-ripened tomatoes in many groceries.

Yield: *4 to 6 servings*

Preparation time: *20 minutes*

Spice meter: *Moderately spiced*

1½ tablespoons fresh lemon or lime juice

1½ tablespoons fresh orange juice

2-inch piece ginger, cut into very thin strips

½ teaspoon salt

3 tablespoons olive or vegetable oil

1 Italian or Cubanelle pepper or sweet banana pepper, seeded and thinly sliced

4 to 6 ripe tomatoes, about 1½ pounds, cut into wedges

2 tablepoons fresh chopped basil or mint

Freshly ground coriander or pepper to taste

1 In a medium-sized bowl, combine the lemon juice, orange juice, ginger, and salt. Slowly whisk in the olive oil. Add the sliced pepper and toss to coat evenly. Let the mixture stand for 15 to 20 minutes.

2 Add the tomatoes to the peppers and toss gently. Add the basil and toss. Taste for salt and adjust if necessary. Before serving, grind fresh coriander or pepper over the salad.

Tip: Italian (or Cubanelle) peppers are sweet, but can have a hint of heat. Sweet banana peppers are also known as Hungarian wax peppers. They can range in taste from sweet to mildly hot. These pepper varieties are long, about 6 to 8 inches, and narrow when compared to bell peppers. They can vary in color from green to red to yellowish. If you can't find any of these varieties, substitute a small yellow bell pepper.

Per serving: Calories 137 (From Fat 97); Fat 11g (Saturated 1g); Cholesterol 0mg; Sodium 309mg; Carbohydrate 11g (Dietary Fiber 3g); Protein 2g.

Indonesian Gado Gado

This traditional Indonesian salad can be served warm or cold, as a light main course or a side dish. You will need to prepare the Southeast Asian Peanut Sauce from Chapter 10 ahead of time, as well as one boiled potato and 2 hard-boiled eggs.

Yield: *4 servings as a main course, 6 to 8 as a first course*

Preparation time: *25 minutes*

Cooking time: *5 to 10 minutes*

Spice meter: *Moderately spiced*

1 cup Southeast Asian Peanut Sauce from Chapter 10 at room temperature, or more to taste

½ head iceberg or romaine lettuce leaves, washed and torn

½ pound green cabbage, thinly sliced or shredded

½ pound green beans, cut into 1-inch pieces

2 medium carrots, very thinly sliced

⅓ pound fresh Chinese or Asian bean sprouts

1 boiled potato, cut into cubes

2 hard boiled eggs, quartered

½ English cucumber, thinly sliced

2 scallions, white and green parts, thinly sliced

1 Line a platter or shallow salad bowl with the lettuce leaves.

2 Fit a large pot with a steamer. Add enough water to just reach the steamer. Cover the pot and bring the water to a boil. Add the cabbage, green beans, and carrots and steam until tender but crisp, about 4 to 5 minutes. Alternatively, boil the vegetables in lightly salted water until tender crisp. Cook in batches if necessary.

4 Arrange the cabbage, green beans, and carrots in the center of the platter and top with the bean sprouts. Surround the vegetables with the potato chunks, egg wedges, and cucumber. If not serving immediately, cover and refrigerate.

5 When ready to serve, pour the Southeast Asian Peanut Sauce over the vegetables in the center. Sprinkle the scallions on top.

Variation: *For a heartier main course salad, add 8 to 12 cooked shrimp or 1 to 2 cooked, sliced chicken breast cutlets to the salad before topping it with the peanut sauce. You may want to use more than one cup of the sauce if you add these extra ingredients.*

Per serving: *Calories 390 (From Fat 232); Fat 26g (Saturated 11g); Cholesterol 106mg; Sodium 235mg; Carbohydrate 31g (Dietary Fiber 8g); Protein 15g.*

Tomato Raita

Raita (pronounced RI-tah) is a condiment that's served most often with Indian curries. You can also serve it with grilled or roasted meat, poultry, or seafood.

Yield: *4 to 6 servings, about 1½ cups*

Preparation time: *15 minutes, plus 30 minutes chilling time*

Spice meter: *Mildly spiced*

1 cup plain yogurt

1 plump clove garlic, pressed or minced

½ teaspoon sugar

¼ teaspoon salt

⅛ teaspoon cumin

Pinch of paprika

2 medium tomatoes, seeded and finely chopped

2 teaspoons fresh minced cilantro or mint (optional)

1 In a bowl, combine all the ingredients except the tomatoes and cilantro or mint. Stir to mix.

2 Add the tomatoes and stir gently. Cover and refrigerate for a minimum of 30 minutes. Before serving, stir in the cilantro.

Variation: Make cucumber raita by replacing the tomato with ½ to ¾ of a peeled, seeded, and diced cucumber.

Per serving: Calories 55 (From Fat 11); Fat 1g (Saturated 1g); Cholesterol 4mg; Sodium 194mg; Carbohydrate 8g (Dietary Fiber 1g); Protein 4g.

Chapter 12

Light Fare

In This Chapter

- Making hors d'oeuvres and snacks
- Making soups

The recipes in this section can be served as starters, snacks, light meals, or alongside drinks or cocktails. Most can be put together quickly or made well ahead of serving time.

Souper Ideas

You've made a pot of soup or perhaps a stew or curry and want to keep it for later in the week or freeze it. It's very important to handle food properly to prevent bacterial growth. Don't fret — you can take a few easy steps to prevent any potential contamination.

Chilling

When you're not going to use the soup right away, chilling it down properly is essential. Don't just let it sit on the back of the stove, but putting any hot food directly into the refrigerator or freezer is unwise. Residual heat can raise the temperature inside the fridge, and items can spoil. It's important to chill soups, stews, or curries quickly and refrigerate or freeze the item as soon as it's cooled. Left at room temperature for too long, food becomes a breeding ground for bacteria. These easy steps can help you keep food safe and tasting its best.

✔ An ice-water bath makes soup cool down quickly so that you can store it. To cool soup, fill a kitchen sink one-third full with very cold water. Add a few trays of ice cubes to the water to make it frigid. Put the pot directly into this ice-water bath, but be careful that the water doesn't spill over into the pot. Use a ladle or spoon to stir the soup, stew, or curry until it cools down and is lukewarm — cool enough that you can poke your (clean) finger in it and it doesn't feel hot.

✔ Transfer the cooled broth or soup to another container that it fills almost completely (with about ½ inch to 1 inch to spare) and cover the container.

✔ If you've made soup in a stainless steel or enamel-coated pot, you can put the covered pot in the fridge for a few hours or overnight, after it's cooled, and then transfer the soup to a more suitable container the next morning.

✔ Broth, curries, stews, and meat, poultry, vegetable, and creamy soups can be refrigerated for up to three days. Vegetable purees and legume soups can be refrigerated for up to four days.

The right container

What's the best vessel in which to store soup? Here's a breakdown:

✔ For refrigerator storage, use a stainless steel, plastic, porcelain, or glass container, covered with a tight-fitting lid or plastic wrap. Promptly refrigerate or freeze cooled soup.

✔ For freezer storage, use self-sealing freezer bags or freezer-proof plastic containers with lids that have a tight seal.

✔ Don't store soup in aluminum or cast iron because these materials will impart an unpleasant or metallic taste to the food.

Freeze it

Freezing is the most convenient way to store leftovers for future meals. These practical tips can help you freeze soups correctly:

✔ When the soup is cooled, you can transfer it to freezer-proof containers.

✔ Use containers that are the right size — individual portions for quick meals and pint-size or quart-size containers for larger batches.

✔ Food expands when it freezes. Ideally, soup should nearly fill its container. Ladle soup into the container so that a gap of ½ inch to 1 inch remains at the top.

✔ Close the container, open it partially to release any trapped or excess air, and then seal it well. If using self-sealing bags, fill the bag about halfway to two-thirds full, release as much air as you can, and then seal.

Thawing

You can thaw soup in several different ways. They all work equally well, but some are faster.

- Thaw overnight in the refrigerator.

- Thaw in the microwave, following the directions that came with your microwave.

- Thaw uncovered on the counter until the soup is softened and mostly liquid, and then reheat or finish thawing in the refrigerator.

If the lid has popped off a container in the freezer, you probably overfilled the container and the food may have freezer burn. The surface will look cracked and possibly parched, with a few ice crystals on top. Food with freezer burn tastes odd and should be discarded.

Don't let already thawed food stand at room temperature for hours or bacteria may begin to form. Refrigerate it until you're ready to reheat or cook it.

Reheating

You can reheat soups in a number of ways, including these:

- Reheat over medium heat, stirring occasionally.

- Bring soup up to a boil to kill any bacteria that may have accumulated if it has been stored improperly, and then reduce the heat and simmer.

- If any ingredients start to stick to the pot, stir and reduce the heat to medium-low.

- When reheating, add extra liquid if you see the soup has become too thick.

Appetizing Tips

Wow your guests by putting into practice a few of these helpful hints:

- When serving fresh bread alongside a dip, cover it with a moist, not wet, paper towel to prevent the bread from drying out.

    Toasted bread or croûtes are already dried and shouldn't be covered with a moist towel. Instead, handle them in the same way as crackers.

✔ Serve an assortment of crackers, not just one type. Many kinds are available — whole wheat, buttery rounds, thin wafers, seasoned and flavored crackers, and crisp rye flatbread types. Arrange the crackers by type on a platter.

✔ Put dips and spreads in small bowls of a complementary color, but keep them covered with plastic wrap until serving time so that the top of the dip doesn't discolor or dry out. If you want, you can set the bowls in the center of the platter and arrange crackers, bread, or chips around them.

Tangy Yogurt Dip

Use as a dip for chips, crackers, or raw vegetables or as dipping sauce for skewered or grilled chicken, lamb, or shrimp. For a richer texture, use half yogurt and half sour cream.

Yield: *6 servings, about 1¼ cups*

Preparation time: *15 minutes; 30 minutes chilling time*

Spice meter: *Moderately spiced*

1 cup plain yogurt	½ teaspoon ground cumin
4 scallions, white and green parts, thinly sliced	½ teaspoon ground coriander
1 plump clove garlic, finely minced or pressed	⅛ teaspoon white or freshly ground black pepper
1 teaspoon minced fresh ginger	Pinch of turmeric
½ jalapeno or serrano, seeded and minced, or Tabasco to taste	¼ cup minced cilantro leaves or parsley

Combine all the ingredients in a bowl. Cover and refrigerate and let stand for 30 minutes before serving.

Variation: *Substitute 1 teaspoon of the Moroccan Spice Mix from Chapter 9 for the coriander, cumin, and white pepper.*

Per serving: *Calories 32 (From Fat 13); Fat 1g (Saturated 1g); Cholesterol 5mg; Sodium 22mg; Carbohydrate 3g (Dietary Fiber 0g); Protein 2g.*

Curried Nuts

Store the Curried Nuts in a closed container. They keep for up to a month in the refrigerator. This recipe can be doubled.

Yield: _About 2 cups_

Preparation time: _5 minutes_

Cooking time: _15 minutes_

Spice meter: _Moderately spiced_

4 cups water

2 cups nuts of your choice: pecans, walnuts, whole almonds, or peanuts

3 tablespoons sugar

½ to ¾ teaspoon crushed red pepper flakes

Peanut oil for frying

½ heaping teaspoon homemade or good-quality curry powder

½ teaspoon salt, or to taste

¼ to ½ teaspoon cayenne, or to taste (optional)

_1_ Bring the water to a boil in a saucepan over medium heat. Add the nuts. Return the water to a boil and cook for 1 to 2 minutes. Immediately drain the nuts well in a colander or strainer.

_2_ Put the nuts in a bowl with the sugar and crushed red pepper flakes and toss while the nuts are still hot, coating them evenly.

_3_ In a small bowl, combine the curry powder, salt, and cayenne. Set aside.

_4_ In a medium-sized skillet over medium heat, heat about 1 inch of peanut oil. Heat the oil until it's hot, about 350 degrees. Test by frying a nut — if the oil sizzles, it's ready. Fry the remaining nuts in batches, if necessary, until the nuts are lightly golden.

_5_ With a slotted spoon, transfer the nuts to a large strainer or colander set over a bowl. Allow any excess oil to drain off into the bowl and discard the oil.

_6_ Put the drained nuts into a clean bowl and toss them with the curry powder, salt, and cayenne mixture.

Variation: _Replace the curry powder with chili powder._

Per serving: _Calories 265 (From Fat 236); Fat 26g (Saturated 3g); Cholesterol 0mg; Sodium 146mg; Carbohydrate 9g (Dietary Fiber 3g); Protein 3g._

Roasted Eggplant Paté

Eggplant paté!? Though it may sound a bit exotic and unusual, eggplant paté is actually very popular. It's quite standard fare in the Mediterranean. The most well-known version, called baba ganoush, hails from the Middle East. In this recipe, the eggplant is roasted and then blended with spices and lightly toasted walnuts, which give the paté a lovely flavor and texture. Serve this Mediterranean-inspired treat as a snack or part of a light meal with crackers, toasted bread or croûtes, or pita.

Yield: *6 to 8 servings*

Preparation time: *10 minutes*

Cooking time: *40 to 50 minutes; 30 minutes cooling time*

Spice meter: *Mildly spiced*

1¼ pounds eggplants, about 2 medium, halved

2 plump cloves garlic, minced

1¼ teaspoons ground cumin

¾ to 1 teaspoon salt, or to taste

¼ teaspoon freshly ground black pepper

3 tablespoons fresh lemon juice or white wine vinegar

½ cup chopped walnuts, toasted in a dry skillet

3 tablespoons chopped fresh flat-leaf parsley

⅓ cup extra virgin olive oil

1 Preheat the oven to 375 degrees. Lightly spray a baking sheet with nonstick cooking spray. Place the eggplants, skin side down, on the baking sheet and bake until the flesh is soft, about 40 to 50 minutes. Set on a rack to cool completely, about 30 minutes.

2 Scoop out the flesh of the eggplant with a spoon. You should have about 1 cup. Put the eggplant flesh in the bowl of a food processor fitted with a metal blade. Pulse until the eggplant is coarsely chopped.

3 Add the garlic, cumin, salt, pepper, lemon juice, and walnuts and process until blended. Add the parsley and pulse to mix.

4 With the machine running, pour the olive oil through the tube and process until the mixture is smooth. Add additional olive oil if the paste is too thick. Transfer to a serving bowl and serve at room temperature.

Variation: *Substitute chopped hazelnuts for the walnuts.*

Tip: *Garnish the eggplant paté with a sprinkle of red — cayenne, paprika, or crushed red chile flakes — and a bit of green — a small sprig of fresh flat-leaf parsley, or chopped parsley.*

Per serving: *Calories 151 (From Fat 126); Fat 14g (Saturated 2g); Cholesterol 0mg; Sodium 222mg; Carbohydrate 6g (Dietary Fiber 2g); Protein 2g.*

Hummus

This Middle Eastern treat, made from pureed chickpeas and ground sesame seed paste, is scented with garlic and cumin. Serve it as a dip with warm pita bread. This dish can be made ahead and refrigerated. Before serving, let it soften at room temperature for approximately 1 hour.

Yield: *6 servings*

Preparation time: *15 minutes*

Spice meter: *Moderately spiced*

16-ounce can chickpeas, drained and rinsed

¼ cup fresh lemon juice

⅓ cup tahini

2 cloves garlic, finely minced or pressed

4 tablespoons olive oil

Water as needed

1 teaspoon ground cumin

Cayenne pepper, crushed red pepper flakes, or ground cumin for garnish

Parsley sprig for garnish (optional)

1 In a food processor fitted with a metal blade, combine the chickpeas, lemon juice, tahini, garlic, and 3 tablespoons of the olive oil. Puree into a smooth paste, adding a bit of water as needed to make the paste smooth and easy to spread.

2 Transfer the hummus to a serving bowl. Drizzle the remaining 1 tablespoon of olive oil on top. Sprinkle with cayenne, crushed red pepper flakes, or ground cumin. Garnish with a sprig of parsley.

Variation: *Make a tahini sauce or dip. Omit the chickpeas. Increase the tahini to ½ cup and the lemon juice to ⅓ cup. Use 3 tablespoons of olive oil and 3 tablespoons of plain yogurt. Combine the tahini, lemon juice, olive oil, yogurt, garlic, and cumin. Stir in a pinch of cayenne and garnish, if you want, with parsley. Serve with toasted pitas, or as a salad or sandwich dressing, or with burgers, kebabs, lamb chops, chicken, or roasted vegetables. The tahini sauce keeps, covered and refrigerated, for 2 weeks.*

Per serving: Calories 225 (From Fat 150); Fat 17g (Saturated 2g); Cholesterol 0mg; Sodium 101mg; Carbohydrate 16g (Dietary Fiber 3g); Protein 5g.

Crostini and croûtes — fancy toast

Patés, dips, and pepperonata can all be served with thin slices of toasted French or Italian bread. The Italians call them *crostini;* the French call them *croûtes.* By any name, they're easy to make. Preheat the oven to 400 degrees. Slice Italian or French bread into ¼-inch slices. Brush the bread on both sides with olive oil and arrange the slices on a baking sheet. Bake, turning once, until the bread is lightly golden on both sides. This should take about 10 to 12 minutes.

Mediterranean Spiced Black Olives

In the Mediterranean, olives are oven marinated with spices for extra flavor. In this recipe, they're steeped with garlic, cumin, fennel, chile, and lemon, all of which are traditional Mediterranean flavors. These olives are marvelous on their own or in salads. Keep them on hand to use in place of ordinary olives.

Yield: *10 to 14 servings, about 1½ quarts*

Preparation time: *15 minutes, plus 1 week standing time*

Spice meter: *Moderately spiced*

1 pound unpitted kalamata, niçoise, or Italian black olives, drained well

1 lemon, washed and thinly sliced

4 whole cloves garlic, peeled

1 teaspoon cumin seeds

1 teaspoon fennel seeds, mustard seeds, or black peppercorns

1 to 2 jalapenos or serranos, minced, or 1 teaspoon crushed red chile flakes

6 sprigs fresh thyme or lemon thyme

2 to 3 cups olive oil

1 In a 1½-quart jar or container, put a layer of one-third of the olives, lemon, and garlic. Add one-third of the cumin seeds, fennel seeds, jalapeno, and thyme. Repeat the layering twice more. Pour in the olive oil, making sure that it covers the olives and spices by approximately two inches.

2 Cover the jar and refrigerate. Let it stand for one week before opening. The olives last for up to 2 months in the refrigerator.

Cook's Fact*: Unripe olives are green; ripe olives are black. Greek kalamata and French niçoise olives are two popular imported ripe olives.*

Warning: *After opening the jar, make sure that there's always enough olive oil in it to completely cover the olives; otherwise, the olives can go bad.*

Per serving: *Calories 265 (From Fat 236); Fat 26g (Saturated 3g); Cholesterol 0mg; Sodium 146mg; Carbohydrate 9g (Dietary Fiber 3g); Protein 3g.*

Spiced Pepperonata

Pepperonata is a delicious spread made from roasted bell peppers. It's often a part of Italian antipasto platters. This version is accented with a touch of spices — garlic and chile. You may use only one color of bell pepper or a combination of colors. Serve with thinly sliced toasted bread or croûtes.

Yield: *6 servings*

Preparation time: *15 to 20 minutes*

Cooking time: *10 to 30 minutes, plus 30 to 45 minutes standing time*

Spice meter: *Mildly spiced*

4 medium red, yellow, or orange bell peppers, about 1 pound total	*¼ to ½ teaspoon crushed red pepper flakes, or to taste*
⅓ cup extra virgin olive oil	*¼ teaspoon freshly ground black pepper, or to taste*
2 to 3 plump cloves garlic, pressed or finely minced	*2 tablespoons chopped flat-leaf parsley*
½ teaspoon salt, or to taste	

1 Put the whole peppers on a preheated grill, on a rack 2 to 3 inches below a preheated broiler, or on a sturdy rack set over the flame of a gas burner on the stove. Roast the peppers, turning them after they've charred and until they're blackened evenly on the outside. This may take 10 to 30 minutes, depending on which method you use.

2 Put the peppers in a paper or plastic bag and close tightly. When the peppers are cool enough to handle, peel off the skin with your fingers. Cut the peppers in half, then remove and discard the seeds and stem. Cut out the ribs.

3 Cut the peppers into thin strips, then again crosswise into tiny cubes.

4 Put the finely chopped pepper cubes into a bowl. Add the remaining ingredients and stir to blend evenly. Let stand for 30 to 45 minutes to let the flavor develop fully. Taste for seasoning and adjust.

Cook's Fact: *Roasting vegetables deepens the color and intensifies the flavor of the veggies. Because the water in the vegetables evaporates, the natural sugar in the vegetables becomes more concentrated and the veggies taste sweeter.*

Per serving: *Calories 128 (From Fat 108); Fat 12g (Saturated 2g); Cholesterol 0mg; Sodium 196mg; Carbohydrate 5g (Dietary Fiber 2g); Protein 1g.*

Pro antipasto

Antipasto is a mainstay of the Italian table. An hors d'oeuvre, it can be served cold, at room temperature, or hot. Antipasti (the plural of antipasto) are platters featuring an assortment of hors d'oeuvres, cold meats, and cheeses. They're a lovely way to present snacks or a light meal to family and friends.

Make your own antipasti platter using the recipes in this chapter. Include items like the Mediterranean Spiced Black Olives, Roasted Eggplant Paté, and Spiced Pepperonata. The Spiced Roasted Vegetables in Chapter 16 are another good addition. Add some cheese, such as slices of fresh mozarella drizzled with olive oil and garnished with chopped basil, provolone, or nutty-flavored fontina. If you want, supplement the platter with a selection of Italian cold meats, such as thinly sliced salami, pepperoni, or prosciutto.

Zesty Cheddar Spread

This spiced version of pimento cheese, a favorite from the American Deep South, can be piped onto crackers or raw vegetables, used as a sandwich spread or a topping for a bagel, or used to fill an omelet.

Yield: *1 pound*

Preparation time: *15 minutes; 1 hour chilling time*

Spice meter: *Moderately spiced to hot and spicy*

½ pound softened cream cheese or Neufchatel cheese

½ pound sharp or extra-sharp grated cheddar cheese

¼ cup drained canned pimentos or diced jarred pimentos

¼ cup drained, sliced, canned jalapeno peppers

¼ teaspoon cayenne

¼ teaspoon paprika

¼ teaspoon ground cumin or curry powder

1 plump clove garlic, pressed, or ⅛ teaspoon garlic powder

2 scallions, white part only, minced

1 In a food processor fitted with a metal blade, combine the cream cheese and cheddar cheese and pulse to blend. Alternatively, combine the cream cheese and cheddar cheese in a medium bowl and stir to mix evenly.

2 Add the remaining ingredients and pulse or stir to mix well.

3 Transfer the mixture to a bowl, cover, and refrigerate until the mixture becomes firm, at least 1 hour.

Variation: Substitute chopped black olives or additional chopped scallions for the jalapenos.

Per serving: Calories 109 (From Fat 87); Fat 10g (Saturated 6g); Cholesterol 30mg; Sodium 152mg; Carbohydrate 1g (Dietary Fiber 0g); Protein 5g.

Black Bean Dip

Serve this tangy dip with tortilla chips and Tomato Salsa (Chapter 11). You can stir a few tablespoons of salsa into the dip, if you want.

Yield: *8 servings*

Preparation time: *10 minutes*

Spice meter: *Moderately spiced to hot and spicy*

2 cups cooked or canned black beans

2 tablespoons lime juice

1 tablespoon red wine vinegar

3 to 4 scallions, white part only

2 plump cloves garlic, minced

2 jalapeno or serrano chiles, seeded and minced

½ teaspoon cumin

⅛ teaspoon allspice

3 tablespoons chopped cilantro

Salt to taste

1 Combine the beans, lime juice, vinegar, and scallions in a food processor fitted with a metal blade. Pulse until the mixture is pureed. If it's too thick, add a tablespoon or two of water.

2 Add the garlic, chiles, cumin, and allspice and pulse to blend.

3 Transfer the bean puree to a bowl. Stir in the cilantro. Taste for salt and add if necessary. If you're using canned beans, you may not need the salt.

Tip: If you're using canned beans, make sure you put them in a colander or sieve, rinse them under cold running water, and drain them well before using them in the recipe.

Per serving: Calories 63 (From Fat 3); Fat 0g (Saturated 0g); Cholesterol 0mg; Sodium 75mg; Carbohydrate 12g (Dietary Fiber 4g); Protein 4g.

Sunset Butternut Soup

This soup, which is also called *haleem,* is scented with fragrant spices — ginger, cinnamon, and nutmeg. It is traditionally eaten in the evenings to break the Muslim Ramadan fast, which lasts from sunrise to sunset. It is perfect as a starter or a light meal during autumn and winter. It also freezes well. A picture of this soup appears in the color section of this book.

Yield: *6 servings*

Preparation time: *15 to 20 minutes*

Cooking time: *35 to 40 minutes*

Spice meter: *Mildly spiced*

2 tablespoons butter or margarine

1 medium onion, chopped

1 medium red bell pepper, chopped

1 large carrot, chopped

½-inch piece fresh ginger, minced

1 plump clove garlic, minced

½ serrano or jalapeno chile, seeded and minced, or ⅛ to ¼ teaspoon cayenne (optional)

1 bay leaf

½ teaspoon ground cinnamon

¼ teaspoon freshly grated or ground nutmeg or ground cardamom

⅛ teaspoon ground cloves

1 Granny Smith apple, peeled, cored, and chopped

4 cups chicken or vegetable broth

1¾ pounds butternut squash, peeled, seeded, and cut into 1½ inch chunks, about 3½ to 4 cups

¾ to 1 teaspoon salt, or to taste

2 to 3 tablespoons chopped cilantro

1 In a large pot, melt the butter over medium-low heat. Add the onion, bell pepper, and carrot and cook, stirring often, until the onion is translucent, about 5 to 7 minutes. Add the ginger, garlic, chile, and bay leaf and cook, stirring for 1 minute. Add the cinnamon, nutmeg, and cloves and cook, stirring often, for 1 minute. Add the apple and cook, stirring occasionally, until softened slightly, about 3 minutes.

2 Add the chicken broth and butternut and simmer, partially covered, until the vegetables are tender, about 25 to 30 minutes.

3 Remove the bay leaf. With a slotted spoon, transfer the vegetables and apple to a food processor. Reserve the broth. Puree the vegetables and apple until smooth. Alternatively, if you have a hand blender, leave the soup in the pot and blend.

4 Return the puree and reserved broth to the pot. Heat thoroughly over medium heat, about 5 minutes. Garnish with chopped cilantro.

Tip: *If the soup is too thick, thin it with additional broth or apple juice or cider.*

Per serving: *Calories 122 (From Fat 61); Fat 7g (Saturated 3g); Cholesterol 14mg; Sodium 969mg; Carbohydrate 15g (Dietary Fiber 4g); Protein 2g.*

Indian-Spiced Lentil Soup

Lentils absorb the flavor of the spices in this warming soup. The recipe is based on one of the cornerstones of Indian cooking — dal — which can be made with dried split peas or lentils. The soup freezes well.

Yield: *6 servings*

Preparation time: *15 to 20 minutes*

Cooking time: *50 to 60 minutes*

Spice meter: *Moderately spiced*

2 tablespoons butter or vegetable oil

2 medium onions, chopped

2 plump cloves garlic, minced

½-inch piece fresh ginger, minced

2 teaspoons ground cumin

1½ teaspoons ground coriander

½ teaspoon turmeric

½ teaspoon brown or black mustard seeds (optional)

½ teaspoon crushed red pepper flakes, or to taste

¼ teaspoon freshly ground black pepper

8 cups chicken or vegetable broth

1 pound brown lentils, picked over, rinsed, and drained

1 tomato, peeled, seeded, and chopped, or ½ cup canned chopped tomatoes

1 tablespoon fresh lemon juice

½ to 1 teaspoon salt, or to taste

1 In a large soup pot, melt the butter over medium-low heat. Add the onion and cook, stirring occasionally, until translucent, about 5 to 7 minutes. Add the garlic and ginger and cook, stirring, for 1 minute. Add the cumin, coriander, turmeric, mustard seeds, crushed red pepper flakes, and black pepper. Cook, stirring, for 1 minute. Do not allow the spices to burn.

2 Increase the heat to medium. Add the broth, lentils, and tomato. Cover and bring the liquid to a boil.

3 Reduce the heat to medium-low. Simmer, partially covered, until the lentils are tender, about 35 to 45 minutes.

4 Puree in batches in a food processor or blender. Alternatively, if you have a hand blender, leave the soup in the pot and blend.

5 Add the lemon juice and salt and stir to mix. Reheat before serving.

Variation: *Instead of the dry spices in the recipe, add 1½ tablespoons homemade or commercial curry powder after cooking the onions, ginger, and garlic. Serve with a dollop of plain yogurt, if you like.*

Per serving: *Calories 364 (From Fat 94); Fat 10g (Saturated 4g); Cholesterol 17mg; Sodium 2,051mg; Carbohydrate 49g (Dietary Fiber 19g); Protein 22g.*

Mexican Tomato Soup

This is a chunky soup, but you can puree it or make it creamy as directed in the variations. To thin the soup, add additional chicken broth or cream. The soup freezes well.

Yield: *6 servings*

Preparation time: *15 minutes*

Cooking time: *45 to 50 minutes*

Spice meter: *Moderately spiced to hot and spicy*

2 tablespoons olive oil	⅛ teaspoon ground cloves
1 medium onion, chopped	1½ cups chicken broth
2 plump cloves garlic, minced	28-ounce can chopped tomatoes
1 to 2 jalapenos, seeded and minced	1 bay leaf
¾ teaspoon ground cumin	¼ teaspoon dried oregano
¼ teaspoon ground cinnamon	½ to ¾ teaspoon salt, or to taste

1 Heat the olive oil in a medium-sized pot over medium heat. Add the onion and cook, stirring occasionally, until the onion is translucent, about 5 minutes. Add the garlic and jalapeno and cook, stirring, for 1 minute. Add the cumin, cinnamon, and cloves and cook, stirring for 30 seconds.

2 Add the broth, tomatoes, bay leaf, and oregano. Simmer, partially covered, for 40 to 45 minutes. Remove the bay leaf with a slotted spoon and season the soup with salt.

Variation: *Create a pureed spiced tomato soup. Puree in batches in a food processor or blender until smooth. Alternatively, if you have a hand blender, leave the soup in the pot and blend.*

Variation: *Make a creamy spiced tomato soup. Decrease the broth to 1 cup and cook. Puree the soup as in the pureed version. Add ½ to ¾ cup half-and-half or cream and reheat over medium heat.*

Per serving: Calories 86 (From Fat 51); Fat 6g (Saturated 1g); Cholesterol 1mg; Sodium 613mg; Carbohydrate 8g (Dietary Fiber 3g); Protein 2g.

Part IV

From the Main Course to the Finish Line

The 5th Wave — By Rich Tennant

"OK Cookie-your venison in lingdonberry sauce is good, as are your eggplant soufflé and the risotto with foie gras. But whoever taught you how to make a croquembouche should be shot!"

In this part . . .

In this large part, I present spicy recipes for chicken, meat, seafood, vegetables, potatoes, grains, pasta, quick breads, sweets, and beverages — everything from main dishes to side dishes to desserts.

Chapter 13

Chicken

* *

In This Chapter

▶ Being safe with chicken

▶ Making great dishes with chicken

* *

Chicken is one of the most versatile of all foods. A wide range of spice combinations are able to complement chicken. In this chapter, you find a wealth of international and classic recipes.

Handling Chicken

When handling raw chicken, make sure you follow these basic hygiene procedures to prevent any contamination:

✔ Check the sell-by date. If you don't plan to use it before the date, remove the chicken from the packaging and wrap it in freezer wrap. Mark the item with the date and contents. It's best to use the chicken within 2 months of freezing to maintain the proper flavor and texture. Technically, in a freezer that's set at 0 degrees, (you can buy a freezer thermometer to test the temperature), you can keep chicken for up to 6 to 8 months.

✔ Thaw frozen chicken overnight in the refrigerator or follow the directions that came with your microwave for defrosting chicken.

✔ Whether the chicken is defrosted or fresh, whole or in parts, wash it and pat it dry with a paper towel.

✔ After working with chicken, wash your cutting board, knife, and hands with hot, soapy water and rinse well.

✔ When the thickest part of the chicken is pierced with an instant-read thermometer, baked, roasted, and grilled chicken parts should reach a temperature of 160 degrees. The juices should run clear.

Here are a few other handy tips for preparing chicken easily:

✔ When substituting boneless chicken breasts for whole parts, decrease the cooking time. Cook the chicken until it is tender and doesn't have any hint of pink in its juices or flesh. When substituting whole parts for boneless chicken breasts, increase the cooking time and cook the chicken until the juices run clear when the chicken part is pierced in the thickest part. The exact time depends on the size of the boneless breast or chicken part.

✔ To cut chicken cutlets into cubes or strips, freeze the chicken for 15 to 30 minutes and then cut.

It's often cheaper to buy whole chicken rather than boneless filets or parts. Figure 13-1 shows you how to cut up a whole chicken. All you need is a good, sharp chef's knife and a cutting board.

CUTTING A CHICKEN INTO PARTS

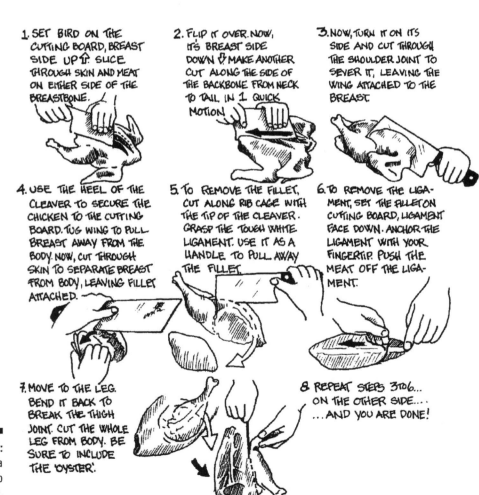

1. SET BIRD ON THE CUTTING BOARD, BREAST SIDE UP. SLICE THROUGH SKIN AND MEAT ON EITHER SIDE OF THE BREASTBONE.

2. FLIP IT OVER. NOW, IT'S BREAST SIDE DOWN & MAKE ANOTHER CUT ALONG THE SIDE OF THE BACKBONE FROM NECK TO TAIL IN 1 QUICK MOTION.

3. NOW, TURN IT ON ITS SIDE AND CUT THROUGH THE SHOULDER JOINT TO SEVER IT, LEAVING THE WING ATTACHED TO THE BREAST.

4. USE THE HEEL OF THE CLEAVER TO SECURE THE CHICKEN TO THE CUTTING BOARD. TUG WING TO PULL BREAST AWAY FROM THE BODY. NOW, CUT THROUGH SKIN TO SEPARATE BREAST FROM BODY, LEAVING FILLET ATTACHED.

5. TO REMOVE THE FILLET, CUT ALONG RIB CAGE WITH THE TIP OF THE CLEAVER. GRASP THE TOUGH WHITE LIGAMENT. USE IT AS A HANDLE TO PULL AWAY THE FILLET.

6. TO REMOVE THE LIGA- MENT, SET THE FILLET ON CUTTING BOARD, LIGAMENT FACE DOWN. ANCHOR THE LIGAMENT WITH YOUR FINGERTIP. PUSH THE MEAT OFF THE LIGA- MENT.

7. MOVE TO THE LEG. BEND IT BACK TO BREAK THE THIGH JOINT. CUT THE WHOLE LEG FROM BODY. BE SURE TO INCLUDE THE 'OYSTER'.

8. REPEAT STEPS 3 TO 6... ON THE OTHER SIDE.... ...AND YOU ARE DONE!

Figure 13-1: Cutting a chicken into parts.

Cooking Chicken

It's easy to cook chicken so it remains tender and succulent if you follow these guidelines:

- ✔ When the thickest part of the chicken is pierced with an instant-read thermometer, baked, roasted, broiled, and grilled chicken parts should reach a temperature of 160 degrees for breasts and 165 for legs. The juices should run clear. If you're unsure, you can cut into the chicken slightly with a paring knife and check that there is no pink meat.

- ✔ Chicken parts are cooked through at different times. White or breast meat cooks faster than dark meat or legs. Separating whole chicken legs into thighs and drumsticks will make them cook more quickly. Wings take much less to cook than other parts.

Broiling and grilling

Broiling and grilling chicken parts is an inexact science because chicken parts vary in size. You can pre-cook the chicken partially in a 350-degree oven for about 20 minutes before placing it on a grill or under a broiler. That way the chicken or marinade won't char as quickly. On a grill, you might want to use only one kind of part, but if you want variety, start the dark meat before of the breasts, and put the wings on last. Remove those pieces that are cooked through first, and keep them warm on a plate covered with foil.

- ✔ **To broil chicken:** Place the chicken, 6 to 8-inches from the heat source, on a two-piece broiler tray so the fat drips away. Broil skin-side down first. After the time suggested in the recipe, usually about 10 to 15 minutes, turn the chicken pieces. You need to turn wings sooner than that. Cook the chicken, turning a few times until it is cooked through. Baste as indicated in the recipes.

- ✔ **To grill chicken:** Cook over a coals that have medium heat, not when over a hot fire. Grill the chicken skin-side up first. After the time suggested in the recipe, usually about 10 to 15 minutes, turn the chicken pieces, but turn wings sooner than that. Cook the chicken, turning a few times until it is cooked through. Baste as indicated in the recipes. Occasionally, rotate the position of the chicken parts on the grill as they cook because different areas of the grill are hotter than others.

Using parts versus cutlets

Boneless chicken breast cutlets cook quickly, about 3 to 4 minutes per side. When substituting boneless chicken breasts for whole parts, decrease the cooking time but cook the chicken until it is tender and without any hint of pink in its juices or flesh.

When substituting whole parts for boneless chicken breasts, increase the cooking time and cook the chicken until when the juices run clear when the chicken part is pierced in the thickest part or test with an instant read thermometer. Exact time changes depends on the size the chicken parts, but if you bake them, they should take about 40 to 45 minutes. If you are simmering them in a sauce, such as in Indian Chicken Curry, brown the chicken pieces first in skillet with a vegetable oil or butter, turning them so all the sides are lightly golden, and then remove the chicken pieces and set them aside. Make the sauce and add the chicken pieces. They should simmer in the sauce for about 40 to 45 minutes.

Down-Home Barbecued Chicken

Barbecued chicken basted in a tomato-based barbecue sauce is a perennial American favorite. Make sure you have extra sauce to serve on the side. Check out this recipe on the seventh page of the color section.

Yield: *4 servings*

Preparation time: *5 minutes*

Cooking time: *30 to 40 minutes*

Spice meter: *Moderately spiced*

2½ to 3 pounds chicken parts

1 cup Tangy Tomato Barbecue Sauce from Chapter 10 or commercial barbecue sauce, plus extra, about 1 cup for serving on the side

Preheat the grill or broiler. Broil skin-side down or grill skin-side up, basting occasionally with the sauce. Cook about 10 to 15 minutes then turn and cook, basting occasionally and turning once or twice more, until the chicken is cooked through. The juices should run clear when pierced with the tip of a paring knife. The cooking time should be about 30 to 45 minutes depending on the size of the parts. Serve with extra barbecue sauce on the side.

Variation: Cook the chicken in your oven. Preheat the oven to 350 degrees. Baste the chicken with a little barbecue sauce. Bake, basting occasionally with the sauce, until the juices run clear when the chicken is pricked with a fork, about 40 to 45 minutes. If the chicken isn't crispy on top, preheat the broiler. Baste the chicken once more and broil the chicken, skin-side up, until the skin is lightly browned, about 5 minutes. Serve with extra barbecue sauce on the side.

Variation: Make barbecued chicken in chile adobo. Marinate the chicken for 6 to 24 hours in Chile Adobo Sauce (Chapter 10). Remove the chicken from the marinade and barbecue the chicken on the grill or bake it in the oven as directed in the recipe.

Per serving: *Calories 376 (From Fat 169); Fat 19g (Saturated 5g); Cholesterol 149mg; Sodium 632mg; Carbohydrate 13g (Dietary Fiber 1g); Protein 38g.*

Chinese-Spiced Baked Chicken

Scented with orange, soy, ginger, and five-spice powder, this is a delightful alternative to plain baked chicken. Serve with Plum Salsa (Chapter 11) if you want.

Yield: *4 servings*

Preparation time: *15 minutes; 1 to 4 hours marinating time*

Cooking time: *45 to 50 minutes*

Spice meter: *Mildly to moderately spiced*

⅓ cup soy sauce

1 teaspoon dark sesame oil

Juice and finely grated zest of one medium orange

2 tablespoons dry sherry

1 plump garlic clove, minced

1-inch piece fresh ginger, minced

1 teaspoon Chinese five-spice powder (optional)

2 scallions, white and green parts, sliced

3 to 3½ pound chicken, cut up, or chicken parts

1 In a shallow baking dish, combine all the ingredients except the chicken.

2 Add the chicken to the marinade and toss to coat evenly. Marinate in the refrigerator for 1 to 4 hours, turning occasionally.

3 Preheat the oven to 350 degrees. Remove the chicken from the marinade and put the chicken, skin-side up, on a foil-lined baking sheet or broiler rack. Bake the chicken, basting occasionally, until the juices run clear when the chicken is pricked with a fork, about 40 to 45 minutes.

4 If the chicken isn't crispy on top, preheat the broiler. Baste the chicken once more and broil the chicken, skin-side up, until the skin is lightly crispy and browned, about 5 minutes.

Cook's Fact: *Chinese five-spice powder is available in most supermarkets, Asian groceries, and specialty stores. You can easily make your own (see Chapter 2).*

Per serving: *Calories 427 (From Fat 210); Fat 23g (Saturated 6g); Cholesterol 178mg; Sodium 1,491mg; Carbohydrate 5g (Dietary Fiber 1g); Protein 46g.*

Grilled Lime-Cumin Chicken Cutlets

You can put this simple and straightforward dish together in a flash. Marinate the chicken while you're preparing any side dishes. If you want, make a terrific sandwich by serving the cutlets on rolls.

Yield: *4 to 6 servings*

Preparation time: *10 minutes; 15 to 30 minutes marinating time*

Cooking time: *10 minutes*

Spice meter: *Mildly to moderately spiced*

1½ teaspoons ground cumin

1 teaspoon ground coriander

1½ teaspoon minced fresh ginger

¼ teaspoon white pepper, black pepper, or cayenne

2½ tablespoons fresh lime or lemon juice

2 teaspoons vegetable oil

4 to 6 boneless chicken breast halves, about 1½ pounds

1 In a shallow dish, combine all the ingredients except the chicken.

2 Add the chicken breast halves and turn to evenly coat in the marinade. Marinate in the refrigerator for 15 to 30 minutes, turning once.

3 Preheat the grill or broiler. Grill the chicken until it's lightly browned on one side, then turn and grill until lightly browned and cooked through, about 3 to 4 minutes per side.

Tip: *Serve the chicken with any of the following: Southeast Asian Peanut Sauce (Chapter 10), Papaya, Mango, or Pineapple Salsa or the fruity pico de gallo variation (Chapter 11), Plum Salsa (Chapter 11), Tomato Salsa (Chapter 11), or Gingered Tomato Salad (Chapter 11).*

Per serving: Calories 175 (From Fat 69); Fat 8g (Saturated 2g); Cholesterol 69mg; Sodium 59mg; Carbohydrate 1g (Dietary Fiber 0g); Protein 24g.

Gingered Roast Chicken

The spice mixture can be rubbed on the skin of the chicken or slipped under loosened skin. After the spices are added, roast the chicken to perfection. Serve with Plum Salsa (Chapter 11) if you want.

Yield: *4 to 6 servings*

Preparation time: *20 minutes; 2 to 24 hours marinating time*

Cooking time: *1 to 1¼ hours*

Spice meter: *Mildly spiced*

2 tablespoons fresh lime or lemon juice

2½ tablespoons olive oil

1½ tablespoons soy sauce

2 tablespoons prepared mustard

1 tablespoon chopped chives or minced flat-leaf parsley

1 teaspoon chopped fresh thyme or ½ teaspoon dried thyme leaves

1-inch piece fresh ginger, minced

2 plump cloves garlic, minced

¼ teaspoon cayenne (optional)

¼ teaspoon white pepper

3 to 3½ pound whole chicken

1 In a bowl, combine all the ingredients except the chicken.

2 Put the chicken in a large roasting pan. Rub the marinade all over the chicken. Alternatively, starting with the breast, carefully slip your fingers under the skin to loosen it, trying not to rip the skin. Put the marinade under the skin and rub gently to coat the meat evenly, a process that makes the chicken more moist. Smear any remaining marinade on the outside of the chicken. Marinate in the refrigerator for at least 2 hours or up to 24 hours.

3 Preheat the oven to 450 degrees. Place the chicken, breast side up, on a rack in a roasting pan and bake. After 15 minutes, reduce the temperature to 350 degrees. Bake until a meat thermometer inserted into the thigh registers 160 degrees or until the juices run clear when the thigh is pierced with a small knife, about an additional 40 to 45 minutes.

4 Remove the chicken from the roasting pan. Tip the chicken so the cavity points downward to let the juices from the cavity run into the pan. Place the chicken on a carving board and let it rest for 10 minutes before carving.

Variation: *This recipe can also be made with chicken parts. Bake in a preheated oven at 350 degrees. The cooking time will be slightly less than when roasting a whole chicken. Depending on what parts you use, you should cook the parts about 40 to 45 minutes. Test to be sure that the juices run clear.*

Per serving: *Calories 320 (From Fat 185); Fat 21g (Saturated 5g); Cholesterol 119mg; Sodium 404mg; Carbohydrate 2g (Dietary Fiber 0g); Protein 30g.*

Mediterranean-Spiced Chicken with Olives

Some dishes benefit from a blend of both spices and herbs. The pleasing combination in this recipe gives baked chicken a deliciously sweet and fragrant flavor. Leftovers are superb cold.

Yield: *6 servings*

Preparation time: *25 minutes; 2 to 24 hours marinating time*

Cooking time: *45 to 50 minutes*

Spice meter: *Moderately spiced to mildly hot*

6 chicken breasts

3 tablespoons brown sugar

½ teaspoon salt

⅔ cup dry white wine

¼ cup honey

1-inch piece of orange or lemon zest, white pith removed

2 teaspoons minced fresh ginger, about ¾-inch piece

2 plump cloves garlic, minced

¼ teaspoon cayenne

¼ teaspoon ground cinnamon

¼ cup chopped flat-leaf parsley

½ teaspoon minced fresh thyme or ¼ teaspoon dried thyme leaves

1 teaspoon fresh minced oregano or ½ teaspoon dried

½ bay leaf, crushed

24 black olives, preferably kalamata or Italian, pitted

Fresh chopped parsley for garnish

1 Rub the chicken breasts on both sides with 1½ tablespoons of the brown sugar, then sprinkle with salt. Place the chicken, skin-side down, in a shallow baking dish.

2 In a bowl, combine the remaining 1½ tablespoons of brown sugar with the white wine, honey, orange or lemon zest, ginger, garlic, cayenne, cinnamon, 2 tablespoons of the parsley, the thyme, oregano, and bay leaf.

3 Pour the mixture over the chicken. Add the olives. Marinate for 2 to 24 hours, as time permits. Preheat the oven to 350 degrees.

4 Turn the chicken skin-side up. Bake the chicken, basting occasionally with the sauce, until the juices run clear when the chicken is pricked with a fork and the skin is lightly browned, about 45 minutes.

5 Divide the chicken and olives among plates and spoon a tablespoon or two of the sauce over each. Garnish with the remaining fresh parsley. Serve with the extra sauce on the side.

Tip: *To crumble a bay leaf, hold it between your fingers and rub it into small pieces.*

Per serving: *Calories 309 (From Fat 105); Fat 12g (Saturated 3g); Cholesterol 82mg; Sodium 513mg; Carbohydrate 21g (Dietary Fiber 0g); Protein 30g.*

ed Fruit Salad (Chapter 11)

Sunset Butternut Soup (Chapter 12); Caraway,
Cheese, and Bacon Beer Bread (Chapter 18) *Spices
from top: caraway, whole nutmeg, cayenne*

Pasta Puttanesca (Chapter 17)

**Vegetarian Bean Chili (Chapter 16); Cumin-Chile Corn Muffins
(Chapter 18)** *Seasonings, clockwise, from top left: white pepper,
cumin, pure chile powder, dried Greek oregano*

Spicy Crab Cakes with Cilantro Sauce;
Fish Veracruz (both in Chapter 15)

Beef (or Pork) Stew with Juniper and Chile
Powder (Chapter 14) *Spice: juniper berries*

Down-Home Barbecued Chicken (Chapter 13); Roasted Potatoes with Garlic and Cumin (Chapter 17) *Spices front: cumin seeds;*

Nut Biscotti with Aniseed; Old-Fashioned
Gingerbread (both in Chapter 18); Mulled Red
Wine (Chapter 19) *Spices: cinnamon, whole cloves*

Jerk Chicken

This spicy chicken is a Jamaican favorite. The longer you marinate the chicken, the more flavorful the taste. Wear latex or rubber gloves when touching the jerk marinade with your hands. Using a spatula or basting brush is a good idea. Serve with Papaya, Mango, or Pineapple Salsa (Chapter 11). Pineapple is the best with this dish. The Gingered Tomato Salad (Chapter 11) is also a good accompaniment.

Yield: *4 to 6 servings*

Preparation time: *15 minutes; 2 to 24 hours marinating time*

Cooking time: *30 to 40 minutes*

Spice meter: *Hot and spicy*

1 recipe Jamaican Jerk Sauce (Chapter 10) or commercial jerk sauce

3½ to 4 pounds chicken parts

1 Put the chicken in a shallow dish that's large enough to hold the pieces in one layer. Spread the jerk sauce on both sides of the chicken. Marinate in the refrigerator for a minimum of 2 hours or overnight.

2 Preheat the grill or broiler. Broil skin-side down or grill skin-side up, basting occasionally with the sauce. Cook about 10 to 15 minutes then turn and cook, basting occasionally and turning once or twice more, until the chicken is cooked through. The juices should run clear when the meat is pierced with the tip of a paring knife. Total cooking time should be about 30 to 45 minutes, depending on the size of the parts.

Variation: *Alternatively, bake the chicken in a preheated oven at 350 degrees until the juices run clear when the meat is pieced with the tip of a paring knife, about 40 to 45 minutes. Brown the chicken, if necessary, under the broiler or on a grill.*

Per serving: *Calories 366 (From Fat 191); Fat 21g (Saturated 5g); Cholesterol 139mg; Sodium 402mg; Carbohydrate 7g (Dietary Fiber 1g); Protein 35g.*

Yakitori

Yakitori, Japan's traditional chicken kebab, is marinated in teriyaki sauce. It can be grilled or broiled.

Yield: *4 servings as a main course, 8 servings as a first course*

Preparation time: *30 minutes; 20 to 60 minutes marinating time*

Cooking time: *10 minutes*

Spice meter: *Mildly spiced*

1½ pounds boneless chicken breasts

¾ cup Teriyaki Sauce (Chapter 10) or commercially available sauce

2 scallions, white and green parts, sliced

1 Cut the chicken into 1 to 1½ inch strips.

2 In a shallow dish, combine the chicken strips and teriyaki sauce and toss to coat evenly. Cover and marinate in the refrigerator for 20 to 60 minutes, turning the chicken once or twice.

3 Remove the chicken from the marinade but reserve the marinade for basting. Thread the chicken onto 8 skewers.

4 Preheat the grill or broiler. Grill or broil, basting with some of the marinade and turning the skewers occasionally, until the chicken is cooked through, about 7 to 10 minutes.

Variation: *Make chicken teriyaki. Instead of cutting the chicken into strips, marinate whole chicken cutlets in the refrigerator for 30 to 60 minutes. Grill or broil until the chicken is cooked through, about 3 to 5 minutes per side.*

Per serving: *Calories 289 (From Fat 86); Fat 10g (Saturated 3g); Cholesterol 103mg; Sodium 1,810mg; Carbohydrate 10g (Dietary Fiber 0g); Protein 38g.*

Skewer it

Skewers come in a variety of lengths, from 6 inches to 12 inches, and can be made of stainless steel, chrome-plated steel, or bamboo. If you're using bamboo skewers, soak them in water for at least 30 minutes before using. That way they shouldn't burn when you put them on the grill or under the broiler.

Southeast Asian Chicken Saté

This popular skewered chicken, versions of which are eaten in Thailand and Vietnam, is marinated and then grilled or broiled. Serve it with dipping sauce such as the Southeast Asian Peanut Sauce in Chapter 10 or the Plum Salsa in Chapter 11. For a side dish, try the Spiced Carrot and Pineapple Sambal (Chapter 11) or the Pickled Cucumber and Carrot Salad (Chapter 11).

Yield: *4 servings as a main course, 8 servings as a first course*

Preparation time: *20 minutes; 1 hour marinating time*

Cooking time: *10 minutes*

Spice meter: *Moderately spiced to hot and spicy*

1½ pounds boneless chicken breasts, cut into thin strips or cubed

3 tablespoons unsweetened coconut milk or plain yogurt

1 tablespoon fresh lime or lemon juice

1 plump clove garlic, pressed or minced

2 stalks fresh lemon grass, thinly sliced, or 2 to 3 tablespoons dried

1 teaspoon ground coriander

¾ teaspoon ground cumin

½ teaspoon cayenne or ground chile pepper powder

1 Cut the chicken into 1 to 1½ inch strips.

2 In a shallow dish, combine all the ingredients except the chicken and stir to mix. Add the chicken to the marinade and toss to coat evenly. Cover and marinate in the refrigerator for 1 hour, turning the chicken once or twice.

3 Remove the chicken from the marinade. Reserve the marinade for basting. Thread the chicken onto 8 skewers.

4 Preheat the grill or broiler. Grill or broil, basting with some of the marinade and turning the skewers occasionally, until the chicken is cooked through, about 7 to 10 minutes.

Tip: *Unsweetened coconut milk is available canned. Cover and refrigerate any leftovers.*

Variation: *Make shrimp saté. Use 1½ pounds of peeled and deveined shrimp instead of chicken. Marinate for 30 minutes and then cook until pink on both sides, about 3 to 4 minutes. Serve with Papaya, Mango, or Pineapple Salsa (Chapter 11) or with Southeast Asian Peanut Sauce (Chapter 11).*

Per serving: *Calories 721 (From Fat 468); Fat 52g (Saturated 22g); Cholesterol 103mg; Sodium 373mg; Carbohydrate 19g (Dietary Fiber 5g); Protein 50g.*

Thai Chicken Curry

This classic curry, made with unsweetened coconut milk, gets its spicy punch from Thai curry paste. Serve it with rice.

Yield: *4 to 6 servings*

Preparation time: *20 minutes*

Cooking time: *20 to 30 minutes*

Spice meter: *Moderately spicy to hot and spicy*

1 tablespoon vegetable oil

2 to 3 tablespoons Thai red or green curry paste (Chapter 9) or commercial Thai curry paste

1¾ cups unsweetened coconut milk

1 to 2 stalks lemon grass, bruised and cut into 1-inch pieces

1 to 2 Thai lime leaves (optional)

2 pounds boneless skinless chicken breasts, cut into strips

¾ cup frozen peas, thawed

2 tablespoons Thai fish sauce or soy sauce

1 In a deep skillet or stewpot over medium heat, heat the vegetable oil. Add the Thai curry paste and cook, stirring constantly, until the aroma is very strong, about 3 to 5 minutes.

2 Add the coconut milk, lemon grass, and lime leaves and simmer for 3 minutes.

3 Add the chicken. Simmer until the chicken is cooked through, about 10 to 15 minutes.

4 Stir in the peas and Thai fish sauce and simmer for 3 to 5 minutes or until the peas are heated through.

Warning: *Coconut milk does not freeze well. Refrigerate any leftovers and reheat on the stove or in a microwave.*

Per serving: *Calories 342 (From Fat 180); Fat 20g (Saturated 14g); Cholesterol 84mg; Sodium 564mg; Carbohydrate 8g (Dietary Fiber 2g); Protein 34g.*

Indian Chicken Curry

This traditional rendition of curry can be made several hours to a day ahead and reheated. Serve with basmati rice, chutney, and Tomato Raita (Chapter 11) or the Gingered Tomato Salad (Chapter 11). Indian curries are often served with a variety of condiments, which each diner can use to garnish his or her food. The condiments include chutney, chopped onions mixed with chopped coriander, raisins, shredded coconut, and sliced banana.

Yield: *4 to 6 servings*

Preparation time: *20 minutes*

Cooking time: *40 to 45 minutes*

Spice meter: *Moderately hot to hot and spicy*

2 tablespoons vegetable oil

1 medium onion, chopped

3 plump cloves garlic, minced

1-inch piece fresh ginger, minced

2 to 3 tablespoons homemade or good-quality curry powder

1½ to 1¾ pounds boneless, skinless chicken breasts, cut into thin strips or cubed

1½ cups peeled and seeded chopped fresh tomatoes or one 14½-ounce can chopped tomatoes

½ to ⅔ cup chicken broth or water

Homemade or commercial chutney for garnish

1 In a stewpot or large deep skillet, heat the vegetable oil over medium heat. Add the onion and cook until it's translucent, about 5 to 7 minutes. Add the garlic and ginger and cook, stirring constantly, for 1 minute. Add the curry powder and cook, stirring constantly, for 1 minute.

2 Add the chicken and tomatoes and cook, stirring often, until the chicken turns white. Add ½ cup of the broth and simmer, uncovered, for 15 minutes.

3 Reduce the heat to medium-low and partially cover the pot. Simmer until the chicken is cooked through, the liquid is slightly reduced, and the flavors are blended, about 20 minutes more. Check and see if the sauce is too thick and add the additional broth or water. Serve with rice and chutney on the side.

Tip: *You'll need to add more broth or water if you are making the curry ahead, but do so before reheating.*

Cook's Fact: *Chutney is the traditional accompaniment to Indian curries. You can find it bottled in the condiment section of most supermarkets. Mango chutney is one popular type. You can also make the Papaya, Mango, or Pineapple Salsa variation for fresh chutney (Chapter 11) or try it with Plum Salsa (Chapter 11).*

Per serving: *Calories 189 (From Fat 72); Fat 8g (Saturated 1g); Cholesterol 63mg; Sodium 144mg; Carbohydrate 5g (Dietary Fiber 1g); Protein 24g.*

Tandoori Chicken Cutlets

No one I know has an authentic Indian clay tandoori oven in his or her house. You'll probably have to be satisfied with grilling or broiling, but the taste is still terrific. Tandoori chicken is marinated in yogurt and spices. Normally, it's characterized by a red color, which you can duplicate by adding a few drops of red food coloring to the yogurt mixture. You can serve it with any fruit salsa in Chapter 11 or with the Gingered Tomato Salad from Chapter 11.

If you prefer to use chicken breasts on the bone instead of the boneless breasts that are called for in this recipe, you can marinate the chicken up to 24 hours and cook as directed in Down-Home Barbecued Chicken in this chapter.

Yield: *4 to 6 servings*

Preparation time: *15 minutes; 2 to 6 hours marinating time*

Cooking time: *10 minutes*

Spice meter: *Moderately spiced*

1 cup plain yogurt	*½ teaspoon salt*
2 plump cloves garlic, pressed or minced	*¼ teaspoon turmeric*
½-inch piece fresh ginger, minced	*⅛ teaspoon ground cloves or 2 whole cloves*
1 teaspoon ground cumin	*¾ teaspoon garam masala (optional)*
1 teaspoon ground coriander	*1¾ pounds boneless, skinless chicken breast halves, about 4 to 6 halves total*
½ to ¾ teaspoon cayenne, or to taste	
½ teaspoon paprika	

1 In a shallow dish, combine all the ingredients except the chicken and stir. Add the chicken and toss to coat evenly. Cover and marinate in the refrigerator fo 2 hours to 6 hours, turning the chicken several times.

2 Preheat the grill or broiler. Grill, basting occasionally with the yogurt sauce, until the chicken is cooked through, about 3 to 4 minutes per side.

Variation: *Combine the yogurt with 1 to 1½ tablespoons prepared or homemade curry powder, ½ teaspoon paprika, and the salt. Stir to combine. Use this as your sauce for a simple, quick alternative.*

Variation: *Make tandoori shrimp. Instead of using chicken, marinate 1½ pounds cleaned medium or large shrimp in the yogurt mixture for 1 to 3 hours. Stir-fry in a hot skillet over medium to medium-high heat until the shrimp begins to curl and turn pink, about 3 to 4 minutes, or broil or grill for 3 to 4 minutes.*

Per serving: *Calories 250 (From Fat 56); Fat 6g (Saturated 2g); Cholesterol 118mg; Sodium 312mg; Carbohydrate 3g (Dietary Fiber 0g); Protein 43g.*

Chapter 14

Meat

In This Chapter

▶ Beef, pork, and veal recipes

▶ Roasts, grills, stews, kebabs, meatloaves, and more

Any meat, whether it's ground beef, steaks, lamb, pork roasts, ribs, or veal, is tastier when well seasoned. In this chapter, I present a collection of recipes from all corners of the globe. Meats are scented with spices, rubbed with spices, or simply accented with robust or mildly aromatic flavors.

Meat Matters

Food safety is a big issue these days, especially when it comes to buying and handling meat. Take these guidelines to heart:

✔ Check the sell-by date and use the meat or freeze it by that date. When freezing, take the meat out of the store packaging and then wrap it in foil or plastic wrap and also freezer wrap. Doing so prevents freezer burn, which will change not only the taste but also the texture of meat. Remember to label and date the package.

✔ Thaw frozen meat overnight in the refrigerator or follow the instructions for thawing meat in your microwave. Don't thaw meat at room temperature.

✔ If meat has a strong or unpleasant odor, discard it.

Most of us are concerned about eating too much fat, and beef and pork do contain their fair share of fat. Keep these tips in mind for keeping your meat lean and tasty.

> ✔ Buy good quality meat and trim it of most of the excess visible fat before you begin to cook it.
>
> ✔ Leave the strands of fat that run through the meat, known as marbling. They make the meat more tender.

Steak au Poivre

This classic French dish is always a hit with steak lovers. Serve it as is or with one of the two quick and easy sauces from the upcoming sidebar "Saucing the steak."

Yield: *4 to 6 servings*

Preparation time: *5 to 10 minutes*

Cooking time: *10 minutes*

Spice meter: *Mildly to moderately spiced*

4 to 6 boneless steaks, such as shell, sirloin, or filet, about 4 to 6 to ounces each, trimmed of visible fat around the edges

⅓ cup whole black or mixed peppercorns, coarsely crushed, or 4 tablespoons cracked black or mixed peppercorns

2 teaspoons kosher salt

1½ teaspoons butter

2 teaspoons olive oil

1 Rub each steak on both sides with the peppercorns. Press the peppercorns into the steak with the heel of your palm. Season both sides of the meat lightly with salt.

2 Over medium-high heat, heat a heavy skillet, preferably cast iron. The skillet needs to be large enough to hold all the steaks without crowding them. Use more than one skillet if necessary. Add the butter and olive oil and tilt the pan to coat evenly.

3 When the pan is hot, add the steaks and sear, allowing them to brown completely on one side before turning them. The steaks should cook about 3 to 4 minutes per side for rare, slightly longer for medium — about 5 to 6 minutes. Check for doneness by touch or by poking the meat with the tip of a paring knife. When they are cooked to your liking, serve immediately.

Per serving: *Calories 228 (From Fat 121); Fat 13g (Saturated 4g); Cholesterol 59mg; Sodium 417mg; Carbohydrate 2g (Dietary Fiber 0g); Protein 24g.*

Southwestern Flank Steak

This tasty steak should be sliced on the bias, which is simply to cut the meat on a slight angle as opposed to straight up and down. This will keep the meat more tender. It's best cooked rare to medium, not well-done.

Yield: *4 to 6 servings*

Preparation time: *10 to 15 minutes; 30 to 60 minutes marinating time*

Cooking time: *10 minutes*

Spice meter: *Mildly to moderately spiced*

¼ cup fresh lemon or lime juice

2 tablespoons soy sauce or water

2 tablespoons olive oil

1 clove garlic, minced or pressed

¼ to ½ teaspoon chili powder

¼ teaspoon ground cumin

¼ teaspoon black pepper

¼ teaspoon dried oregano

⅛ to ¼ teaspoon cayenne or ground chile pepper powder

1½ pounds flank or skirt steak, top round steak, or London broil

1 In a flat shallow dish, combine the lemon juice, soy sauce, olive oil, garlic, chili powder, cumin, pepper, oregano, and cayenne.

2 Add the steak to the marinade and turn to coat. Marinate for at least 30 minutes or refrigerate and marinate up to 1 hour.

3 Preheat the broiler or grill. Remove the meat from the marinade and pat it dry with paper towels. Broil about 6 inches from the heat, approximately 3 to 4 minutes per side for rare, 5 to 6 minutes per side for medium. Test for doneness with a knife or by using an instant-read thermometer. The temperature should be 125 to 130 degrees for rare to medium rare, 140 to 145 degrees for medium.

4 Let the steak rest for about 3 to 5 minutes before slicing on the diagonal against the grain.

Tip: Trim any excess fat from around the edge of the meat with a sharp knife; leave any marbling or veins of fat that run through the steak intact. Choose a piece of meat that's thick enough for grilling, a minimum of ½ to ¾ inch thick.

Per serving: *Calories 228 (From Fat 121); Fat 13g (Saturated 4g); Cholesterol 59mg; Sodium 417mg; Carbohydrate 2g (Dietary Fiber 0g); Protein 24g.*

Saucing the steak

Steak au Poivre, or any plain pan-sautéed steak, can be complemented by either of these flavorful sauces. They're easy to prepare and turn the ordinary into something special.

✔ **Deglazed Red Wine Sauce:** Remove the steaks from the pan. Pour ⅓ cup dry red wine into the pan. Scrape the bottom of the pan to loosen the brown bits and let the liquid reduce by half. Add 2 tablespoons of butter and swirl or stir until it melts. Pour the sauce over the meat and serve.

✔ **Brandy Cream Sauce:** Cook the steaks for slightly less time than you otherwise would, as they will continue to cook while standing. Set the cooked steaks aside. In the same skillet in which you sautéed the steaks, add 1 minced shallot and cook, stirring, for 15 to 20 seconds. Add ¼ cup brandy to the pan and ignite it. When the flames die down, add ½ to ⅔ cup cream. Stirring often, cook the cream until the cream is reduced by half, about 3 minutes. Add an optional 1 tablespoon cracked peppercorns or 2 tablespoons canned green peppercorns, drained of their liquid. Pour the sauce over the meat or serve the sauce on the side.

Beef and Bean Chili

A pot of spicy chili is welcome whatever the weather — hot or chilly. This chunky version is made with beef cubes. Serve it with rice, cornbread, or warmed flour tortillas. This recipe freezes well.

Yield: *6 servings*

Preparation time: *30 minutes*

Cooking time: *1½ to 2 hours*

Spice meter: *Hot and spicy*

2 pounds trimmed beef chuck, cut into 1½ inch cubes

1½ teaspoons salt

3 tablespoons vegetable oil

1 medium onion, chopped

1 medium green bell pepper, chopped

3 cloves garlic, chopped

3 to 4 tablespoons chili powder, or to taste

1 teaspoon ground cumin

¼ to ½ teaspoon cayenne, or to taste

1½ cups tomato puree or canned crushed tomatoes

¾ cup mild-flavored beer or water

1½ cups cooked red kidney beans or pinto beans or one 16-ounce can red kidney beans or pinto beans, rinsed and drained

Grated Monterrey Jack cheese or cheddar cheese or sour cream for garnish

1 Season the beef with ¾ teaspoon of the salt. In a stewpot over medium heat, heat 1½ tablespoons of the vegetable oil. Lightly brown the meat on all sides, in batches if necessary, adding an additional ½ tablespoon vegetable oil as necessary. With a slotted spoon, transfer the meat to a plate and set aside.

2 In the same stewpot, still over medium heat, heat the remaining 1 to 1½ tablespoons of vegetable oil. Add the onion and green bell pepper and cook, stirring occasionally, until the onion is translucent and the peppers are softened, about 5 minutes. Add the garlic and cook, stirring, for 1 minute. Add the chili powder, cumin, and cayenne and cook, stirring often, for 1 to 2 minutes.

3 Return the beef to the pot and stir, coating the meat with the spices. Add the tomato puree and beer. Reduce the heat to medium-low. Simmer, uncovered, until the beef is tender, about 1 to 1½ hours.

4 Add the kidney beans and the remaining ¾ teaspoon salt and simmer, uncovered, for 15 to 20 minutes. If too much liquid has evaporated, add a little extra when you add the beans.

Variation: Try this recipe with cubed pork shoulder or cubed leg of lamb instead of beef.

Per serving: Calories 513 (From Fat 293); Fat 33g (Saturated 10g); Cholesterol 103mg; Sodium 935mg; Carbohydrate 21g (Dietary Fiber 7g); Protein 35g.

Indonesian Beef Saté

Saté can be served as a main dish or as an appetizer with Southeast Asian Peanut Sauce. Pickled Cucumber and Carrot Salad (Chapter 11) or Spiced Carrot and Pineapple Salad (Chapter 11) are excellent accompaniments.

Yield: *4 servings as a main course, 8 servings as a first course*

Preparation time: *20 minutes; 1 to 2 hours marinating time*

Cooking time: *10 minutes*

Spice meter: *Moderately spiced to hot and spicy*

1½ pounds lean round steak, cut into thin strips or cubed

1 tablespoon lime or lemon juice

2 tablespoons soy sauce

1 teaspoon dark or Chinese sesame oil

2 teaspoons dark brown sugar

2 plump cloves garlic, pressed or minced

½-inch piece fresh ginger, minced

2 scallions, white and green parts, thinly sliced

¼ teaspoon freshly ground black pepper

¼ teaspoon cayenne

One recipe Southeast Asian Peanut Sauce (Chapter 10)

1 Cut the beef into 1 to 1½ inch strips.

2 In a shallow dish, combine the lime juice, soy sauce, sesame oil, sugar, scallions, garlic, ginger, pepper, and cayenne. Stir to mix. Add the beef to the marinade and toss to coat. Cover and marinate in the refrigerator for 1 to 2 hours, turning the meat once or twice.

3 Remove the meat from the marinade, but reserve the marinade for basting. Thread the beef onto 8 skewers.

4 Preheat the grill or broiler. Grill or broil, basting with some of the marinade and turning the skewers occasionally, until the beef is cooked through to the desired doneness, about 7 to 10 minutes. Serve with Southeast Asian Peanut Sauce (Chapter 10) for dipping.

Variation: *Make pork saté. Use 1½ pounds trimmed, lean boneless pork loin or tenderloin, cut into thin strips, and follow the recipe. You can serve pork saté with a dipping sauce of Southeast Asian Peanut Sauce (Chapter 10) or with Plum Salsa (Chapter 11).*

Per serving: *Calories 256 (From Fat 66); Fat 7g (Saturated 2g); Cholesterol 106mg; Sodium 594mg; Carbohydrate 5g (Dietary Fiber 0g); Protein 41g.*

Brazilian Picadillo

Picadillo (pee-kah-DEE-yoh) is popular in many Latin American and Caribbean countries. You can serve picadillo with rice or use it as a filling for tortillas or tacos. This recipe calls for beef, but picadillo can be made with any ground meat, such as pork, turkey, and chicken. This recipe freezes well.

Yield: _4 to 6 servings_

Preparation time: _15 to 20 minutes_

Cooking time: _40 to 45 minutes_

Spice meter: _Moderately spiced_

2 tablespoons olive oil

1 medium onion, chopped

1 clove garlic, minced

1 jalapeno pepper, seeded and minced, or ¾ to 1 teaspoon ground jalapeno chile pepper powder

1½ pounds lean ground beef

1¼ cups chopped canned tomatoes with juices

1 tablespoon white wine or cider vinegar

¼ teaspoon dried oregano

½ teaspoon ground cinnamon

¼ teaspoon ground cumin

⅛ teaspoon ground cloves

¼ teaspoon freshly ground black pepper

½ cup chopped pitted black or pitted green olives

⅓ cup raisins

Salt to taste, about ¼ to ½ teaspoon

_1_ In a large skillet over medium heat, heat the olive oil. Add the onion and cook, stirring occasionally, until the onion is translucent, about 5 minutes. Add the garlic and jalapeno and cook, stirring constantly, for 1 minute. If you're using ground jalapeno chile pepper powder, add it in Step 3 along with the other spices.

_2_ Add the ground beef and cook, stirring occasionally to prevent lumps, until the beef is browned thoroughly, about 7 minutes.

_3_ Add the tomatoes, vinegar, oregano, cinnamon, cumin, cloves, black pepper, olives, and raisins. Stir. Reduce the heat to medium-low. Cover partially and simmer for 25 to 30 minutes. If the picadillo becomes too dry, add a little water. Taste for salt and add if necessary.

Variation: _Make picadillo stuffed peppers. Preheat the oven to 375 degrees. Lightly spray a baking dish with nonstick cooking spray. Cut 3 large bell peppers in half lengthwise; remove the core, seeds, and ribs. Fill the 6 pepper halves evenly with picadillo. Bake until the peppers are tender when pierced with a paring knife, about 1 to 1¼ hours, spooning some of the pan juices over the top after about 40 minutes baking time. If you want, top the peppers with tomato sauce or grated cheddar cheese and bake about 5 minutes longer, until the sauce is heated or the cheese is melted._

Per serving: _Calories 301(From Fat 161); Fat 18g (Saturated 6g); Cholesterol 75mg; Sodium 327mg; Carbohydrate 13g (Dietary Fiber 2g); Protein 23g._

Coriander-Spiced Burgers

These burgers feature the spices in South Africa's beef sausage, *boerewors*. Serve them on buns with chutney or any salsa, such as those in Chapter 11, instead of ketchup. For convenience, you can make the patties, wrap them individually, and freeze them.

Yield: *6 servings*

Preparation time: *15 minutes; 2 to 3 hours marinating time*

Cooking time: *15 minutes*

Spice meter: *Moderately spiced*

2½ teaspoons coriander seeds	¼ teaspoon freshly grated or ground nutmeg
1 pound lean ground beef	¼ teaspoon white pepper
½ pound ground pork or ground chuck	⅛ teaspoon ground allspice or cloves
1½ tablespoons white wine vinegar	½ to ¾ teaspoon salt, or to taste

1 Over medium heat, toast the coriander in a dry skillet, stirring occasionally. Grind the coriander and set aside.

2 In a medium bowl, combine the beef, pork, vinegar, coriander, nutmeg, pepper, allspice, and salt. Using your hands, mix well. Cover and refrigerate for 2 to 3 hours.

3 Preheat a broiler or grill. Shape the beef and pork mixture into 6 patties, one-quarter pound each.

4 Broil or grill the burgers, turning after each side browns. Cook until the meat is medium to medium-well and no longer pink, about 12 to 15 minutes.

Tip: *When toasting spices, remove the pan from the heat immediately after the spices become fragrant and have darkened slightly.*

Per serving: *Calories 218 (From Fat 124); Fat 14g (Saturated 5g); Cholesterol 75mg; Sodium 255mg; Carbohydrate 1g (Dietary Fiber 0g); Protein 21g.*

Cape Malay Bobotie

Pronounced "babooty," bobotie is traditional fare in the Western Cape province of South Africa. This recipe is a unique and wonderfully spicy way to prepare ground meat.

Yield: *6 servings*

Preparation time: *20 minutes*

Cooking time: *1¼ to 1½ hours*

Spice meter: *Moderately spiced*

3 slices white bread, torn into pieces

½ cup milk, heated

2 tablespoons vegetable oil

2 medium onions, chopped

2 cloves garlic, minced

1 to 1½ tablespoons homemade good-quality curry powder

½ teaspoon turmeric

¼ teaspoon ground cinnamon

1 teaspoon salt

¼ teaspoon freshly ground black pepper

1¾ pounds lean ground beef

2 tablespoons fresh lemon juice

½ cup raisins

2 tablespoons apricot jam or mango chutney

1 tablespoon brown sugar

3 eggs

2 bay leaves, broken in half

1 cup milk

1 Preheat the oven to 350 degrees. Lightly butter a shallow 2-quart baking dish.

2 Put the bread in a small bowl and pour the milk over it, then set aside.

3 Heat the vegetable oil in a deep, medium-sized skillet over medium heat. Add the onions and cook, stirring occasionally, until the onions are tender, about 10 minutes. Add the garlic and cook, stirring often, for 1 minute. Add the curry powder, turmeric, and cinnamon, and cook, stirring constantly, for 1 minute. Add ½ teaspoon of the salt and the pepper.

4 In a large bowl, combine the bread, onion-spice mixture, ground beef, lemon juice, raisins, apricot jam, brown sugar, and 1 egg. Using your hands, mix well.

5 Spread the mixture in the prepared pan and smooth the top. Bury the bay leaves in the meat mixture at even intervals. Cover with aluminum foil and bake until the mixture is firm, about 45 to 55 minutes.

6 In a liquid measuring cup, lightly beat the milk, the remaining 2 eggs, and the remaining ½ teaspoon of salt.

7 Take the bobotie from the oven. Remove the aluminum foil and pour the topping from Step 6 on top of the partially baked bobotie.

8 Return the bobotie to the oven and bake, uncovered, on the middle rack of the oven until the topping is set and lightly browned, about 20 to 30 minutes.

Variation: Some cooks make this dish with ground lamb instead of beef.

Per serving: Calories 470 (From Fat 215); Fat 24g (Saturated 8g); Cholesterol 202mg; Sodium 611mg; Carbohydrate 31g (Dietary Fiber 2g); Protein 33g.

Tex-Mex Meatloaf

A new twist on an American favorite, this meatloaf combines both spices and herbs. Serve with Tomato Salsa (Chapter 11), chili sauce, or your favorite condiment.

Yield: *8 servings*

Preparation time: *20 minutes*

Cooking time: *1¼ to 1½ hours*

Spice meter: *Moderately spiced*

4 slices white bread	*½ cup chopped fresh parsley*
½ cup scalded milk	*2 to 2½ tablespoons chili powder*
1 pound ground beef	*2 teaspoons ground cumin*
½ pound ground veal	*1¼ teaspoons salt, or to taste*
½ pound lean ground pork	*1 teaspoon dried oregano*
2 eggs	*½ to 1 teaspoon cayenne, or to taste*
1 medium onion, chopped	*½ teaspoon freshly ground black pepper*
2 plum tomatoes, peeled, seeded and diced	*½ teaspoon ground allspice (optional)*
3 plump cloves garlic, minced	

1 Preheat the oven to 350 degrees. Place the bread in a medium bowl. Pour the scalded milk over the bread and let the bread soak in the milk until it absorbs all the liquid.

2 In a large bowl, combine the bread with any remaining liquid with all the remaining ingredients. Using your hands, gently mix the ingredients together evenly. Take care not overwork the meat.

3 Put the mixture in a 9-x-5-inch loaf pan, mounding it slightly on top. Bake until the meat is cooked through and firm to the touch, about 1¼ to 1½ hours. An instant-read thermometer inserted into the center of the meatloaf should read 160 degrees. Carefully pour off any obvious excess fat. Let the meatloaf stand on a rack for 10 to 15 minutes before slicing.

Tip: To scald milk, heat it in a saucepan over medium-low to medium heat until it nearly comes to a boil. No skin should form on the top.

Variation: Instead of making a meatloaf, make meatballs by shaping the mixture into balls that are approximately 1½ inches in diameter. To cook: Preheat the oven to 400 degrees. Put the meatballs on a baking sheet sprayed with nonstick cooking spray and bake until cooked through, about 15 minutes.

Per serving: Calories 277 (From Fat 129); Fat 14g (Saturated 5g); Cholesterol 129mg; Sodium 551mg; Carbohydrate 12g (Dietary Fiber 2g); Protein 24g.

Beef or Pork Stew with Juniper and Chile Powder

This hearty one-pot dish is perfect for autumn and winter meals. If you want to make the stew hot and spicy, add ½ teaspoon crushed red chile flakes 15 minutes before serving. This recipe freezes well, and you can see it on the sixth page of the color section.

Yield: *6 to 8 servings*

Preparation time: *30 minutes*

Cooking time: *1¼ to 1½ hours*

Spice meter: *Moderately spiced*

1 teaspoon salt

½ teaspoon freshly ground black pepper

2 pounds beef chuck or round or pork shoulder or a combination of each cut into 1½ inch cubes

3 tablespoons olive oil or vegetable oil

2 leeks, washed well and thinly sliced

1 medium onion, chopped

2 red, yellow, or green bell peppers, thinly sliced

1 plump clove garlic, minced

1 to 1½ tablespoons mild to medium ground chile pepper powder, such as ground ancho, Anaheim, or mild New Mexican

1½ teaspoons juniper berries, lightly crushed

1 teaspoon minced fresh thyme or ½ teaspoon dried thyme leaves

1½ cups chopped or crushed tomatoes

1¾ cups beef broth or water

1 orange, seeded and quartered

1 cup frozen corn kernels (optional)

2 tablespoons chopped fresh parsley for garnish

1 In a stewpot over medium heat, heat 1 tablespoon of the olive oil. Add the leeks and onion and cook, stirring occasionally, until the onions are translucent, about 5 minutes. Add the bell peppers and cook, stirring occasionally, for 3 to 5 minutes. Add the garlic and cook, stirring constantly, for 1 minute. Remove the vegetables and set aside.

2 Season the meat with salt and black pepper. In the same stewpot, heat the remaining olive oil. Working in batches, brown the meat on all sides.

3 Return all the beef to the pot. Add ground chile pepper powder and stir. Cook for 1 to 2 minutes. Add the reserved vegetables and the juniper berries, thyme, tomatoes, broth, and orange wedges. Reduce the heat to medium-low. Cover partially and simmer for 45 minutes.

4 Add the corn and simmer, partially covered, for an additional 30 to 45 minutes or until the meat is tender. Add more water or broth if necessary. Before serving, remove the orange wedges and stir in the parsley.

Tip: *Serve with crusty bread, cornbread, warmed flour tortillas, mashed potatoes, or mashed sweet potatoes.*

Per serving: *Calories 274 (From Fat 152); Fat 17g (Saturated 5g); Cholesterol 67mg; Sodium 567mg; Carbohydrate 9g (Dietary Fiber 2g); Protein 22g.*

Beef or Pork Adobo

Serve this traditional Mexican dish of spicy marinated meat with warmed flour tortillas. You will need to make the Chile Adobo Sauce from Chapter 10 ahead of time. This recipe freezes well.

Yield: *4 to 6 servings*

Preparation time: *10 minutes; 3 to 24 hours marinating time*

Cooking time: *1 to 1¼ hours*

Spice meter: *Hot and spicy*

1 recipe Chile Adobo Sauce (Chapter 10)

2 to 3 tablespoons vegetable oil or olive oil

2 pounds beef round or pork loin, cut into thin ½-inch long strips

½ cup water, beef broth, or orange juice

1 Put the meat in a large flat baking dish. Pour the Chile Adobo Sauce over the meat and toss to coat. Cover and refrigerate for 3 to 24 hours.

2 Remove the meat from the marinade, but reserve it. In a large skillet over medium heat, heat the vegetable oil. Add the meat and cook, stirring occasionally, until all the meat is browned.

3 Reduce the heat to medium-low. Add the reserved marinade and the water, broth, or juice to the pan. Cover partially and simmer for 1 hour or until the meat is very tender. Thin with additional liquid if the sauce becomes too thick while simmering.

Tip: Make it a wrap! Put some of the beef or pork adobo in warmed flour tortillas, top with sour cream, grated cheddar, or Jack cheese and some sliced pitted olives, and wrap.

Per serving: Calories 351 (From Fat 217); Fat 24g (Saturated 7g); Cholesterol 96mg; Sodium 300mg; Carbohydrate 3g (Dietary Fiber 1g); Protein 29g.

Spicy Roast Pork

In this recipe, the roast is marinated with fragrant spices. It's an unusual but delicious way to prepare pork. Serve with the Plum Salsa from Chapter 11. Alternatively, baste every 10 minutes during the last 30 minutes of roasting with the orange currant glaze in the variation.

Yield: *6 servings*

Preparation time: *15 minutes; 1½ to 24 hours marinating time*

Cooking time: *1½ hours*

Spice meter: *Moderately spiced*

3 plump cloves garlic, minced

1-inch piece fresh ginger, minced

¾ teaspoon dry English mustard

½ to 1 teaspoon cayenne or ground chile pepper powder

½ teaspoon ground cardamom

½ teaspoon freshly ground black pepper

¼ teaspoon ground cinnamon

¼ teaspoon turmeric

⅛ teaspoon ground cloves

2 tablespoons soy sauce

2 tablespoons white or red wine vinegar

3 pounds boneless pork loin roast, trimmed of most fat

1 In a small bowl, combine all the ingredients except the pork, and stir to mix.

2 Prick the pork all over with a fork and place it in a shallow baking dish. Rub the spice mixture evenly on the meat. Cover and marinate in the refrigerator for 1½ hours or overnight.

3 Preheat the oven to 350 degrees. Remove the meat from the refrigerator and let it stand at room temperature for 20 to 30 minutes before roasting.

4 Bake the pork until a meat or instant-read thermometer registers 160 degrees, about 1½ hours. After the roast is cooked, let the meat stand for 10 to 15 minutes before carving.

Variation: *Make orange currant glaze. In a small saucepan over medium-low heat, combine ¾ cup currant jelly, ⅓ cup orange juice, and 3 tablespoons white or red wine vinegar, stirring until the jelly is melted. Combine 1 tablespoon cornstarch and 1 tablespoon water and stir well. Add the cornstarch mixture to the jelly mixture and stir. Cook until the sauce thickens only slightly, about 2 minutes. Reheat the sauce over low heat, as necessary, to keep it runny enough for basting. Serve heated orange currant sauce on the side.*

Variation: *Make grilled or broiled spiced pork tenderloin. Rub the spice mixture in Step 1 on two 1 to 1½ pound pork tenderloins and then marinate for 2 to 24 hours. Broil or grill the tenderloins, turning often, until they're browned on all sides and their internal temperature on an instant-read thermometer is between 150 and 155 degrees, about 10 to 15 minutes. They will still be slightly pink inside. Let them stand for 10 minutes before slicing. Note that while they stand the temperature should rise to 155 to 160 degrees. Serve with Plum Salsa (Chapter 11).*

Per serving: *Calories 368 (From Fat 149); Fat 17g (Saturated 6g); Cholesterol 138mg; Sodium 443mg; Carbohydrate 2g (Dietary Fiber 0g); Protein 49g.*

Fragrantly Spiced Maple Spareribs

Although the marinating time is long, these ribs are easy to prepare. They can be partially cooked ahead of time and finished just before you plan to serve them. They've always been a hit on my family's table.

Yield: *4 servings*

Preparation time: *15 minutes; 6 to 24 hours marinating time*

Cooking time: *1¼ hours*

Spice meter: *Mildly spiced*

3½ pounds lean pork spareribs

½ cup maple syrup

3 tablespoons soy sauce

2 tablespoons dry sherry

3 cloves garlic, minced

½-inch piece fresh ginger, minced

¼ teaspoon ground allspice (optional)

1 Cut the spareribs into serving-size portions. Place the spareribs in a large flat glass, ceramic, or stainless steel pan.

2 In a small bowl, combine the maple syrup, soy sauce, sherry, garlic, ginger, and allspice. Pour the marinade over the ribs, turning the ribs to coat them evenly. Cover loosely and refrigerate for at least 6 hours or overnight, turning the ribs occasionally in the marinade.

3 Preheat the oven to 325 degrees. Remove the ribs from the marinade and place them curved side up on a foil-lined broiler pan. Reserve the marinade.

4 Bake until the ribs are tender, about 1 hour, brushing every 20 minutes with reserved marinade. The ribs can be cooked ahead to this point.

5 Preheat the broiler. Baste the ribs with marinade. Place the broiler rack 4 to 6 inches from the heat source. Broil, turning once or twice until the ribs are lightly browned, about 5 to 10 minutes.

Warning: *Because of the sugar content in the maple syrup, check the ribs often while broiling to make sure they don't burn. If they do, lower the oven rack so the ribs are not as close to the heat. It's fine if the ribs have a few dark or slightly charred spots.*

Per serving: *Calories 788 (From Fat 484); Fat 54g (Saturated 20g); Cholesterol 214mg; Sodium 959mg; Carbohydrate 29g (Dietary Fiber 0g); Protein 45g.*

Hot and Spicy Roasted Ribs

These ribs absorb the flavor of the tangy dry rub. They're absolutely scrumptious.

Yield: *4 servings*

Preparation time: *15 minutes; 2 to 24 hours marinating time*

Cooking time: *1¼ hours*

Spice meter: *Moderately spiced to hot and spicy*

3½ pounds lean pork spareribs

2 tablespoons paprika

1 tablespoon light brown sugar

1 teaspoon salt

1 teaspoon garlic powder

¾ teaspoon onion powder

½ teaspoon dried thyme leaves

½ teaspoon cumin

½ teaspoon celery seeds (optional)

½ teaspoon cayenne, or to taste

½ teaspoon white or black pepper

1 recipe Tangy Tomato Barbecue Sauce (Chapter 10) or bottled barbecue sauce

1 Cut the spareribs into serving size portions. Place the spareribs in a large flat glass, ceramic, or stainless steel pan.

2 In a small bowl, make a spice mix by combining the paprika, sugar, salt, garlic powder, onion powder, thyme, celery seeds, cayenne, and pepper.

3 Rub the spice mix on both sides of the ribs and place the ribs in a single layer on a broiler pan or roasting pan. Cover loosely and refrigerate for 2 hours or overnight.

4 Preheat the oven to 325 degrees. Bake until the ribs are tender and nearly cooked through, about 1 hour. The ribs can be cooked ahead to this point.

5 Preheat the broiler. Broil, turning the ribs once until the ribs are lightly browned, about 10 to 15 minutes. Serve with barbecue sauce on the side.

Tip: *Before broiling, you can baste the ribs with some of the barbecue sauce.*

Per serving: *Calories 701 (From Fat 489); Fat 54g (Saturated 20g); Cholesterol 214mg; Sodium 768mg; Carbohydrate 7g (Dietary Fiber 1g); Protein 45g.*

Spice Islands Lamb Stew

This simple, Malaysian-influenced lamb stew is imbued with aromatic spices. It can be served with plain or spiced rice or with boiled, mashed, or roasted potatoes. Serve with chutney or with the Plum Salsa from Chapter 11. This recipe freezes well.

Yield: *6 to 8 servings*

Preparation time: *15 minutes*

Cooking time: *1½ to 2 hours*

Spice meter: *Moderately spiced to hot and spicy*

3 to 4 tablespoons vegetable oil	*½ teaspoon freshly ground black pepper*
3 pounds lean lamb, cut into 1½ inch cubes	*½ teaspoon ground allspice*
2 medium onions, sliced	*½ teaspoon ground mace*
4 plump cloves garlic, minced	*1 cup hot water*
1 jalapeno, seeded and minced	*2 tablespoons fresh lemon juice*
2 bay leaves	*1 teaspoon freshly grated nutmeg*
6 cloves	*½ teaspoon salt, or to taste*

1 In a stewpot over medium heat, heat 1½ tablespoons of the vegetable oil. Brown the lamb in batches, adding more vegetable oil as necessary. Set the browned lamb aside on a plate.

2 Add additional vegetable oil if necessary and heat, then add the onions to the pot. Cook, stirring occasionally, until the onions are softened, about 7 minutes. Add the garlic and jalapeno and cook, stirring often, for 1 to 2 minutes. Add the bay leaves, cloves, black pepper, allspice, and mace. Stirring constantly, cook until the spices are fragrant, 1 to 2 minutes.

3 Return the lamb to the pot, layering it on top of the onions and spices, but do not stir. Add ½ cup of the hot water. Reduce the heat to medium-low. Cover and simmer until the lamb is tender, about 1 to 1½ hours. Add more water if necessary, but do not stir the mixture.

4 Add the remaining water and the lemon juice, nutmeg, and salt. Stir and simmer for an addditional 10 to 15 minutes.

Tip: Lamb from the shoulder or leg is best for stewing.

Per serving: Calories 295 (From Fat 132); Fat 15g (Saturated 4g); Cholesterol 115mg; Sodium 244mg; Carbohydrate 3g (Dietary Fiber 0g); Protein 36g.

Curried Lamb Kebabs

These fabulous kebabs from South Africa are marinated in a curried sweet-and-sour sauce. After you've tasted them, you won't be able to get enough! Serve with the Gingered Tomato Salad from Chapter 11 and the Spiced Rice with Almonds from Chapter 17.

Yield: *4 servings, 8 skewers*

Preparation time: *25 minutes; 2 to 24 hours marinating time*

Cooking time: *15 minutes*

Spice meter: *Moderately spiced to hot and spicy*

½ cup smooth apricot jam

⅓ cup white wine vinegar

¼ cup water

4 whole cloves

1 bay leaf

2 cloves garlic, minced

½ inch piece fresh ginger, minced

2 tablespoons good-quality curry powder

1 teaspoon ground coriander

1 teaspoon ground allspice or cinnamon

½ teaspoon ground cumin

¼ teaspoon freshly ground black pepper

2 medium onions, peeled and quartered

1½ to 1¾ pounds lean lamb from leg, cut into 1-inch cubes

1 In a medium saucepan, combine all the ingredients except the onions and lamb. Over medium heat, bring the mixture to a boil. Reduce the heat to low and simmer for 5 minutes. Cool the marinade completely before using.

2 Place the lamb cubes and onions in a large shallow glass or stainless steel baking dish. Pour the marinade over the top and toss to coat evenly. Cover and refrigerate for 2 to 24 hours, tossing the meat several times.

3 Separate the onion wedges into pieces. Alternately, thread the lamb and onions onto 8- to 10-inch bamboo or metal skewers.

4 Preheat the broiler or grill. Grill or broil the kebabs, basting and turning them occasionally. Cook until the lamb is slightly pink inside, about 12 to 15 minutes.

Cook's Fact: *This recipe is a traditional dish of the Cape Malays in Cape Town, South Africa, where the kebabs are known as lamb sosaties.*

Per serving: *Calories 376 (From Fat 93); Fat 10g (Saturated 3g); Cholesterol 109mg; Sodium 105mg; Carbohydrate 36g (Dietary Fiber 3g); Protein 36g.*

Indian Rogan Josh

Rogan Josh is a classic lamb curry from Kashmir is accented with a range of spices, tomatoes, and yogurt. Serve this delicious dish with chutney.

Yield: *6 servings*

Preparation time: *20 minutes*

Cooking time: *1½ to 1¾ hours*

Spice meter: *Hot and spicy*

2 tablespoons vegetable oil

2 pounds trimmed, lean lamb from leg or shoulder, cut in 1½ inch cubes

1 medium onion, thinly sliced

4 plump cloves garlic, chopped

1-inch piece fresh ginger, minced

4 cloves

½ cinnamon stick

6 cardamom pods, bruised

1 teaspoon ground coriander

1 teaspoon ground fennel

¼ teaspoon turmeric

1 bay leaf

1 teaspoon paprika

1 to 2 teaspoons cayenne or ground red chile pepper powder, or to taste

1½ cups beef or chicken broth

½ cup plain yogurt

1 In a large stewpot over medium heat, heat 1 tablespoon of the vegetable oil. Pat the lamb dry with paper towels. Brown the lamb in batches, if necessary. With a slotted spoon, transfer the lamb to a plate and set aside.

2 In the same stewpot, heat the remaining vegetable oil. Add the onion and reduce the heat to medium-low. Cook, stirring occasionally, until the onion is very soft, about 10 to 15 minutes.

3 Add the garlic and ginger and cook, stirring for 1 minute. Add the cloves, cinnamon stick, cardamom, coriander, fennel, tumeric, and bay leaf and cook, stirring constantly, for 1 minute. Add the paprika and cayenne and cook, stirring constantly, for 1 minute. Add the broth and bring to a gentle boil.

4 Return the lamb to the pot. Cover partially and simmer until the lamb is tender, about 1 to 1½ hours.

5 Add the yogurt and simmer until it's heated through, about 5 minutes. Serve with rice and chutney on the side.

Variation: *Substitute 2 to 3 tablespoons good-quality curry powder for the cloves, cinnamon stick, cardamom, coriander, fennel, and turmeric. Reduce the amount of cayenne to ¼ to ½ teaspoon, or to taste. In Step 3, after sautéing the garlic and ginger, add the curry powder, bay leaf, paprika, and cayenne and cook, stirring constantly, for 1 minute.*

Tip: *You can make this ahead through Step 4. Add the yogurt when reheating before serving.*

Per serving: *Calories 278 (From Fat 125); Fat 14g (Saturated 4g); Cholesterol 99mg; Sodium 335mg; Carbohydrate 3g (Dietary Fiber 1g); Protein 33g.*

Hungarian Veal Goulash with Mushrooms

The delicate flavor of this dish, which is also known as *veal paprikash*, comes from Hungarian sweet paprika. It's rich and quite delicious. Make it when you want to splurge. This recipe freezes well.

Yield: *6 servings*

Preparation time: *15 minutes*

Cooking time: *1½ to 1¾ hours*

Spice meter: *Mildly spiced*

3 to 4 tablespoons butter or margarine

1 medium onion, diced

2 cloves garlic, minced

2½ pounds trimmed, boneless veal shoulder, cut into 1½ inch cubes

1 teaspoon salt

all-purpose flour for dusting the meat, about ¼ to ⅓ cup

1½ tablespoons Hungarian sweet paprika

⅓ cup dry white wine

1 cup beef or chicken broth

6 ounces white mushrooms, sliced

¾ to 1 cup sour cream or nonfat sour cream

Minced fresh flat-leaf parsley for garnish, about 2 tablespoons

1 In a stewpot over medium heat, melt 1 tablespoon of the butter. Add the onion and cook, stirring occasionally, until the onion is translucent, about 5 minutes. Add the garlic and cook, stirring constantly, for 2 minutes. Transfer the onions to a plate and set aside.

2 Pat the meat dry with paper towels. Season the meat with salt and lightly dust it with flour, shaking off any excess. In the same stewpot over medium heat, melt 1 tablespoon butter. Working in batches, lightly brown the veal on all sides. Transfer the browned meat to a plate. Add additional butter between batches, up to 1 tablespoon, as necessary.

3 Return the veal to the pot. Add the paprika, stirring constantly to coat the meat evenly. Pour in the wine and scrape the bottom to loosen any brown bits; cook for 2 to 3 minutes. Add the broth and reserved onions.

4 Reduce the heat to medium-low. Cover and simmer until the meat is tender and the sauce is reduced, about 1¼ to 1½ hours.

5 Meanwhile, in a small skillet over medium-low heat, melt the remaining tablespoon of butter. Add the mushrooms and cook, stirring occasionally, until the mushrooms are softened. Set aside.

6 When the veal is tender, add the mushrooms and stir in the sour cream. Simmer until everything is heated through, about 5 minutes. Do not let the sauce boil. Garnish with parsley.

Tip: *Don't feel like opening a bottle of white wine? Substitute dry white vermouth, which lasts almost indefinitely after it's opened.*

Per serving: *Calories 383 (From Fat 205); Fat 23g (Saturated 12g); Cholesterol 182mg; Sodium 662mg; Carbohydrate 6g (Dietary Fiber 1g); Protein 38g.*

Chapter 15

Seafood

Seafood is enhanced by a variety of spices. You might think that seafood, unlike meat and poultry, should be seasoned with very light spices, but in this chapter, you'll find international recipes from a range of countries — from India, to North Africa, to Mexico to Japan — that dispel this more conventional approach to seafood cookery. These easy-to-prepare recipes are accented with an array of spices, such as cumin, ginger, garlic, chiles, curry, and spice rubs, that complement the bounty of the sea.

Fish Facts

The quality of any seafood dish depends on the freshness of the seafood. When purchasing fresh fish, buy it from a store with a high turnover. If you shop at a fish market and the market doesn't have what you're looking for, fishmongers can often suggest a substitute that has similar texture and taste.

Remember these facts when making a seafood recipe:

✔ Buy fresh seafood from a reputable store.

✔ Fresh seafood should not smell overly fishy.

✔ Approximately 1½ to 2 pounds of fish should serve 4 to 6 people. Cut the fish into equal serving-size pieces or buy 4 to 6 individual pieces totaling the weight.

✔ Thaw frozen seafood in the refrigerator.

✔ Don't overcook seafood: Fish will become dry and flaky and shellfish will become tough and rubbery.

✔ As a general rule, seafood should be marinated for up to 30 minutes. However, you will find a few recipes that call for marinating time of up to 1 hour.

Tuna or Salmon Teriyaki

This traditional Japanese marinade is perfect for most fish steaks. I recommend tuna or salmon, but you can also substitute swordfish.

Yield: *4 servings*

Preparation time: *10 minutes; 15 to 30 minutes marinating time*

Cooking time: *10 minutes*

Spice meter: *Mildly spiced*

¾ cup Teriyaki Sauce (Chapter 10) or commercially bottled teriyaki sauce

2 scallions, white and green parts, sliced

1½ to 2 pounds tuna or salmon steaks, about 1 inch thick

1 In a shallow dish, combine the teriyaki sauce and scallions. Add the fish and turn to coat evenly. Cover and marinate in the refrigerator for 15 to 30 minutes, turning the fish once or twice.

2 Remove the fish from the marinade. Reserve the marinade for basting.

3 Preheat the grill or broiler. Grill or broil, basting occasionally and turning once, about 3 to 5 minutes per side until the fish is cooked through and is firm but not flaky.

Variation: *Cut the fish into 1½ to 2-inch cubes. Alternately thread the fish onto skewers with pieces of raw onion, bell pepper, or pineapple. Marinate for 20 to 40 minutes. Grill or broil, basting and turning the skewers occasionally, until the fish is cooked through, about 9 to 12 minutes.*

Variation: *Marinate London Broil or any steaks such as sirloin or filet in the teriyaki sauce for 1 hour. Grill or broil, basting occasionally, until the meat is cooked through to your taste: rare, medium-rare, or medium.*

Per serving: *Calories 294 (From Fat 73); Fat 8g (Saturated 2g); Cholesterol 63mg; Sodium 2,133mg; Carbohydrate 12g (Dietary Fiber 0g); Protein 40g.*

Fish Veracruz

This tasty dish from south of the border features fish in a tomato sauce that's spiked with garlic, chiles, cumin, cinnamon, and black olives. It appears on the fifth page of the color section.

Yield: *4 to 6 servings*

Preparation time: *20 minutes*

Cooking time: *30 minutes*

Spice meter: *Moderately spicy to hot and spicy*

2 tablespoons olive oil

1 medium onion, thinly sliced

2 cloves garlic, minced

1 to 2 jalapenos or serranos, seeded and minced

½ teaspoon ground cumin

⅛ to ¼ teaspoon ground cinnamon

⅛ teaspoon ground cloves

2 cups fresh, peeled, or canned chopped tomatoes

½ teaspoon freshly ground black pepper

1 tablespoon fresh lime juice

1 teaspoon sugar

⅓ cup pitted black olives

Salt to taste

1½ pounds firm white fish filets, such as snapper, grouper, monkfish, or cod, about 1inch thick, cut into serving-size pieces

2 tablespoons minced cilantro

1 Heat the olive oil in a large skillet over medium heat. Add the onion and cook, stirring occasionally, until the onion is translucent, about 5 minutes. Add the garlic and jalapenos and cook, stirring, for 1 minute. Add the cumin, cinnamon, and cloves and stir for 30 seconds.

2 Add the tomatoes, black pepper, lime juice, sugar, and olives. Cover partially and simmer for 15 minutes. Add salt to taste.

3 Add the fish to the sauce, spooning some sauce over each piece. Cook over medium heat until the fish is white and cooked through, about 8 minutes. The sauce should be gently bubbling; adjust the heat if it's too high or too low. Garnish with cilantro before serving.

Cook's Fact: *Cilantro leaves are also called Chinese parsley or coriander leaves.*

Per serving: *Calories 149 (From Fat 60); Fat 7g (Saturated 1g); Cholesterol 28mg; Sodium 203mg; Carbohydrate 6g (Dietary Fiber 1g); Protein 17g.*

Southeast Asian Fried Flounder or Sole

This simple dish can be served plain, with lemon, or with any of the salsas from Chapter 11.

Yield: *4 to 6 servings*

Preparation time: *10 minutes; 30 to 60 minutes marinating time*

Cooking time: *10 minutes*

Spice meter: *Moderately spiced*

¼ cup unsweetened canned coconut milk

2 tablespoons fresh lemon or lime juice

1½ teaspoons soy sauce

1 plump clove garlic, thinly sliced into thirds lengthwise

2 lemon grass stalks, sliced (optional)

1½ pounds flounder or sole filets

⅓ cup all-purpose flour

½ teaspoon ground cumin

½ teaspoon ground coriander

½ teaspoon cayenne

2 tablespoons peanut oil or vegetable oil

Cilantro sprigs for garnish

Lime or lemon wedges for garnish

1 In a shallow dish that's large enough to hold all the filets, combine the coconut milk, lemon juice, soy sauce, garlic, and lemon grass and stir to mix.

2 Add the filets to the dish. Cover and marinate in the refrigerator for 30 to 60 minutes.

3 In a small bowl, combine the flour, cumin, coriander, and cayenne and stir to mix.

4 Remove the fish from the marinade and pat it dry with paper towels. Dredge or dip both sides of the filets in the flour mixture, shaking off any excess.

5 In a large nonstick skillet, heat the peanut oil over medium heat. Add the filets and cook until lightly golden, about 4 to 5 minutes per side. Cook in batches if necessary; keep finished pieces warm by transferring them to an ovenproof plate, covering them loosely with foil and placing the plate in a low oven, heated to about 150 to 200 degrees. Garnish with cilantro and lime or lemon wedges.

Variation: *This recipe works equally well with boneless chicken cutlets that have been placed between two pieces of waxed paper and pounded thin with a meat pounder. Feel free to add a couple of tablespoons of sesame seeds or desiccated grated coconut to the flour.*

Per serving: *Calories 190 (From Fat 67); Fat 7g (Saturated 2g); Cholesterol 53mg; Sodium 156mg; Carbohydrate 11g (Dietary Fiber 1g); Protein 20g.*

Roasted Moroccan Monkfish

For this dish, you need to make Moroccan Spice Mix (Chapter 9). Serve with Coriander Plum Chutney (Chapter 11) if you want.

Yield: *4 to 6 servings*

Preparation time: *10 minutes*

Cooking time: *20 to 25 minutes*

Spice meter: *Moderately spiced*

1 tablespoon fresh lemon juice

2 tablespoons olive oil

1½ tablespoons Moroccan Spice Mix (Chapter 9)

½ teaspoon salt

1 to 1½ pounds monkfish filets, rinsed and dark membrane removed

1 Preheat the oven to 425 degrees. Using olive oil, lightly coat a baking dish that's large enough to hold the fish. Set aside.

2 In a medium bowl or flat shallow dish, combine the lemon juice, remaining olive oil, Moroccan Spice Mix, and salt.

3 Add the fish to the bowl and turn it to coat it evenly in the spice rub.

4 Place the fish in the prepared baking dish, the nicest side up. Roast uncovered for 10 minutes, basting occasionally with any pan juices. Cover with aluminum foil and roast until the monkfish is cooked through in the thickest part, about 10 to 15 minutes longer.

Variation: Substitute Cajun Spice Rub (Chapter 9) or 1½ tablespoons coarsely ground black or mixed peppercorns for the Moroccan Spice Mix.

Per serving: Calories 151 (From Fat 78); Fat 9g (Saturated 1g); Cholesterol 27mg; Sodium 311mg; Carbohydrate 2g (Dietary Fiber 1g); Protein 16g.

Spicy Crab Cakes with Cilantro Sauce

A touch of curry and a hint of cayenne makes these crab cakes sparkle with flavor. You can see them on the fifth page of the color section. You make full-size or mini crab cakes, which are a bit easier to turn when cooking. The mini cakes also can be served as an appetizer for 6 people. Serve them with the Cilantro Sauce or with any salsa in Chapter 11. The cakes freeze well; wrap them individually.

Yield: *4 to 6 servings*

Preparation time: *25 minutes; 15 to 30 minutes refrigeration*

Cooking time: *10 minutes*

Spice meter: *Mildly spiced*

1 pound lump crabmeat, cleaned	*½ to 1 teaspoon curry powder*
¼ cup cracker crumbs	*⅛ teaspoon cayenne*
1 egg, lightly beaten	*⅛ teaspoon freshly ground white pepper*
3 tablespoons mayonnaise	*Flour or cornmeal for dredging the cakes, about ⅓ cup*
3 scallions, white part only, chopped	
2 tablespoons chopped chives	*3 tablespoons olive oil or vegetable oil*
½ teaspoon salt	

Cilantro Sauce

⅓ cup plus 1 tablespoon orange juice	*1 teaspoon ground coriander*
¼ cup fresh lemon juice	*½ teaspoon ground cumin*
1⅓ cups loosely packed fresh cilantro leaves	*⅔ cup olive oil*

1 Pick through the crabmeat and remove any cartilage. In a medium bowl combine the crabmeat and cracker crumbs. Stir in the egg, mayonnaise, scallions, parsley, salt, curry, cayenne, and pepper.

2 Refrigerate the crab mixture for 15 to 30 minutes or until it's firm enough to form into cakes.

3 Meanwhile, prepare the cilantro sauce. In a blender, combine the orange juice, lemon juice, cilantro, coriander, and cumin and pulse until the cilantro is chopped. With the motor running, pour the olive oil into the blender in a steady stream and blend. Remove the sauce from the blender and set aside at room temperature; stir well before serving.

4 Shape the crab mixture into 4 to 6 cakes. You can also shape them into 12 to 14 ½-inch mini cakes. When you're ready to cook, dredge or dip each cake on both sides in a little flour or cornmeal.

5 In a large nonstick skillet, heat the olive oil over medium heat. Add the crab cakes and cook until lightly browned, carefully turning once, about 5 minutes per side for large cakes or 2 to 3 minutes per side for mini cakes. Serve with the sauce.

Variation: Substitute dry English mustard for the curry powder and chopped parsley for the chives. Serve with cilantro sauce, any salsa from Chapter 11, or tartar sauce and lemon wedges.

Per serving: Calories 356 (From Fat 239); Fat 27g (Saturated 4g); Cholesterol 120mg; Sodium 595mg; Carbohydrate 8g (Dietary Fiber 1g); Protein 20g.

Masala Fish

This flavorful recipe with an Indian twist is excellent for any firm fish steak. Try it with tuna, swordfish, or salmon. Serve with any of the salsas from Chapter 11.

Yield: 4 to 6 servings

Preparation time: 15 minutes; 1 hour marinating time

Cooking time: 10 minutes

Spice meter: Moderately spicy

2 teaspoons curry powder

½ teaspoon ground cumin

½ teaspoon ground coriander

½ teaspoon ground turmeric

⅛ to ¼ teaspoon cayenne

1 clove garlic pressed or ¼ teaspoon garlic powder

2 tablespoons fresh lemon juice juice

2 tablespoons peanut oil or vegetable oil

1½ to 2 pounds tuna, swordfish, salmon, or other fish steaks, about 1 inch thick

Fresh lime or lemon wedges for garnish

1 In a small bowl combine the curry powder, cumin, coriander, turmeric, and cayenne and stir to mix. Add the garlic, lemon juice, and peanut oil and stir to form a paste.

2 Spread the mixture evenly on both sides of the fish steaks. Cover loosely and marinate in the refrigerator for 1 to 2 hours.

3 Preheat the broiler and lightly spray a broiler pan with nonstick cooking spray.

4 Arrange the fish on the broiler pan. Broil, turning once, until the fish is cooked through, about 4 to 5 minutes per side. The fish should offer no resistance when it's pierced with a knife, but it should not be flaky. Serve garnished with lime or lemon wedges.

Tip: The fish can also be cooked on a preheated grill.

Per serving: Calories 140 (From Fat 70); Fat 8g (Saturated 2g); Cholesterol 30mg; Sodium 70mg; Carbohydrate 1g (Dietary Fiber 0g); Protein 16g.

Shrimp

Fresh versus frozen: Which should you buy? If you live where shrimp is harvested locally or you have a fabulous seafood shop, of course, you can and should buy it fresh. Otherwise, for the recipes in this book, frozen will work just as well.

When buying fresh shrimp, go to a shop whose seafood department has a high turnover (this generally means the seafood will be very fresh). The store should not have an overly "fishy" odor, a sign that the seafood might not be at its peak. Preferably fresh shrimp should be kept on ice in the store display case and should not have yellowed or blackened shells.

Frozen shrimp should show no signs of freezer burn, such as excessive ice crystals, or look dried out, or chalky. Thaw frozen shrimp overnight in the refrigerator or at room temperature for about half an hour. Then cook it immediately (or wrap it and refrigerate it until you're ready to cook).

Shrimp, whether fresh or frozen and thawed, must be deveined before you prepare it. Sometimes you can buy it already shelled and deveined, a timesaving shortcut, but most often, the shrimp is precooked and best eaten in shrimp cocktails. If you do use store-prepared shrimp, (which we all do when we're in a rush), in the recipes in this book, you'll be reheating cooked shrimp in the sauce, and you'll have to watch that it doesn't get tough from overcooking. Use a lower heat than suggested and let the shrimp simmer gently in the sauce.

Make your own shrimp broth

Full of shrimp flavor, use this simple broth in Shrimp Curry in this chapter or in any recipe where shrimp or fish broth is called for, such as soups or sauces. It's quick, (about 30 minutes from start to finish), and very easy (little hands-on time) to prepare. You should have about 1½ quarts. Freeze any leftovers in ice cube trays and then pop the cubes into a self-sealing plastic bag and keep them in the freezer. Frozen, the broth should last for up to 2 months.

6 cups canned low-sodium chicken broth

shells from ½ to 1 pound of shrimp

1 celery stalk, coarsely chopped

1 small carrot, coarsely chopped

1 small onion, peeled and halved

1. In a large saucepan over medium heat, combine the broth, shrimp shells, celery, carrot, and onion. Bring to a gentle boil and immediately reduce the heat to medium-low so that the liquid barely bubbles. Simmer for 20 to 30 minutes.

2. Strain the broth and discard the solids. Use the broth immediately or cool, uncovered, by placing the pot in an ice bath and stirring the broth. Refrigerate it and use within 2 days or freeze.

To devein shrimp, first peel them as shown in Figure 15-1. (Save the shells if you're going to make shrimp broth, which is covered in an upcoming sidebar.) With a sharp paring knife, make a shallow slit along the back of the shrimp. With the tip of the knife, loosen, remove, and discard the dark vein, as shown in Figure 15-2.

Wash any utensils that you've used in preparing raw seafood, such as cutting boards and knives, with hot, soapy water.

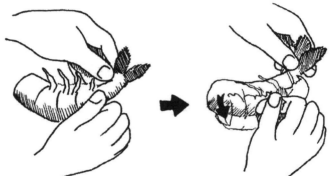

HOLD THE SHRIMP BY THE TAIL WITH ONE HAND. USE THE THUMB AND FOREFINGER OF THE FREE HAND TO GRASP THE SHRIMP'S LEGS AND EDGE OF SHELL.

PULL THE LEGS AND SHELL OFF THE SHRIMP. THEY SHOULD EASILY SLIP OFF IN ONE PIECE.

Figure 15-1: Peeling shrimp: The first step before deveining.

☆ LEAVE THE TAIL INTACT FOR A FANCIER PRESENTATION OR PULL OFF FOR A COMPLETELY NAKED SHRIMP.

PEELING SHRIMP

Figure 15-2: Removing that icky mud vein.

HOLD THE SHRIMP UNDER COLD, RUNNING WATER.

MAKE A SHALLOW SLIT WITH A KNIFE DOWN THE SHRIMP'S BACK ALONG THE LINE OF THE VEIN.

WASH THE VEIN AND GRIT AWAY WITH THE WATER.

DEVEINING SHRIMP

Shrimp in Chile Adobo Sauce

If you have the Chile Adobo Sauce from Chapter 10 on hand, this is a quick meal to make. Serve the shrimp with rice or with warmed flour tortillas.

Yield: *4 to 6 servings*

Preparation time: *5 minutes; 15 to 60 minutes marinating time*

Cooking time: *15 minutes*

Spice meter: *Hot and spicy*

1 recipe Chile Adobo Sauce(Chapter 10)

2 to 3 tablespoons vegetable or olive oil

1¾ pounds shelled and de-veined medium shrimp

¼ cup water or orange juice

Chopped fresh cilantro for garnish

1 Put the shrimp in a large flat baking dish. Pour the Chile Adobo Sauce over the shrimp and toss to coat. Cover and refrigerate for 15 to 60 minutes.

2 Remove the shrimp from the marinade. Set the marinade aside. In a large skillet over medium heat, heat the vegetable oil. Add the shrimp and cook, stirring frequently, until all the shrimp begin to turn opaque, about 2 minutes.

3 Reduce the heat to medium-low. Add the reserved marinade and water to the pan. Cover partially and simmer for about 10 minutes. Garnish with cilantro.

Warning: *Do not overcook the shrimp or they will become tough.*

Per serving: *Calories 189 (From Fat 92); Fat 10g (Saturated 1g); Cholesterol 188mg; Sodium 466mg; Carbohydrate 3g (Dietary Fiber 1g); Protein 21g.*

Shrimp Curry

This basic shrimp curry can be made hotter by adding a seeded, minced jalapeno when you add the garlic and ginger. Serve with rice and chutney.

Yield: *4 to 6 servings*

Preparation time: *20 minutes*

Cooking time: *35 to 40 minutes*

Spice meter: *Hot and spicy*

2 tablespoons peanut oil or vegetable oil

2 medium onions, chopped

2 plump cloves garlic, minced

½ inch-piece fresh ginger, minced

1½ to 2 tablespoons good-quality curry powder

½ cup chicken broth, shrimp broth, or water

2 teaspoons fresh lime or lemon juice

1½ cups chopped, peeled, and seeded tomatoes or canned tomatoes with their juices

3 tablespoons cream or half-and-half (optional)

1¾ pounds shelled and deveined medium shrimp

1 Heat the peanut oil in a large, deep skillet over medium heat. Add the onions and cook, stirring occasionally, until the onions are tender, about 10 minutes. Add the garlic and ginger and cook, stirring constantly, for 1 minute. Add the curry powder and cook, stirring, for 1 to 2 minutes.

2 Add the broth, lime juice, and tomatoes. Reduce the heat to medium-low. Cover and simmer for 10 to 15 minutes. Add the cream and simmer until heated through, about 3 minutes.

3 Add the shrimp and cook, uncovered, until the shrimp is pink and curled, about 3 to 5 minutes. Do not overcook the shrimp.

Variation: *Substitute canned, unsweetened coconut milk for the broth or water, but omit the cream.*

Per serving: *Calories 165 (From Fat 55); Fat 6g (Saturated 1g); Cholesterol 189mg; Sodium 232mg; Carbohydrate 6g (Dietary Fiber 2g); Protein 21g.*

Shrimp in West African Peanut Sauce

The combination of peanuts, tomatoes, coconut, and spices is typical of West African and Brazilian cuisine. In this recipe, the shrimp is poached in a tangy sauce.

Yield: *4 servings*

Preparation time: *20 minutes*

Cooking time: *35 to 40 minutes*

Spice meter: *Hot and spicy*

2 tablespoons peanut oil or vegetable oil

5 scallions, white part only, sliced

1 medium onion, chopped

1 small red bell pepper, chopped

1 plump clove garlic, minced

½-inch piece fresh ginger, minced

1½ cups chopped tomatoes

½ teaspoon crushed red chile flakes

½ teaspoon ground cumin

½ teaspoon paprika

½ teaspoon freshly ground black pepper

½ teaspoon salt

3 tablespoons peanut butter

1 cup unsweetened canned coconut milk

1½ pounds shelled and deveined medium shrimp

Chopped peanuts for garnish

Chopped fresh cilantro for garnish

1 Heat the peanut oil in a large skillet over medium heat. Add the scallions, onion, and bell pepper and cook, stirring occasionally, until the vegetables are tender, about 10 minutes.

2 Add the garlic and ginger and cook, stirring constantly, for 1 minute. Add the tomatoes, crushed red chile flakes, cumin, paprika, black pepper, and salt and cook for 5 minutes. Add the peanut butter; stir until blended evenly. Add the coconut milk and cook until the sauce begins to thicken slightly, about 15 to 20 minutes.

3 Add the shrimp and cook, uncovered, until the shrimp is pink and curled, about 3 to 5 minutes. Do not overcook the shrimp.

Tip: *You can make your own natural peanut butter by grinding unsalted roasted peanuts in a food processor fitted with a metal blade. If it's too thick, add a little peanut oil and pulse to combine.*

Per serving: Calories 399 (From Fat 240); Fat 27g (Saturated 13g); Cholesterol 242mg; Sodium 642mg; Carbohydrate 11g (Dietary Fiber 3g); Protein 31g.

Chapter 16

Vegetables and Legumes

In This Chapter

▶ Making vegetable side dishes

▶ Making vegetarian main dishes

*W*hether they're served as a side or a main dish, vegetables and legumes can be full of flavor. Spices give the most ordinary vegetables and legumes a delightful taste and add that special something that makes your meal stand out as a winner. Remember to consider the entire menu when selecting a vegetable accompaniment and make sure that it complements the other dishes that you'll be serving.

Veggie Basics

Good-quality produce is the key to any vegetable dish. Here are a few tips for buying veggies and a few simple steps to take when preparing them to be cooked.

- ✔ Check all produce for signs of spoilage, such as mildew, mold, and bruising.

- ✔ Touch produce to see if it's firm. There shouldn't be any soft spots or cracks in the skin.

- ✔ Store vegetables in the crisper section of your fridge. Don't refrigerate tomatoes, potatoes, onions, or winter squash such as butternut or acorn. Leave these veggies at room temperature.

- ✔ Wash vegetables in cold water and drain in a colander. Leafy vegetables and asparagus require more than one washing. Greens, such as collards, spinach, and Swiss chard, must be washed several times. Soak them in a sink filled with cold water and swish the leaves, allowing the grit to sink to the bottom. Remove the leaves and repeat until no grit is left. Cut out the tough stems toward the bottom to reduce cooking time.

- ✔ Root vegetables such as carrots and parsnips may require scrubbing with a vegetable brush.

- ✔ Mushrooms, (like strawberries,) can be wiped with a damp towel or with a soft mushroom brush. You can also rinse them quickly and then pat them dry with a dry towel.

- ✔ Pare vegetables such as carrots, parsnips, and celery with a vegetable peeler. Read recipes before paring winter squash and potatoes.

Prepping Veggies

Chopping up vegetables isn't the most rewarding experience. After all, wouldn't you rather be cooking and eating than prepping vegetables? But if you know the right techniques, you'll get through the drudgery a little more quickly and ultimately end up with a nicer-looking presentation.

Pull out your sharpened chef's knife and cutting board and practice the following techniques:

- ✔ Chopping: As you secure the food on the cutting board, make sure your fingers are curled under with fingertips facing in toward your palm and away from the blade, as shown in Figure 16-1.

- ✔ Julienne cutting: Cut the ingredient into even slices, stack the slices, and then slice vertically through the stack to create thin strips, as shown in Figure 16-2. This technique is also called matchstick cutting.

- ✔ Dicing: Cut the ingredient into long strips using the julienne technique. Then cut across the strips to create cubes (see Figure 16-3). To mince food, use the same technique but keep your cuts closer together.

- ✔ Roll cutting: Make a diagonal slice across the tip of the vegetable. Then roll it a quarter turn and make another diagonal slice along the same angle as the first cut. Roll another quarter turn and cut again (see Figure 16-4). Keep repeating until you're done.

Figure 16-1: Curl your fingers away from the blade when slicing.

SAFE FINGER PLACEMENT WHEN SLICING

MATCHSTICK/JULIENNE CUTTING

Figure 16-2:
The right way to make even matchstick cuts.

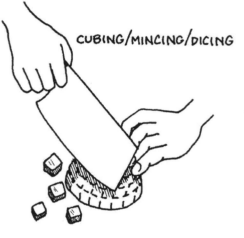

CUBING/MINCING/DICING

Figure 16-3:
Cubing and mincing require the same technique. The only difference is the size of the cut.

ROLL CUTTING

Figure 16-4:
A good way to cut cylindrical vegetables.

Spiced Roasted Vegetables

These flavorful vegetables can be served as a side dish or as a first course or salad. They're great on a buffet table — at room temperature (which is my preference), warm, or chilled. Although there are several ingredients and steps, the veggies are surprisingly easy to make. You can roast the vegetables a day ahead, toss with the dressing, and refrigerate them.

Yield: *6 to 8 servings*

Preparation time: *20 minutes*

Cooking time: *40 minutes, plus cooling time, if desired*

Spice meter: *Mildly spiced*

Spiced Olive Oil

¼ cup extra virgin olive oil

3 cloves garlic, peeled and lightly smashed

¾ teaspoon cumin seed

½ teaspoon cracked black pepper

1 serrano chile, halved

2 sprigs fresh thyme

Roasted Vegetables

1 medium eggplant, sliced ¼-inch thick and cut into half-moons

1 large or 2 medium onions, quartered

2 small zucchini, cut lengthwise into ¼-inch thick long pieces

2 medium red, yellow, or green bell peppers, seeded, ribs removed, and quartered

1 large tomato, cored

½ cup black olives or Mediterranean Spiced Black olives (Chapter 12)

2 tablespoons balsamic vinegar

2 plump cloves garlic, pressed or minced

1¼ teaspoons salt, or to taste

½ teaspoon freshly ground black pepper, plus pepper to taste

2 tablespoons extra virgin olive oil

2 tablespoons chopped flat-leaf parsley

1 Combine the olive oil, garlic, cumin seed, cracked black pepper, serrano, and thyme in a small saucepan and heat over medium-low heat for 5 to 10 minutes. Alternatively, combine the ingredients in a microwave-proof liquid measuring cup and heat for 1 minute on medium power. Let the spiced oil stand for 20 minutes.

2 Preheat the oven to 425 degrees. Combine the eggplant, onions, zucchini, and bell peppers in a large roasting pan. Season the vegetables with 1 teaspoon of the salt. Pour the spiced oil, with the spices included, over the vegetables and toss to coat evenly. Put the tomato in the center of the pan and roll it to coat with the spiced oil. Roast until the vegetables are very tender, about 30 minutes, stirring the vegetables once or twice. Remove all the vegetables except the onion to a platter, but set the tomato aside. Break the onion up into individual sections and roast for an additional 10 minutes, then arrange it on the platter.

3 When the tomato is cool enough to touch, remove the skin. Break up the tomato with a spoon or fork and stir it into the vegetables on the platter. Scatter the olives on top.

4 Combine the balsamic vinegar, garlic, the remaining ¼ teaspoon salt, and the pepper in a small bowl. Drizzle in the olive oil while beating with a fork or whisk. Pour the dressing over the vegetables. Garnish with parsley and freshly ground black pepper.

Tip: *You can roast vegetables with any spiced olive oil. Chapter 5 has numerous recipes for spiced oils.*

Per serving: Calories 147 (From Fat 103); Fat 11g (Saturated 2g); Cholesterol 0mg; Sodium 445mg; Carbohydrate 11g (Dietary Fiber 3g); Protein 2g.

Braised Cumin-Coriander Carrots

Spiced with the complementary duo of cumin and coriander, these carrots are sweet and delicious. Note that older, large carrots take longer to cook than baby carrots.

Yield: *4 servings*

Preparation time: *10 minutes*

Cooking time: *15 minutes*

Spice meter: *Mildly spiced*

1 pound carrots, peeled and cut in ¼ inch slices, or 1 pound baby carrots, peeled and trimmed

1½ tablespoon butter

⅓ cup water or orange juice

1 teaspoon sugar

¼ teaspoon ground cumin

¼ teaspoon ground coriander

1½ tablespoons chopped fresh cilantro or flat-leaf parsley

1 In a large pot over medium heat, combine the carrots, butter, water, sugar, cumin, and coriander. When the water boils, reduce the heat to medium-low, cover and simmer for 5 minutes.

2 Uncover and raise the heat to medium. Continue cooking, stirring occasionally, until the carrots are tender and the liquid is evaporated, about 7 to 10 minutes depending on the size of the carrots. Toss the carrots with the cilantro and serve.

Variation: *Omit the cumin and coriander. In Step 1, add ½ cinnamon stick and 5 lightly bruised cardamom pods along with the carrots, butter, water, and sugar. Follow the recipe as directed. Remove the whole spices after cooking. Replace the cilantro with chopped fresh parsley or mint.*

Per serving: Calories 88 (From Fat 33); Fat 4g (Saturated 2g); Cholesterol 10mg; Sodium 59mg; Carbohydrate 13g (Dietary Fiber 3g); Protein 2g.

Spicy Green Beans

Liven up ordinary green beans by spiking them with cumin, chiles, mustard seeds, and coconut — like some Indian and Southeast Asian cooks do.

Yield: *4 servings*

Preparation time: *10 minutes*

Cooking time: *10 minutes*

Spice meter: *Moderately spiced to hot and spicy*

1 pound green beans, trimmed and cut into ½-inch lengths	*1 jalapeno or serrano, seeded and minced (optional)*
2 tablespoons vegetable oil	*¾ teaspoon cumin seeds*
¼ teaspoon brown or black mustard seeds	*¼ cup shredded coconut*
5 scallions, white part only, sliced	

1 Have a large bowl of iced water ready and set aside. In a large saucepan over high heat, cook the green beans in lightly salted water until they're tender but crisp, about 5 minutes. Drain the beans in a colander or sieve and immediately plunge them into the ice water. When the beans are cold, transfer them to a plate and pat them dry with a paper towel.

2 Heat the vegetable oil in a large skillet over medium heat. Add the mustard seeds and scallions. When the mustard seeds begin to crackle, add the jalapeno and cumin seeds and cook, stirring constantly, for 1 minute. Add the coconut and cook, stirring constantly, for 1 minute.

3 Add the green beans and cook, stirring often, for 2 to 3 minutes. The beans are done when they're heated through.

Cook's Fact: *The process of partially cooking vegetables in lightly salted boiling water is known as blanching. The salt in the water sets the color so it remains bright. Immersing vegetables in iced water is known as refreshing, a procedure that halts the cooking process and keeps the vegetables tender-crisp. These two processes are used when vegetables are to be cooked a second time or reheated quickly. Most fine restaurants prep vegetables in this way so that the veggies take little time to prepare when an order is placed by patrons.*

Per serving: *Calories 131 (From Fat 83); Fat 9g (Saturated 3g); Cholesterol 0mg; Sodium 23mg; Carbohydrate 12g (Dietary Fiber 4g); Protein 2g.*

Garlicky Broccoli Stir-Fry

This recipe highlights garlic, but it also features a blend of predominantly Chinese flavors. The broccoli in this recipe doesn't need to be cooked beforehand. However, feel free to use frozen or leftover cooked broccoli — just note that it will take less time to cook.

Yield: *4 to 6 servings*

Preparation time: *15 minutes*

Cooking time: *10 minutes*

Spice meter: *Moderately spiced*

1½ to 2 pounds broccoli	*1 teaspoon minced fresh ginger*
2 tablespoons peanut oil	*1 teaspoon five-spice powder or ½ teaspoon crushed red chile flakes (optional)*
½ cup orange juice	
½ cup chicken broth or water	*1 teaspoon Chinese or Asian sesame oil*
3 to 4 plump cloves garlic, minced	*2 teaspoons soy sauce*

1 Slice the broccoli stalks into coin-size pieces and separate the florets into small sections. Set the broccoli aside.

2 In a large, deep skillet or wok, heat the peanut oil over medium-high heat. Add the broccoli and cook, stirring often, until the broccoli is bright green, about 5 minutes.

3 Add the orange juice, broth, garlic, ginger, and five-spice powder. Simmer until most of the liquid is evaporated, about 5 minutes.

4 Add the sesame oil and soy sauce and toss the broccoli to blend the ingredients evenly. Serve immediately.

Variation: For a non-Chinese version, omit the ginger and five-spice powder in Step 3 as well as the sesame oil and soy sauce in Step 4. Add salt to taste before serving.

Per serving: *Calories 92 (From Fat 54); Fat 6g (Saturated 1g); Cholesterol 0mg; Sodium 226mg; Carbohydrate 8g (Dietary Fiber 3g); Protein 4g.*

Gingered Zucchini or Summer Squash

In summer, when zucchini is plentiful, who doesn't look for a new way to cook it? This spectacular recipe takes the commonplace squash to new heights.

Yield: *4 to 6 servings*

Preparation time: *10 to 15 minutes*

Cooking time: *10 to 15 minutes*

Spice meter: *Mildly to moderately spiced*

1 tablespoon butter

2 tablespoons vegetable oil or olive oil

3 scallions, white part only, thinly sliced

½ inch piece fresh ginger, finely minced or grated

1 plump clove garlic, minced

½ teaspoon homemade or good-quality curry powder (optional)

2 pounds zucchini, coarsely grated or sliced into very thin rounds or half-moons

½ teaspoon salt

¼ teaspoon freshly ground black pepper

1 tablespoon chopped fresh mint or flat-leaf parsley (optional)

1 In a large skillet over medium heat, melt the butter with the vegetable oil and heat. Add the scallions, ginger, garlic, and curry powder and cook, stirring almost constantly, for 1 to 2 minutes.

2 Add the zucchini and cook, stirring often, until the squash is tender and just begins to turn golden, about 7 to 10 minutes. Add the salt and pepper and stir. Stir in the mint and serve.

Tip: *To cut down on preparation time, grate the zucchini using a shredding disk in a food processor.*

Per serving: *Calories 82 (From Fat 60); Fat 7g (Saturated 2g); Cholesterol 5mg; Sodium 200mg; Carbohydrate 5g (Dietary Fiber 2g); Protein 2g.*

Mashed Spiced Butternut

Butternut, like pumpkin, is enhanced by spices such as cinnamon, ginger, and nutmeg. Here it is steamed with whole spices that scent the butternut and then pureed like mashed potatoes, spiced, and tossed with butter. The butternut can be cubed the day before and refrigerated in a covered container This recipe freezes well.

Yield: *4 to 6 servings*

Preparation time: *15 to 20 minutes*

Cooking time: *15 minutes*

Spice meter: *Mildly spiced*

2 to 2½ pounds butternut squash, peeled and cut into -1-inch cubes, about 4½ to 5 cups

6 cardamom pods, crushed slightly with the back of a knife

4 whole cloves

4 whole coriander seeds

2 cinnamon sticks, broken

2 slices fresh ginger, unpeeled

2 bay leaves

2 tablespoons butter

⅓ cup milk or orange juice, warmed

¼ teaspoon ground cinnamon

⅛ teaspoon ground nutmeg or allspice

Salt to taste, about ¾ teaspoon

1 In a medium bowl, combine the butternut, cardamom, cloves, coriander, cinnamon, ginger, and bay leaves.

2 In a large pot fitted with a steamer, bring water to a boil over high heat. Add the butternut and spice mixture and steam until tender, about 15 minutes. Remove the whole spices with a slotted spoon and discard.

3 Transfer the butternut to a bowl. Mash the butternut with a masher. Alternatively, puree the butternut in the bowl of a food processor fitted with a metal blade.

4 Add the butter, milk, ground cinnamon, nutmeg, and salt and stir to mix. Reheat if necessary.

Tip: *Peel the butternut with a vegetable peeler. Slice it in half, lengthwis,e and scoop out the seeds, then cut it into cubes. If necessary, cut off the narrow end before slicing the seed-bearing section in half.*

Per serving: *Calories 79 (From Fat 39); Fat 4g (Saturated 3g); Cholesterol 12mg; Sodium 301mg; Carbohydrate 10g (Dietary Fiber 3g); Protein 1g.*

Braised Red Cabbage with Caraway, Apples and Bacon

You can use green or Savoy cabbage if you prefer in this northern European–inspired dish.

Yield: *4 servings*

Preparation time: *15 to 20 minutes*

Cooking time: *15 minutes*

Spice meter: *Mildly spiced*

2 tablespoons butter

1¼ pounds red cabbage, cored and shredded (about 1 medium-size cabbage)

2 medium apples, peeled, cored, and thinly sliced

¼ cup dry white wine

⅓ cup chicken broth or water

½ teaspoon caraway seeds

½ teaspoon salt

2 to 3 strips bacon, cooked and crumbled

1 Melt the butter in a large deep skillet over medium heat. Cook the cabbage, stirring occasionally, until it begins to soften, about 3 minutes.

2 Add the apples and cook, stirring, for 3 minutes.

3 Add the wine, broth, caraway, and salt. Cover and reduce the heat to medium-low. Simmer until the cabbage and apples are tender, about 7 to 10 minutes. Stir in the crumbled bacon and heat thoroughly.

Warning: *If you're out of white wine, don't use cooking wine — it's full of salt. Instead, substitute dry white vermouth, extra broth, or water.*

Per serving: *Calories 139 (From Fat 73); Fat 8g (Saturated 4g); Cholesterol 19mg; Sodium 435mg; Carbohydrate 16g (Dietary Fiber 4g); Protein 3g.*

Tomato preparation

To peel a tomato, cut an X in the skin on the bottom of the tomato without piercing the flesh. Immerse the tomato in a pot of boiling water for 20 seconds and remove it with a slotted spoon. Peel the skin with the tip of a paring knife (or just use your fingers). It should slip off easily.

To seed a tomato, cut out the core at the top and then slice the tomato in half. Squeeze the seeds out or flick them out with your finger.

How to Peel, Seed, and Chop Tomatoes

1. Insert paring knife diagonally — Cut out stem

2. Cut a shallow "x" on the bottom

3. Drop into boiling water for about 20 seconds or so

4. Remove with a long-handled fork — Immerse in Cold water

5. Starting at the "x," peel off the skin. Easy! (Peel peaches and apricots the same way.)

6. cut in half

7. Squeeze! Seeds ooze out

8. chop into desired size.

Greens with Mustard Seeds, Onions, and Tomatoes

Collards or turnip greens can stand up to the strongly flavored Indian combination of mustard seeds, ginger, and chiles.

Yield: *4 to 6 servings*

Preparation time: *15 minutes*

Cooking time: *20 to 30 minutes*

Spice meter: *Moderately spiced to hot and spicy*

3 tablespoons vegetable oil

1 medium onion, thinly sliced

¼ teaspoon black or brown mustard seeds

1 jalapeno, seeded and minced, or ½ teaspoon crushed red chile flakes

1-inch piece fresh ginger, minced

2 plump cloves garlic, minced

1½ pounds collard or turnip greens, washed, trimmed, and chopped

½ cup water or chicken broth

1½ teaspoons sugar

1 medium tomato, peeled, seeded, and chopped

Lemon wedges for garnish

1 In a large skillet over medium heat, heat 1 tablespoon of the vegetable oil. Add the onion and cook, stirring occasionally, until the onion is translucent, about 5 minutes.

2 Add the remaining vegetable oil and heat. Add the mustard seeds. When they start to crackle, add the jalapeno, ginger, and garlic. Cook, stirring often, for 1 minute. Add the greens. Cook, stirring occasionally, until the greens begin to soften, about 5 to 10 minutes depending on the toughness of the stem and the type of green that you use.

3 Add the water, sugar, and tomato. Cover and reduce the heat to medium-low. Simmer until the greens and tomatoes are just tender and most of the liquid is absorbed, about 10 to 15 minutes, depending on the toughness of the stem. Serve with lemon wedges.

Variation: *A medium head of common green or Savoy cabbage, about 1 pound, cored and thinly sliced, can be substituted. Note that the cooking times will alter slightly.*

Per serving: *Calories 114 (From Fat 70); Fat 8g (Saturated 1g); Cholesterol 0mg; Sodium 98mg; Carbohydrate 10g (Dietary Fiber 4g); Protein 3g.*

Fragrantly Spiced Spinach

The spice mix for this dish is based on the classic French spice combination, *quatre épices*. There's a recipe for quatre épices in Chapter 2. If you have some handy, substitute ½ teaspoon quatre épices for the white pepper, cinnamon, nutmeg, and cloves in this recipe.

Yield: *4 to 6 servings*

Preparation time: *10 minutes*

Cooking time: *5 to 10 minutes*

Spice meter: *Mildly spiced*

1¼ to 1½ pounds spinach, washed and trimmed

2½ tablespoons butter

3 to 4 plump scallions, minced, white part only, or 1 shallot, minced

½ teaspoon finely minced fresh ginger

¼ teaspoon white pepper

⅛ teaspoon ground cinnamon

⅛ teaspoon freshly grated or ground nutmeg

Pinch of ground cloves

2 teaspoons lemon juice

Salt to taste, about ¼ teaspoon

1 In a large pot of lightly salted boiling water, cook the spinach until just tender and bright green, about 2 minutes. Drain well in a sieve and set aside.

2 Over medium-low heat, melt the butter in a skillet. Add the scallions and cook until tender, stirring occasionally, about 3 to 4 minutes. Add the ginger, white pepper, cinnamon, nutmeg, and cloves and cook, stirring for 1 minute. Add the lemon juice and salt.

3 Add the spinach to the pan and toss with tongs until the spinach is coated with the spiced butter and heated thoroughly.

Variation: *This recipe can also be made with Swiss chard. Use 2 pounds Swiss chard, well-washed and trimmed of its tough stem. Boil until just tender, about 5 minutes. Do not add the salt at the end of the recipe because Swiss chard is high in sodium.*

Per serving: *Calories 62 (From Fat 41); Fat 5g (Saturated 3g); Cholesterol 13mg; Sodium 149mg; Carbohydrate 3g (Dietary Fiber 2g); Protein 2g.*

Spiced Lemony Lentils

In this dish, lentils absorb the complex flavors of the seasonings, giving them a pleasantly spiced taste. This dish can be served as a main dish or as a side dish. You can also serve it cold or at room temperature as a legume salad on a bed of baby lettuce or frisee and garnished with chopped tomatoes.

Yield: *4 servings*

Preparation time: *15 minutes*

Cooking time: *20 to 25 minutes*

Spice meter: *Mildly to moderately spiced*

2 tablespoons vegetable oil

1 medium onion, finely chopped

1 cinnamon stick

1 bay leaf

2 plump cloves garlic, minced

1-inch piece fresh ginger, minced

¾ teaspoon ground coriander

½ teaspoon ground cumin

3½ to 4 cups water, vegetable broth, or chicken broth

2 cups brown lentils, picked over, rinsed, and drained

1 tablespoon fresh lemon juice

1 tablespoon freshly grated lemon zest

½ to ¾ teaspoon salt, or to taste

3 tablespoons minced fresh parsley or cilantro

1 In a large saucepan over medium heat, heat the vegetable oil. Add the onion, cinnamon, and bay leaf and cook, stirring occasionally, until the onions are translucent, about 5 minutes. Add the garlic and ginger and cook, stirring often, for 1 minute. Add the coriander and cumin and cook, stirring constantly, for 30 to 45 seconds.

2 Add the water and lentils, bay leaf, and lemon juice. Bring the water to boil. Cover partially and reduce the heat to medium-low. Simmer until the lentils are tender but not mushy, about 15 to 20 minutes. Do not overcook. The liquid should mostly be evaporated.

3 Stir in the lemon zest, salt, and parsley.

Warning: *If too much water boils out before the lentils have finished cooking, add a small amount of water or broth. For this dish, the liquid should be nearly evaporated by the end of the cooking time.*

Variation: *To serve this recipe as a salad, toss the cooled cooked lentils in a little prepared vinaigrette or in an oil and vinegar salad dressing. Make your own dressing by mixing 2 tablespoons of white wine vinegar with ½ teaspoon of salt and ¼ teaspoon pepper, and then whisking this mixture together with 5 to 6 tablespoons of olive oil. Refrigerate any leftover dressing.*

Per serving: *Calories 367 (From Fat 72); Fat 8g (Saturated 1g); Cholesterol 0mg; Sodium 299mg; Carbohydrate 54g (Dietary Fiber 21g); Protein 23g.*

Vegetarian Bean Chili

This spicy vegetarian chili combines beans and vegetables. Check out a picture of it on the fourth page of the color section. Add a few extra veggies if you wish, such as a sliced zucchini or yellow summer squash. This recipe freezes well.

Yield: _6 to 8 servings_

Preparation time: _15 minutes_

Cooking time: _50 to 60 minutes_

Spice meter: _Moderately spicy to spicy hot_

2 tablespoons vegetable oil

1 medium onion, chopped

1 green or red bell pepper, chopped

1 celery stalk, finely chopped

2 medium carrots, finely chopped

1 to 2 jalapenos, seeded and minced, to taste

2 cloves garlic, minced

2 to 3 tablespoons chili powder, or to taste

1 teaspoon cumin

One 14½-ounce can chopped tomatoes

1 to 1½ cups water, vegetable broth, or chicken broth

Two 20-ounce cans of beans, such as black, pinto, pink, or red kidney, drained and rinsed; or 4 cups freshly cooked beans (about 10 ounces dry)

1 teaspoon minced fresh oregano or ½ teaspoon dried

1¼ cups (one 10 ounce package) frozen corn kernels

½ teaspoon salt

2 tablespoons minced cilantro for garnish (optional)

⅓ cup grated cheddar cheese for garnish (optional)

_1_ Heat the vegetable oil in a stewpot over medium heat. Add the onion, bell pepper, celery, and carrots and cook, stirring occasionally, until the vegetables begin to soften, about 5 to 7 minutes.

_2_ Add the jalapeno and garlic and cook, stirring occasionally, for 1 minute. Add the chili powder and cumin and cook, stirring constantly, for 30 seconds. Add the tomatoes, water, beans, and oregano. Reduce the heat to medium-low. Cover partially and simmer until the liquid is slightly reduced, about 30 minutes. If too much liquid has evaporated during cooking, add a bit extra.

_3_ Add the salt and corn and simmer for 10 to 15 minutes. Serve garnished with cilantro and grated cheese.

Tip: _Always rinse canned beans under cold running water, then drain them in a colander or sieve._

Per serving: _Calories 174 (From Fat 43); Fat 5g (Saturated 0g); Cholesterol 0mg; Sodium 325mg; Carbohydrate 27g (Dietary Fiber 9g); Protein 7g._

Legume and dried beans prep

Before doing anything else, pick through lentils, split peas, and dried beans for grit and small stones. Put them in a strainer or colander and then rinse them in a strainer under cold running water.

After picking through the beans and rinsing them, put them in a pot and cover them with several inches of cold water. Soak the beans overnight. If you can't wait overnight, place the beans in a stewpot and cover with 3 inches of water. Over high heat, bring the water to a boil and boil for 2 minutes. Remove the pot from the heat and let stand for 1 hour. Discard the soaking water.

Note: Soaking lentils or split peas isn't necessary.

When cooking the dried beans, use 2 quarts of water for 1 pound of dried beans. Place the beans and water in a large stewpot and bring to a boil. Reduce the heat to medium-low and simmer until the beans are tender, about 1½ to 2 hours. Skim off foam as it appears. Drain the cooked beans in a colander.

Chapter 17

Pasta, Potatoes, and Grains

In This Chapter

▶ Pasta as a first or main course

▶ Potato and grain side dishes

*A*lthough potatoes, grains, and pasta aren't highly flavorful on their own, they don't have to be bland when you serve them. Perk them up by seasoning them with a variety of spices — from fragrant and mild to hot and spicy. Pasta dishes can either be served as a starter or as a main course. The non-pasta recipes in this chapter are marvelous accompaniments to roasted, grilled, or sautéed meat, poultry, or seafood, as well as stews and curries.

Using Your Noodles

One of the most versatile foods there is, pasta is a favorite dish throughout the world. Figure 17-1 shows many of the different sizes and shapes of pastas that you're likely to encounter.

Figure 17-1:
The world
of pasta.

Pasta is easy to prepare, but here are a few cooking tips to help you make the most of your noodles:

- Cook pasta in plenty of lightly salted boiling water. While it's cooking, stir the pasta a few times to prevent the noodles from clumping together.

- Cook the pasta to the *al dente* stage — until it offers only slight resistance when you test a strand by biting it. If pasta is cooked too long, it becomes too soft. Drain pasta in a colander, not a sieve or strainer. Otherwise, the pasta will be over-drained. Droplets of water should cling to the pasta.

- Cool cooked pasta that's going to be used in cold noodle dishes by putting the colander under cold running water and tossing the pasta gently. Run the water until the noodles are cool. Doing so stops the cooking process, keeps the noodles fresh tasting, and prevents them from becoming pasty.

- Fresh pasta cooks very quickly. Add the pasta to a large pot of rapidly boiling salted water (the water will stop boiling rapidly) and stir occasionally. When the water returns to a boil, the pasta should be cooked. Test a strand and drain in a colander.

Quick Fixes

Before I get to the more involved recipes in this chapter, I'd like to give you ideas for whipping up quick and easy pasta dishes:

- **Quick noodle side dish:** Toss cooked, wide egg noodles with butter and poppy seeds.

- **Quick main dish pasta:** Toss either hot or cold cooked pasta with olive oil, chopped fresh garlic, chopped fresh parsley, freshly grated lemon zest, and ¼ to ½ teaspoon crushed red chile flakes. Add chopped pitted black olives, chopped fresh or sun-dried tomatoes, some crumbled bacon, and crumbled goat cheese or freshly grated Parmesan. Top with freshly ground black pepper.

Of course, there are a million variations to each of the recipes above. Don't like poppy seeds? Try an herb or spice that you do like. A quick raid of the pantry might yield surprising and tasty results.

Cold Spiced Noodles with Sesame Oil and Vegetables

Easy and delicious, noodles dishes like this one are on Chinese menus and also can be found in deli salad bar counters. This dish can be made ahead and refrigerated.

Yield: *4 servings as a main course; 6 to 8 servings as a first course*

Preparation time: *10 to 15 minutes*

Cooking time: *10 minutes*

Spice meter: *Moderately spiced to hot and spicy*

⅓ cup soy sauce

3 tablespoons Chinese sesame oil

1½ tablespoons rice wine vinegar

½-inch piece fresh ginger, minced

2 plump cloves garlic, minced

1½ teaspoons crushed Szechuan peppercorns or ¼ to ½ teaspoon crushed red pepper flakes

A few drops Chinese hot chile oil or Tabasco to taste (optional)

12 ounces spaghetti, vermicelli, or dried Asian egg noodles

3 scallions, white and green parts, sliced

¼ cucumber, peeled and cut into matchsticks

1 medium carrot, coarsely grated

1 tablespoon sesame seeds, toasted, or 2 tablespoons chopped roasted peanuts

1 In a pasta serving bowl, combine the soy sauce, sesame oil, rice wine vinegar, ginger, garlic, crushed Szechuan peppercorns, and hot chile oil and set aside.

2 Cook the pasta according to the package directions in a large pot of lightly salted boiling water. Drain the pasta in a colander and rinse the noodles under cold water until they're cool.

3 Combine the pasta with the sauce in a serving bowl and toss to coat evenly. Top with the scallions, cucumber, carrot, and sesame seeds.

Variation: *In Step 3, top the noodles with 1½ cups cooked shrimp along with the other ingredients.*

Per serving: *Calories 464 (From Fat 116); Fat 13g (Saturated 2g); Cholesterol 0mg; Sodium 1,608mg; Carbohydrate 73g (Dietary Fiber 5g); Protein 13g.*

Pasta Puttanesca

This classic Italian pasta dish is quick, easy, and delightfully spicy. It's shown on the third page of the color section.

Yield: *4 to 6 servings as a main course, 8 servings as a first course*

Preparation time: *10 minutes*

Cooking time: *10 minutes*

Spice meter: *Moderately spiced to hot and spicy*

3 tablespoons virgin olive oil

2 anchovy fillets, minced

3 cloves garlic, minced

½ teaspoon crushed red pepper flakes

⅓ cup black olives, preferably kalamata, nicoise, or Italian

1 tablespoon capers

28-ounce can crushed or chopped plum tomatoes with their juices

¼ cup chopped fresh flat-leaf parsley

1 pound spaghetti, fusilli, or linguine

8 fresh basil leaves, torn into small pieces or cut into small thin strips

Freshly ground black pepper to taste, about ¼ teaspoon

1 Heat the olive oil in a large skillet over medium heat. Add the anchovies and cook, stirring, about 1 minute. Add the garlic and crushed red pepper flakes and cook for 1 minute. Stir in the olives, capers, tomatoes, and 2 tablespoons of the parsley. Simmer the sauce for 15 to 20 minutes.

2 Meanwhile, cook the pasta according to the package directions in a large pot of lightly salted boiling water. Drain the pasta in a colander.

3 Add the remaining parsley and basil to the sauce. Add the pasta and toss well.

Cook's Fact: *Capers, the bud of a bush native to the Mediterranean and Asia, are usually sold packed in brine. Before using, rinse them in a strainer under running water to remove the excess salt.*

Tip: *As a garnish, shave some Parmesan cheese over vegetables, salads, and pasta dishes that have an Italian or southern French flair.*

Per serving: Calories 420 (From Fat 92); Fat 10g (Saturated 1g); Cholesterol 1mg; Sodium 580mg; Carbohydrate 70g (Dietary Fiber 6g); Protein 13g.

Indonesian Peanut Noodles with Vegetables

Peanut sauce is often used in Indonesian cooking. Here, it's used in a fabulous pasta dish. Instead of making the peanut sauce in Step 1, feel free to substitute Southeast Asian Peanut Sauce (Chapter 10).

Yield: *4 servings as a main course; 6 to 8 servings as a first course*

Preparation time: *15 minutes*

Cooking time: *10 minutes*

Spice meter: *Moderately spiced to hot and spicy*

Sauce:

½ cup natural or creamy peanut butter, preferably unsweetened

2 tablespoons fresh lime juice

¼ cup light soy sauce

3 tablespoons brown sugar

3 to 4 tablespoons hot water or chicken broth

½ to 1 teaspoon crushed red pepper flakes or 1 to 2 heaping teaspoons sambal oelek or Chinese garlic chile paste

1-inch piece fresh ginger, minced

Noodles:

12 ounces udon, spaghetti, or vermicelli

3 scallions, white and green parts, sliced

1 medium carrot, grated

8 snow peas, strings removed, thinly sliced on an angle

¼ English cucumber, peeled and cut into matchsticks

⅓ cup chopped roasted peanuts

2 tablespoons minced mint or cilantro

1 In a small bowl, combine the peanut butter, lime juice, soy sauce, sugar, water, crushed red pepper flakes, and ginger. Set aside. If the sauce is too thick for your liking, thin with a little extra water or broth.

2 Cook the pasta according to the package directions in a large pot of lightly salted boiling water. Drain the pasta in a colander and rinse the noodles under cold water until they are cool.

3 Have a bowl of iced water ready. Cook the carrots and snow peas in lightly salted boiling water for 1 minute. Do not overcook. Drain in a sieve and immediately plunge the sieve, with the vegetables in it, into the iced water to stop the cooking. You may prepare the vegetables while the pasta is cooking.

4 In a serving bowl, combine the pasta, scallions, carrot, snow peas, and cucumber. Top with the peanut sauce and toss. Garnish with peanuts and mint.

Variation: In Step 3, add 1 to 1½ cups cooked shredded chicken to the pasta and vegetables, and then top with the peanut mixture.

Variation: It's easy to make the classic Chinese dish of cold Chinese noodles in sesame sauce by varying this recipe slightly. Omit the carrots, snow peas, chopped peanuts, and mint. You may substitute tahini or Chinese sesame sauce for the peanut butter, or use the peanut butter. Substitute 2 tablespoons rice wine vinegar for the lime juice. In Step 1, add 2 tablespoons of Chinese sesame oil and 1 to 2 plump cloves garlic, pressed or minced, to the other ingredients for the sauce and combine. Skip Step 3. In Step 4, combine the pasta and sesame sauce and toss. Garnish with the cucumber.

Per serving: Calories 410 (From Fat 199); Fat 22g (Saturated 3g); Cholesterol 0mg; Sodium 854mg; Carbohydrate 42g (Dietary Fiber 4g); Protein 15g.

Spiced Couscous with Currants

A staple of North African cuisine, couscous is granular semolina and is technically a type of pasta, not a grain. The instant variety used in this recipe makes a quick and delicious side dish. It can be served hot or at room temperature as a salad.

Yield: 4 to 6 servings

Preparation time: 10 minutes

Spice meter: Mildly to moderately spiced

1 cup instant couscous	¼ teaspoon ground cumin
½ teaspoon salt	⅛ teaspoon ground cinnamon
1 cup boiling water or chicken broth	⅛ teaspoon cayenne
1½ tablespoon butter	⅓ cup currants, plumped
¼ teaspoon ground coriander	

1 In a medium bowl, combine the couscous, salt, and boiling water and stir.

2 Add the butter, coriander, cumin, cinnamon, and cayenne. Cover and let stand for about 5 minutes, until the couscous is plumped. Fluff with a fork and stir in the currants.

Tip: Not sure how to plump currants? Put the currants in a small bowl. Pour enough boiling water over them to cover them completely. Let them stand for 10 minutes. Drain in a sieve, discarding the water.

Per serving: Calories 157 (From Fat 28); Fat 3g (Saturated 2g); Cholesterol 8mg; Sodium 198mg; Carbohydrate 28g (Dietary Fiber 2g); Protein 4g.

Mashed Vanilla-Scented Sweet Potatoes

Vanilla adds a new dimension to sweet potatoes or yams. This recipe can be made ahead and reheated in a microwave.

Yield: *4 to 6 servings*

Preparation time: *10 minutes*

Cooking time: *About 1 hour*

Spice meter: *Mildly spiced*

2½ pounds sweet potatoes

2½ tablespoons butter

⅓ cup orange juice, heated

½ vanilla bean pod, split and seeds scraped out

Salt to taste, about ¾ teaspoon

Freshly ground white or black pepper to taste, about ¼ teaspoon

1 Preheat the oven to 400 degrees. Bake the sweet potatoes on a baking sheet until they can be easily pierced with the tip of a paring knife, about 50 to 60 minutes, depending on their size.

2 Remove the pulp from the potatoes and discard the skins. In a large bowl, mash the pulp with a potato masher.

3 Melt the butter in a skillet over medium-low heat. Add the orange juice and vanilla seeds and heat until just warm.

4 Add the butter-vanilla-orange mixture to the potatoes. Add the salt and pepper to taste. Stir until smooth.

Variation: Replace the vanilla bean with ¼ teaspoon ground cinnamon and a scant ⅛ teaspoon freshly grated or ground nutmeg.

Per serving: *Calories 169 (From Fat 45); Fat 5g (Saturated 3g); Cholesterol 13mg; Sodium 303mg; Carbohydrate 29g (Dietary Fiber 4g); Protein 2g.*

Roasted Potatoes with Garlic and Cumin

Potatoes stand up to the strong flavors that are in this recipe, which is shown on the seventh page of the color section.

Yield: *4 to 6 servings*

Preparation time: *10 minutes*

Cooking time: *About 45 minutes*

Spice meter: *Moderately spiced to hot and spicy*

1¾ to 2 pounds baby or new potatoes, halved; or regular potatoes, cut into 1½-inch chunks	1 medium to large onion, quartered and thinly sliced
3 tablespoons olive oil	2 cloves garlic, minced
1 teaspoon salt	½ teaspoon crushed red pepper flakes
¼ teaspoon freshly ground black pepper	½ teaspoon cumin seeds (optional)

1 Preheat the oven to 400 degrees. In a roasting pan, toss the potatoes with 1½ tablespoons of the olive oil, salt, and black pepper. Roast the potatoes, turning occasionally, until they're tender and lightly browned, about 35 to 45 minutes.

2 While the potatoes are roasting, make the flavoring. In a small skillet over medium-low heat, heat the remaining 1½ tablespoons olive oil. Add the onion and cook, stirring occasionally, until the onions are lightly golden, about 10 to 15 minutes. Add the garlic, crushed red pepper flakes, and cumin seeds and cook, stirring, for 1 minute. Keep warm or reheat over low heat.

3 When the potatoes are finished, add the onion-spice mixture and toss well.

Variation: *Add 3 strips of crumbled, cooked bacon to the cooked onion spice mixture before tossing it with the potatoes.*

Per serving: *Calories 150 (From Fat 62); Fat 7g (Saturated 1g); Cholesterol 0mg; Sodium 392mg; Carbohydrate 18g (Dietary Fiber 3g); Protein 3g.*

Curried Barley Pilaf

This colorful dish can be served as a hot side dish. Or, if you want, serve it chilled or at room temperature as a salad.

Yield: *4 servings*

Preparation time: *10 minutes*

Cooking time: *45 to 55 minutes*

Spice meter: *Mildly to moderately spiced*

2 tablespoons butter

1 small onion, chopped

½ small red or green bell pepper, chopped (optional)

½-inch piece fresh ginger, minced

1 clove garlic, minced

2 to 3 teaspoons homemade or good-quality curry powder

1 cup medium pearled barley, rinsed and drained

3 to 3½ cups heated chicken broth or water

¾ teaspoon salt

1 tablespoon chopped fresh mint or cilantro (optional)

1 Melt the butter in a saucepan. Add the onion and bell pepper and cook until the vegetables are softened, stirring occasionally, about 5 to 7 minutes. Add the ginger and garlic and cook, stirring constantly, for 1 minute. Add the curry powder and cook, stirring constantly, for 1 minute.

2 Add the barley and cook, stirring constantly, for 1 minute. Add 3 cups of the broth and bring it to a boil.

3 Cover and reduce the heat to medium-low. Simmer gently until the barley is tender and the broth is absorbed, about 35 to 45 minutes. Taste a grain to see when it's tender. Add more liquid if too much has evaporated and the barley is not cooked. If excess liquid is in the pot, remove the covered pot from the heat and let the barley stand for 5 minutes.

4 Season with salt and stir in the mint.

Tip: *If the barley grains stick together, add extra butter and fluff with a fork.*

Variation: *Omit the bell pepper and substitute 1½ cups rinsed and drained basmati or white rice for the barley. Use only 2½ cups broth. Follow the recipe, cooking until the rice is tender and the liquid is absorbed, about 15 to 20 minutes. Test a grain to see if it is tender. Add ½ cup of raisins about 5 minutes before the rice is finished. Omit the mint.*

Per serving: *Calories 266 (From Fat 86); Fat 10g (Saturated 4g); Cholesterol 19mg; Sodium 1,192mg; Carbohydrate 41g (Dietary Fiber 8g); Protein 6g.*

Spiced Rice with Almonds

Spiced rice is served throughout India, Indonesia, the Middle East, South America, and parts of eastern and southern Africa. Spiced rice is a wonderful accompaniment to curries. It also goes well with grilled and roasted meat, poultry, or seafood.

Yield: *4 servings*

Preparation time: *10 minutes*

Cooking time: *20 to 25 minutes*

Spice meter: *Mildly spiced*

3 tablespoons butter or vegetable oil	½ bay leaf
1 small onion, chopped	1½ cups basmati or white rice
½ cinnamon stick	2½ cups heated chicken broth or water
6 cardamom pods, bruised	⅔ cup sliced almonds
½ teaspoon turmeric	

1 In a large saucepot over medium heat, melt 2 tablespoons of the butter. Add the onion and cook until the onions are softened, stirring occasionally, about 5 minutes. Add the cinnamon, cardamom, turmeric, and bay leaf and cook, stirring, for 1 minute.

2 Add the rice and cook, stirring constantly, for 1 minute. Add the broth. Cover and reduce the heat to low.

3 Simmer until the rice is tender and the liquid is absorbed, about 15 to 20 minutes.

4 Meanwhile, in a small skillet over medium-low heat, melt the remaining tablespoon of the butter. Add the almonds and cook, stirring occasionally, until they're lightly browned. Set aside.

5 When the rice is cooked, remove the whole spices and bay leaf and stir in the almonds.

Variation: *Make saffron rice. Saffron imparts flavor along with a yellow color. To use it in this recipe, omit the turmeric. Add 4 to 6 threads of saffron to the broth in Step 2 before covering the pan. Follow the rest of the recipe as directed.*

Per serving: *Calories 471 (From Fat 173); Fat 19g (Saturated 7g); Cholesterol 26mg; Sodium 626mg; Carbohydrate 73g (Dietary Fiber 5g); Protein 8g.*

Chapter 18

Quick Breads and Sweets

In This Chapter

▶ Baking savory and sweet breads and muffins

▶ Making desserts and dessert sauces

*B*aked goods, whether breads, muffins, or cakes, are always tastier when they're accented with a single spice or a combination of spices. Fruit desserts and dessert sauces also take on a lovely flavor when they're scented with spices. In this chapter, you find recipes that present standard ingredient and spice combinations — as well as some delectable but unusual pairings.

Baking Know-How

If you follow these procedures when you bake, you'll be sure to get good results:

✔ Use an oven thermometer to ensure that the oven temperature is correct.

✔ Preheat the oven first, then prepare the baking pan or sheet as prescribed in the recipe and set it aside.

✔ Measure all the ingredients and set them aside before proceeding with recipe steps.

✔ Stir flour or cornmeal before measuring it, then spoon it into a dry measuring cup. Sweep the top of the cup with a butter knife to level it, as shown in Figure 18-1. Don't dip the measuring cup into the flour or you can end up with as much as ¼ cup more flour than if you measure correctly.

✔ Use large eggs in all baking recipes. Other sizes will give either too much or to little liquid to batters.

✔ For texture and flavor, it's best to use whole milk in baking recipes. If you're worried about the fat content, you can get away with using 2 percent milk. Don't use skim; it's too watery.

✔ Do not overmix quick breads or muffins. Most can be mixed by hand with a wooden spoon. The batter is mixed enough when you don't see any patches of dry ingredients. Don't worry about lumps because this type of batter shouldn't be smooth.

✔ As soon as the liquid ingredients and dry ingredients that contain baking soda or baking powder are combined, the rising action begins to take place. Don't let the batter sit at room temperature too long. To get the best result, put the batter in the pan and bake it immediately.

✔ Fill any muffin cups that don't have batter in them halfway with water so that the muffins will bake evenly.

✔ Place the baking pan or sheet on a rack in the lower third of the oven. If your oven has hot spots, turn the pan around halfway through the baking time.

✔ If you're using a glass baking dish or one with a dark finish, reduce the oven temperature by 25 degrees to prevent overbaking.

✔ Test for doneness by inserting a skewer, cake tester, or toothpick into the center. It should come out clean.

✔ Let quick breads cool completely before slicing them with a serrated knife. Muffins and coffee cakes can be served warm.

Accurate Measuring

Figure 18-1:
The proper way to measure flour and other dry ingredients for baking.

Caraway, Cheese, and Bacon Beer Bread

This hearty bread scented with caraway, mustard, and parsley is a delightful addition to breakfast, lunch, or dinner menus. Take a look at it in the color section of the book. It's best fresh, but can be frozen.

Yield: *1 loaf*

Preparation time: *15 minutes*

Cooking time: *50 to 60 minutes*

Spice meter: *Mildly spiced*

3 cups all-purpose flour

1 tablespoon plus 1 teaspoon baking powder

1 tablespoon sugar

½ teaspoon salt

1⅓ cups grated sharp or extra sharp cheddar cheese

6 strips of bacon, crisply cooked and crumbled

2 teaspoons caraway seeds

1¼ teaspoons dry English mustard

⅓ cup chopped parsley

⅓ cup chopped scallions

1½ cups (a 12-ounce bottle) mild-flavored domestic beer at room temperature

1 Preheat the oven to 350 degrees. Lightly spray a 9-x-5-inch loaf pan with nonstick cooking spray and set aside.

2 In a medium bowl, combine all the ingredients except the beer.

3 Make a well in the center of the dry ingredients. Slowly pour in the beer and stir with a wooden spoon until just blended.

4 Pour the batter into the prepared pan. Bake for 50 to 60 minutes or until a toothpick inserted into the center comes out clean. The top of the bread will be lightly golden and have a rough appearance.

Variation: *Make whole wheat beer bread. Use 2 cups white all-purpose flour and 1 cup whole wheat flour.*

Per serving: *Calories 191 (From Fat 56); Fat 6g (Saturated 3g); Cholesterol 16mg; Sodium 354mg; Carbohydrate 26g (Dietary Fiber 1g); Protein 8g.*

Corny ideas

The Cumin-Chile Corn Muffins can be simplified or changed quite easily. If you add any of these additional ingredients, do so after Step 2 of the recipe.

- ✔ **Plain and simple:** Omit the cumin, white pepper, and cayenne.

- ✔ **Sweet citrus spice:** Make the plain and simple version, using 3 to 4 tablespoons of sugar. Add ¼ teaspoon cinnamon, ¼ teaspoon ginger, and ¼ teaspoon allspice or freshly grated or ground nutmeg, and 1 tablespoon freshly grated orange or lemon zest. Serve with honey butter.

- ✔ **Blueberry or cranberry spice:** Make the plain and simple version, using 3 to 4 tablespoons of sugar. Add ¼ teaspoon cinnamon and ¼ teaspoon freshly grated or ground nutmeg. Stir in 1 cup of blueberries or cranberries in Step 4, right before you spread the batter into the pan. Frozen berries work best and help prevent the batter from discoloring.

- ✔ **Tex-Mex:** Make the plain and simple version and add 1 tablespoon chili powder.

- ✔ **With cheese:** Add 1 cup grated Monterey Jack or cheddar cheese.

- ✔ **With jalapenos:** Add ¼ cup drained, canned jalapenos.

- ✔ **With sun-dried tomatoes:** Add ⅓ cup finely chopped reconstituted sun-dried tomatoes.

- ✔ **With ham or bacon:** Add ⅓ cup finely chopped ham or crisply cooked crumbled bacon.

Cumin-Chile Corn Muffins

Served with softened butter, these savory corn muffins are delicious alongside chilis, soups, stews, roasted or fried chicken, and fried seafood. They're shown on the fourth page of the color section. You can also use these muffins as the basis for cornbread stuffing. Some folks like sweeter muffins; you can adjust the sugar to your taste.

Yield: *12 muffins*

Preparation time: *10 minutes*

Baking time: *About 15 minutes*

Spice meter: *Mildly to moderately spiced*

1 cup cornmeal, preferably stone ground

1 cup all-purpose flour

3 teaspoons baking powder

1 to 3 tablespoons sugar, to taste

½ teaspoon salt

1 teaspoon ground cumin

¼ teaspoon cayenne or other ground chile pepper powder

⅛ teaspoon white pepper

1 egg, lightly beaten

1 cup milk

3 tablespoons corn oil, melted butter, or shortening

1 Preheat the oven to 425 degrees. Spray 12 regular-size muffin cups with nonstick cooking spray, or lightly grease them with butter, or line them with paper liners. Set the muffin tray aside.

2 Combine the cornmeal, flour, baking powder, salt, cumin, cayenne, and white pepper in a bowl.

3 In a 2-cup liquid measuring cup, combine the beaten egg and milk and set aside.

4 Add the corn oil to the dry ingredients and stir to mix. Pour the egg-milk mixture into the dry ingredients and stir with a wooden spoon to mix. The batter should be lumpy.

5 Spoon the batter into the prepared muffin cups, making sure they're about ½ full.

6 Bake until a toothpick inserted into the center comes out clean, about 15 to 18 minutes. Cool briefly and then turn the muffins out onto a rack. Serve the muffins with butter while they're still warm.

Variation: *You can make cornbread instead of muffins. Lightly grease an 8- or 9-inch square baking pan instead of muffin cups. In Step 3, use melted butter or shortening instead of corn oil. Spread the batter evenly in the prepared pan in Step 5. In Step 6, bake until a toothpick inserted in the center comes out clean, about 20 to 25 minutes.*

Variation: *Make jumbo muffins. Grease only 6 regular- size muffin cups and fill the cups with batter. Bake about 25 minutes. If you're using a 12-cup pan, remember to fill the empty cups halfway with water so that the muffins bake evenly.*

Variation: *If you want, add a touch of lemon by stirring 1½ teaspoons of freshly grated lemon zest to the dry ingredients.*

Per serving: Calories 134 (From Fat 44); Fat 5g (Saturated 1g); Cholesterol 20mg; Sodium 208mg; Carbohydrate 19g (Dietary Fiber 1g); Protein 3g.

Cinnamon Coffee Cake

There's nothing like this fragrantly spiced cake for breakfast or as a snack in the late afternoon. Traditionally, this streusel-topped cake is made with plain yogurt or sour cream. The batter can also be used for muffins; see the variation for instructions.

Yield: *1 cake; 12 servings*

Preparation time: *15 minutes*

Cooking time: *35 to 40 minutes*

Spice meter: *Mildly spiced*

Nutty Streusel Topping:

¼ cup chopped nuts, such as walnuts, pecans, or hazelnuts

3 tablespoons brown sugar

1 teaspoon ground cinnamon

¼ teaspoon freshly grated or ground nutmeg

Cake:

1½ cups all-purpose flour

2 teaspoons baking powder

½ teaspoon baking soda

1 teaspoon ground cinnamon

¼ teaspoon ground allspice

¼ teaspoon freshly grated or ground nutmeg

½ cup sugar

2 tablespoons butter

2 eggs

⅔ cup plain yogurt or sour cream

1 teaspoon vanilla extract

1 In a small bowl, combine the nuts, brown sugar, cinnamon, and nutmeg. Set aside.

2 Preheat the oven to 350 degrees. Spray an 8-x-8-inch baking pan with nonstick cooking spray.

3 In a medium bowl, combine the flour, baking powder, baking soda, cinnamon, and nutmeg.

4 In another medium bowl or in the bowl of a food processor fitted with a metal blade, combine the sugar and butter. Beat with a mixer or pulse the processor until blended. Add the eggs, yogurt, and vanilla extract and blend.

5 Add the dry ingredients all at once to the wet ingredients in the bowl or food processor. Stir with a wooden spoon or pulse the processor a few times until just blended. The batter will be thick.

6 Spread the batter evenly in the prepared pan. Top evenly with the walnut mixture.

7 Bake until a toothpick inserted into the center comes out clean, about 35 to 40 minutes. Cool on a wire rack for 10 minutes and serve warm or at room temperature.

Cook's Fact: Streusel is a crumbly topping made from sugar, butter, flour, spices, and some- times nuts. It's used on coffee cakes, muffins, pies, and fruit crumbles.

Variation: *Make spiced streusel muffins. Fill muffin tins ½ to ⅔ full and top with the streusel. If all the muffin cups aren't filled with batter, fill any empty cup with water so they bake evenly. Bake until a toothpick inserted into the center comes out clean, about 20 to 25 minutes. Makes 12.*

Variation: *Add fruit to the cake. Before you add the fruit, add optional lemon zest or orange zest in Step 3. If you're adding blueberries, use 1 teaspoon of freshly grated lemon zest; if you're adding cranberries, use 2 teaspoons of orange zest. Stir in 1 cup of blueberries or cranberries in Step 5, right before you spread the batter into the pan. Frozen berries work best and help prevent the batter from discoloring. Top with the streusel and bake.*

Per serving: Calories 159 (From Fat 45); Fat 5g (Saturated 2g); Cholesterol 42mg; Sodium 135mg; Carbohydrate 25g (Dietary Fiber 1g); Protein 4g.

Chocolate Cinnamon Sauce

Nothing beats this sauce over ice cream, alongside cakes, or with brownies à la mode. Covered, it will keep up to 2 weeks in the refrigerator. Reheat leftover sauce in a double boiler or over low heat while stirring frequently.

Yield: *About 1½ cups*

Preparation time: *10 minutes*

Cooking time: *About 10 minutes*

Spice meter: *Mildly spiced*

4 ounces good-quality bittersweet or
semisweet chocolate, chopped

2 tablespoons butter

2 tablespoons water

¼ to ⅓ cup sugar

¼ teaspoon ground cinnamon

½ cup cream or half-and-half

1 In the top of a double boiler over gently simmering water or in a small saucepan over very low heat, combine the chocolate, butter, water, and sugar. Cook, stirring often, until the chocolate is melted and the liquid bubbles gently.

2 Add the cinnamon and stir, then add the cream and stir. Simmer until the cream is heated thoroughly, about 3 minutes. Serve warm or at room temperature. The sauce can be reheated in a double boiler over simmering water or in a microwave.

Variation: *Replace the water with strong coffee, such as expresso, or Kahlua.*

Variation: *Replace the cinnamon with 1 teaspoon vanilla extract.*

Per recipe: Calories 217 (From Fat 135); Fat 15g (Saturated 9g); Cholesterol 29mg; Sodium 7mg; Carbohydrate 20g (Dietary Fiber 2g); Protein 2g.

Old-Fashioned Gingerbread

This gingerbread is easy, economical, and absolutely scrumptious. It's shown on the last page of the color section. The family recipe dates from the days of the great depression in the 1930s. If you like, sprinkle it with a bit of powdered sugar and serve warm. Alternatively, serve with whipped cream or with some Vanilla Sauce (see the recipe later in this chapter). The gingerbread freezes well.

Some gingerbread recipes ask you to cream the butter and sugar; this one uses boiling water to melt the butter. Just make sure you cut the butter in small pieces so that it melts quickly.

Yield: *1 cake; 12 servings*

Preparation time: *10 minutes*

Cooking time: *30 to 35 minutes*

Spice meter: *Moderately spiced*

1½ cups all-purpose flour

½ teaspoon baking powder

½ teaspoon baking soda

1 tablespoon ground ginger

1½ teaspoons ground cinnamon

¼ teaspoon ground cloves

2 tablespoons finely chopped crystallized ginger (optional)

6 tablespoons butter, cut into small pieces

½ cup boiling water

½ cup brown sugar

½ cup unsulphured molasses

1 egg, lightly beaten

1 Preheat the oven to 350 degrees. Lightly butter an 8-x-8-inch square baking pan or spray with nonstick cooking spray.

2 In a small bowl, combine the flour, baking powder, baking soda, ginger, cinnamon, and cloves. Add the crystallized ginger, if you're using it, and stir. Set aside.

3 Put the butter in a medium bowl and pour the boiling water over it. Stir until the butter melts. Add the sugar, molasses, and egg. Stir well with a whisk or wooden spoon.

4 Add the flour mixture to the wet ingredients and stir with a whisk or wooden spoon until the flour is just blended. The batter will be runny.

5 Spread the batter evenly in the prepared pan. Bake for 25 to 30 minutes or until a toothpick inserted into the center comes out clean. Cool on a rack. Once cool, dust the top with confectioners' sugar, if you want.

Tip: *To dust baked goods, put a little confectioners' sugar in a sieve and hold the sieve over the top of the item to be dusted. Gently tap the side of the sieve with one hand while moving the sieve so that the entire surface is lightly and evenly sprinkled with the sugar. You can use the same method to dust desserts with cocoa.*

Cook's Fact: *Crystallized ginger is actually candied ginger. The ginger has been cooked in a sugar syrup.*

Per serving: *Calories 187 (From Fat 57); Fat 6g (Saturated 4g); Cholesterol 33mg; Sodium 84mg; Carbohydrate 31g (Dietary Fiber 1g); Protein 2g.*

Spiced Chocolate Loaf

Enhanced with spices, this dense, chocolatey bread is a treat any time of day. I like to add a little cayenne. It doesn't make the bread hot, it just gives the bread extra zing. Feel free to omit the cayenne if you wish. This freezes well.

Yield: *1 loaf; 12 servings*

Preparation time: *15 minutes*

Cooking time: *45 to 55 minutes*

Spice meter: *Mildly to moderately spiced*

1¾ cup all-purpose flour

½ cup unsweetened cocoa powder

1¼ teaspoons baking soda

1 teaspoon ground cinnamon

½ teaspoon ground ginger

½ teaspoon ground allspice

½ teaspoon salt

⅛ to ¼ teaspoon cayenne, or to taste (optional)

⅛ teaspoon ground cloves

⅔ cup sugar

2 eggs

3 tablespoons butter, melted

1 cup buttermilk

1 Preheat the oven to 350 degrees. Lightly butter a 9-x-5-inch loaf pan or spray with non-stick cooking spray.

2 In a bowl, combine the flour, cocoa powder, baking soda, cinnamon, salt, ginger, allspice, salt, cayenne, and cloves.

3 In a separate bowl, combine the sugar and eggs. Whisk together until the mixture has thickened slightly and is a light lemon color. Whisk in the melted butter.

4 Add half the buttermilk to the wet ingredients, then half the flour mixture, stirring with a wooden spoon after each addition. Repeat with the remaining buttermilk and flour mixture and stir until just blended. The batter will be thick.

5 Put the batter in the prepared pan and spread it evenly with a rubber spatula. Bake for 45 to 55 minutes or until a toothpick inserted into the center comes out clean. Cool in the pan on a rack for 5 minutes. Remove the loaf from the pan and continue cooling on a rack.

Tip: *To make spreading thick batters easier, moisten the spatula with water.*

Variation: *In Step 4, after the buttermilk and flour are blended in completely, add ⅔ cup of either raisins, mini chocolate chips, or chopped nuts (walnuts, pecans, and macadamias work well).*

Per serving: Calories 165 (From Fat 41); Fat 5g (Saturated 2g); Cholesterol 44mg; Sodium 262mg; Carbohydrate 28g (Dietary Fiber 2g); Protein 4g.

Spiced Apple Cake

Serve warm for breakfast or as a snack. Try the cake with whipped cream, vanilla ice cream, or Vanilla Sauce (see the recipe in this chapter) for a simple country-style dessert. Or allow the cake to cool and then sprinkle the top with confectioners' sugar.

Yield: *1 cake; 12 servings*

Preparation time: *15 minutes*

Cooking time: *40 to 45 minutes*

Spice meter: *Mildly spiced*

1 cup all-purpose flour

1 teaspoon baking powder

2¼ teaspoons homemade Pumpkin Pie Spice Mix (Chapter 9) or commerical pumpkin pie spice mix

½ teaspoon salt

8 tablespoons (1 stick) butter or margarine, melted

1 egg, lightly beaten

⅓ cup light brown sugar

⅓ cup sugar

1 teaspoon vanilla extract

2 cups peeled, cored, and coarsely chopped apples, such as Rome, Cortlandt, or MacIntosh

½ cup chopped walnuts (optional)

1 Preheat the oven to 350 degrees. Spray an 8-x-8-inch square pan with nonstick cooking spray and set aside.

2 In a small bowl, combine the flour, baking powder, and Pumpkin Pie Spice Mix and set aside.

3 In medium-size bowl, combine the butter, egg, brown sugar, sugar, and vanilla and stir well.

4 Add the dry ingredients to the wet ingredients and stir with a wooden spoon. Do not overmix. The batter will be quite thick. Stir in the apples and nuts.

5 Spread the mixture evenly in the prepared baking pan. Bake for 40 to 45 minutes or until a toothpick inserted into the center comes out clean. Cool briefly on a rack.

Tip: *Feel free to substitute 1 teaspoon ground cinnamon, ½ teaspoon ground ginger, ½ teaspoon freshly grated or ground nutmeg, and ¼ teaspoon ground allspice for the Pumpkin Pie Spice Mix.*

Per serving: *Calories 179 (From Fat 76); Fat 8g (Saturated 5g); Cholesterol 38mg; Sodium 138mg; Carbohydrate 25g (Dietary Fiber 1g); Protein 2g.*

Nut Biscotti with Anise

These delicious Italian cookies are a wonderful accompaniment to coffee, tea, sorbets, ice cream, and fresh or poached fruit desserts. They can be stored in a covered container for a week or two. Check them out on the last page of the color section.

Yield: *4 dozen cookies*

Preparation time: *20 minutes*

Cooking time: *45 to 50 minutes*

Spice meter: *Mildly spiced*

3½ tablespoons butter, softened	*1¾ teaspoons baking powder*
¾ cup sugar	*1 tablespoon freshly grated lemon zest (optional)*
2 eggs	
1 teaspoon vanilla extract	*1½ teaspoons anise, crushed*
2 cups all-purpose flour	*1 cup chopped nuts, such as almonds or hazelnuts*

1 Preheat the oven to 375 degrees. Spray 2 baking sheets with nonstick spray or lightly butter them with extra butter. Dust both sheets lightly with a small amount of flour and set aside.

2 In a medium bowl, beat the butter and sugar until creamy and fluffy. Add the eggs and beat together. Add the vanilla and beat to combine.

3 In another bowl, combine the flour, baking powder, lemon zest, anise, and nuts. Stir to mix.

4 Add the dry ingredients to the wet ingredients, about one third at a time, stirring to combine after each addition.

5 Divide the dough in half. On a lightly floured surface, roll the dough into two logs about 2 inches in diameter.

6 Shake any excess flour from the baking sheets and transfer one log to each baking sheet. Bake until the logs are lightly golden and show a few cracks on the top, about 30 minutes. Remove from the oven and set on a rack to cool.

7 Reduce the temperature to 250 degrees.

8 When the logs are cool enough to touch, slice the logs on the diagonal with a very sharp or serrated knife. Make 1½- to 2-inch-wide slices.

9 Return the slices to the baking sheets. Bake until the biscotti begins to dry out, about 15 to 20 minutes. Cool on a rack.

Variation: *Replace the anise with 1 teaspoon cinnamon. Replace the nuts with ⅔ cup raisins. Proceed with the recipe as directed.*

Variation: Replace the lemon zest with 1½ teaspoons of freshly grated orange zest.

Warning: If the dough is a little too wet for you to form the log, add an additional tablespoon or two of flour.

Per serving: *Calories 58 (From Fat 22); Fat 2g (Saturated 1g); Cholesterol 8mg; Sodium 17mg; Carbohydrate 8g (Dietary Fiber 0g); Protein 1g.*

Vanilla Sauce

This lovely sauce can be served with ice cream, cakes, bread pudding, or poached fruit. Covered, it keeps up to 2 weeks in the refrigerator. Reheat leftover sauce in a double boiler or over low heat while stirring frequently.

Yield: **About 1¼ cups**

Preparation time: **5 minutes**

Cooking time: **15 to 25 minutes**

Spice meter: **Mildly spiced**

¾ cup heavy cream

6 tablespoons butter

1 vanilla bean or 1 teaspoon vanilla extract

¾ cup cup sugar

Pinch of salt

1 In a saucepan over medium-low heat, combine the cream, butter, and vanilla bean, if you're using a bean. Simmer until the butter is melted. Remove from the heat and let stand for 15 minutes. Remove the vanilla bean.

2 Add the sugar and salt to the pan and cook, stirring often, over medium-low heat until the sugar is melted and the sauce is glossy and slightly thickened, about 5 to 10 minutes. Remove the sauce from the heat. If using vanilla extract, add it now and stir to blend. Serve the sauce while it's warm. This sauce can be reheated in a double boiler over simmering water or in a microwave.

Tip: After infusing, wash the vanilla bean and pat it dry. Wrap it in foil and reserve it for another use.

Variation: Add 4 bruised cardamom pods to the cream along with the vanilla bean and remove them at the same time. You may use either white or brown sugar.

Variation: Add 1 tablespoon of bourbon, rum, or brandy along with the cream in Step 1.

Per recipe: *Calories 303 (From Fat 203); Fat 23g (Saturated 14g); Cholesterol 72mg; Sodium 36mg; Carbohydrate 26g (Dietary Fiber 0g); Protein 1g.*

The proof is in the bread pudding

Served warm with Vanilla Sauce, bread pudding is a simple but delicious dessert. Bread pudding is merely bread cubes topped with a spiced custard and baked. It's a good way to use left-over bread that's becoming stale. It is surprisingly easy to make.

To make bread pudding, preheat the oven to 350 degrees. Butter a 2-quart baking dish. Put 4 to 5 cups of cubed day-old bread (white, French, raisin, or oatmeal) in the prepared dish and set aside. In a bowl, whisk together 3 eggs and ⅔ cup sugar. Add 3 cups milk, 2 teaspoons vanilla, and 1 teaspoon cinnamon and whisk to combine. Pour the custard mixture over the bread and let stand for ½ hour, pushing the bread down occasionally so that it soaks up some of the liquid. Place the pudding dish inside a larger baking pan and pour enough hot water into the baking pan so it reaches about halfway up the pudding dish. Bake until a toothpick inserted into the center comes out clean, about 45 minutes to 1 hour.

You can vary bread pudding by adding ½ to ⅔ cups raisins, chopped pecans, or shredded coconut to the custard or make a chocolate bread pudding by adding two ounces of melted semisweet or bittersweet chocolate to the milk.

Spiced Poached Fruit

This basic recipe works equally well for apples, pears, or dried fruit. Fruit that has been poached in spiced liquid makes a delicious dessert. Poached dried fruit is also good for breakfast or brunch.

Yield: *6 servings*

Preparation time: *10 minutes*

Cooking time: *About 35 minutes*

Spice meter: *Moderately spiced*

1 cup dry red or dry white wine

1½ cups water

½ cup sugar

¼ cup honey

½-inch piece ginger, unpeeled and sliced into coin-size rounds

½ cinnamon stick or ½ teaspoon ground cinnamon

4 whole cloves or ¼ teaspoon ground cloves

½ teaspoon grated nutmeg

2-inch strip fresh lemon or orange zest, white pith removed

1½ pounds peeled and halved apples or pears or ¾ pound dried fruit mix — prunes, apricots, peaches, cherries, cranberries, and so on, about 3 cups

1 In a medium-size saucepan over medium heat, combine the wine, water, sugar, honey, ginger, cinnamon, cloves, nutmeg, and lemon zest. Bring the liquid to a boil.

2 Add the fruit and cook, turning the fruit occasionally until it's tender and easily pierced with a paring knife. This will take 20 to 40 minutes for fresh fruit, depending on the size and ripeness, or 35 minutes for dried fruit.

3 Remove the pan from the stove. Transfer the fruit to a bowl.

4 Return the pan to the stove over medium-high heat and cook the liquid until it's reduced by one-third, about 10 to 15 minutes. Remove the whole spices if you wish. Cool the liquid slightly and pour it over the fruit. Serve warm or chilled.

Tip: Poached fresh fruit will keep in its liquid in a covered container for up to 3 days; poached dried fruit keeps for 3 to 4 weeks. Both should be refrigerated.

Per serving: *Calories 176 (From Fat 4); Fat 0g (Saturated 0g); Cholesterol 0mg; Sodium 1mg; Carbohydrate 46g (Dietary Fiber 2g); Protein 0g.*

Chapter 19

Beverages

In This Chapter

- Holiday beverages
- Warm and cool drinks

Spices aren't just accents for food. Many hot and chilled beverages that are perfect for either summer or winter entertaining can be spiked with spices.

Drink It Up

There are no special tricks to brewing delicious spicy beverages, but here are a few suggestions for ways to make yours stand out.

- Don't let hot beverages that use liquor boil because the alcohol will evaporate. Keep them simmering over low heat.
- Make "virgin" drinks by omitting the liquor.
- Serve drinks in pretty cups or glasses.
- Garnish drinks that contain fruit with a slice of the same fruit. Serve those without fruit with one of the spices that you're using; for example, if a drink contains cinnamon, serve it with a cinnamon stick.

Mulled Red Wine

Mulled red wine is wonderfully spicy way to serve inexpensive wine. You can see it on the last page of the color section of this book. You may or may not sweeten the wine with sugar. It's delicious either way.

Yield: *4 to 6 servings*

Preparation time: *5 minutes*

Cooking time: *About 15 minutes*

Spice meter: *Mildly to moderately spiced*

½ cup water

¼ cup sugar (optional)

8 whole cloves or allspice berries or 4 of each

1 cinnamon stick

1 thinly sliced orange or lemon

1 bottle fruity dry red wine

1 In a saucepan over medium heat, combine the water, sugar, cloves or allspice, cinnamon stick, and orange or lemon. Heat until the sugar dissolves.

2 Add a bottle of dry red wine. Simmer until hot, about 10 to 15 minutes, and serve.

Tip: *Not sure if the wine is dry and fruity? Get a recommendation from the wine merchant. Examples of dry red wines are Merlot and Cabernet sauvignon, but some less expensive table wines would also work in this recipe.*

Warning: *Take care not to let the mixture boil once the wine has been added.*

Per serving: *Calories 92 (From Fat 1); Fat 0g (Saturated 0g); Cholesterol 0mg; Sodium 6mg; Carbohydrate 4g (Dietary Fiber 1g); Protein 0g.*

Hot Spiced Apple Cider

A marvelous winter warm-up, this fragrantly spiced cider can be spiked with brandy or rum.

Yield: *4 to 6 servings*

Preparation time: *5 minutes*

Cooking time: *25 to 30 minutes*

Spice meter: *Mildly to moderately spiced*

1 quart apple cider

3 to 4 whole cloves

8 allspice berries

1 cinnamon stick

⅓ to ½ cup brandy or rum (optional)

1 In a saucepan over medium heat, combine the cider, cloves, allspice berries, and cinnamon stick. Simmer 20 to 30 minutes, but do not boil.

2 Add the brandy or rum if desired and simmer for 5 minutes, but do not boil.

Tip: *If you add brandy or rum and the cider doesn't taste sweet enough, add extra sugar to taste.*

Per serving: *Calories 108 (From Fat 0); Fat 0g (Saturated 0g); Cholesterol 0mg; Sodium 17mg; Carbohydrate 20g (Dietary Fiber 0g); Protein 0g.*

Mexican Hot Chocolate

This traditional Mexican beverage is spiced with cinnamon. For a richer version, replace 1½ cups of the milk with cream.

Yield: *4 to 6 servings*

Preparation time: *5 minutes*

Cooking time: *10 minutes*

Spice meter: *Mildly spiced*

½ cup cream

¼ cup unsweetened cocoa

2 teaspoons ground cinnamon

⅓ cup sugar, or to taste

3½ cups milk

1 In a saucepan over medium-low heat, combine the cream with the cocoa, cinnamon, and sugar. Stir until very smooth.

2 Add the milk and whisk or stir until blended. Heat until hot, about 5 to 7 minutes, and serve.

Tip: You don't need to follow the directions above. Alternatively, combine all the ingredients in a blender or food processor fitted with a metal blade. Pour the mixture into cups and microwave until hot.

Per serving: Calories 209 (From Fat 113); Fat 13g (Saturated 8g); Cholesterol 47mg; Sodium 78mg; Carbohydrate 21g (Dietary Fiber 2g); Protein 6g.

New Orleans Café Brulot

This traditional, festive after-dinner brew is made with coffee, scented with spices and citrus, spiked with brandy, and set alight before it's served. You may garnish each demitasse (a small coffee cup) with orange peel or a cinnamon stick.

Yield: *4 to 6 servings*

Preparation time: *10 minutes*

Cooking time: *5 to 10 minutes*

Spice meter: *Mildly to moderately spiced*

Zest of one orange, cut in one long strip

Zest of one lemon, cut in one long strip

4 teaspoons sugar, or to taste

1 cinnamon stick, broken into pieces

6 allspice berries or whole cloves

½ cup brandy or cognac

2 tablespoons curacao (optional)

2 cups very strong freshly brewed black coffee

1 In a saucepan over medium-low heat, combine the orange and lemon zests, sugar, cinnamon stick, allspice, brandy, and curacao. Stir frequently. When the mixture is warm and the sugar is starting to dissolve, ignite the brandy.

2 Pour the coffee into the pan in a steady stream. Allow the mixture to heat, but do not boil. Serve immediately in demitasse cups.

Tip: *Use a vegetable peeler or citrus zester to remove the zest of the orange and lemon. Try not to get much of the white pith on the zest because the pith has a bitter taste. Remove any white pith from the strip with a sharp paring knife.*

Variation: *Omit the sugar and cognac. Brew the coffee and pour it over the citrus zest and spices. Let the coffee steep for at least one hour. Chill thoroughly. Add sugar and milk or cream to taste. You can spike this cool drink with Kahlua or Tia Maria.*

Per serving: *Calories 35 (From Fat 0); Fat 0g (Saturated 0g); Cholesterol 0mg; Sodium 2mg; Carbohydrate 4g (Dietary Fiber 0g); Protein 0g*

Spiced Iced Tea

This refreshing iced tea is also good when served hot. Use traditional or fruit flavored teas, such as Earl Grey, raspberry, or any one of your favorite blends.

Yield: *4 to 6 servings*

Preparation time: *10 minutes*

Cooking time: *15 to 20 minutes; 1 hour cooling time*

Spice meter: *Mildly spiced*

4 teabags	*6 cardamom pods, bruised*
6 cups cold water	*½-inch piece of ginger, sliced into chunks*
½ cinnamon stick	*⅓ cup sugar, or to taste (optional)*
6 whole cloves or allspice berries	*2 tablespoons fresh lemon juice*

1 Place the teabags in a 1½-quart liquid measuring cup, bowl, jug, or pitcher. If you're using a glass container, put a metal spoon in the pitcher to prevent the glass from cracking. (The spoon allows some of the heat to escape.)

2 In a saucepan over high heat, combine the water, cinnamon, cloves, and cardamom. Bring the water to a boil.

3 Pour the boiling water and spices into the container with the teabags. Add the sugar and lemon juice and let the tea steep for 4 to 5 minutes.

4 Strain the tea into another jar or pitcher or remove the teabags and spices with a slotted spoon. Chill thoroughly in the refrigerator.

Tip: Make sun-brewed iced tea. Combine all the ingredients in a clear glass or plastic jug. Cover the jug and set it in full sunlight until the tea has darkened to your taste. Depending on the strength of the sun in your area, this can take 2 to 4 hours. Strain out the bags and spices. Add the lemon juice and sugar to taste.

Variation: Omit the lemon juice. Substitute 2 cups of milk for 2 cups of the water. Follow the instructions through Step 4 but do not chill. This tea should be served hot.

Per serving: *Calories 4 (From Fat 0); Fat 0g (Saturated 0g); Cholesterol 0mg; Sodium 7mg; Carbohydrate 1g (Dietary Fiber 0g); Protein 0g.*

Bloody Mary Mix

Serve this classic cocktail over ice with a celery stick or wedge of lemon. You can add a shot of vodka or tequila.

Yield: *2 cups*

Preparation time: *5 minutes*

Spice meter: *Moderately spiced*

2 cups tomato juice

2 tablespoons fresh lemon juice, or to taste

¼ teaspoon celery salt

¼ teaspoon garlic salt

½ to 1 teaspoon Tabasco sauce, or to taste

1 teaspoon Worcestershire sauce

Freshly ground black or white pepper to taste

1 tablespoon prepared grated white horseradish

Combine all the ingredients in a bottle or pitcher. Cover the bottle and shake (or stir if using a pitcher) until the mixture is well blended. Refrigerate until serving.

Tip: *If you don't feel like measuring the Tabasco and Worcestershire sauce, add a generous dash and adjust to taste.*

Per serving: Calories 60 (From Fat 1); Fat 0g (Saturated 0g); Cholesterol 0mg; Sodium 1,331mg; Carbohydrate 12g (Dietary Fiber 1g); Protein 2g.

Pairing spicy food and beverages

Traditionally, alcoholic beverages aren't served with spicy food; tea or water are the standard offerings. In restaurants, Chinese and Japanese dishes are most often served with teas such as Chinese Black or Japanese Green Tea. One notable exception is that sake and plum wine are often served with Japanese food.

Today, however, many people enjoy drinking beer and wine with spicy fare. Pilsner-style beer (pale, light lagers) are suitable, and you might want to pair regional beers with food from the same country: Mexican beer with Mexican food or Thai beer with Thai food. Sangria is perfect with Mexican and Spanish fare. Red wines, such as Shiraz or Cabernet blends, and white wines, such as Chardonnay or Sauvignon Blanc, work well with most spicy dishes.

Part V
The Part of Tens

The 5th Wave — By Rich Tennant

"Do I like arugula? I _love_ arugula!! Some of the best beaches in the world are there."

In this part . . .

Every *For Dummies* book ends with top-ten lists, and this one is no exception. I give you ten ways to present and garnish meals and ten Internet and mail-order sources for spices and unusual ingredients.

Chapter 20

Ten Spicy Presentations

In This Chapter

▶ Creating visual appeal

▶ Garnishing ideas

*Y*ou've planned your menu and prepared the food. Now it's time to enter the last phase: the art of presentation. Here's where you, the cook, give the meal your signature touch. Time permitting, you can make your presentation as plain or elegant as you want.

How you set your table establishes the tone of the meal, be it casual or elegant. Tablecloths or dinnerware can reflect the theme, the cultural origins of the menu, or the importance of an occasion. You may choose to serve from a lovely platter, tureen, or bowl, or you may decide to arrange food on each diner's plate.

Regardless of the mood you create, the food itself should be garnished to make it as eye appealing as possible. This doesn't mean the food has to be dressed to kill or that you need to create a complicated or architectural presentation.

Over-garnishing actually detracts from a home-cooked meal. All that's needed is a little thought and a simple garnish — a light dusting of cinnamon on a dessert plate or a light sprinkling of herbs on top of the food, for example. The trick is to use a garnish that complements the flavors and colors in the dish.

Before serving, wipe any spills or drips from your platters, plates, or bowls with a damp cloth or paper towel.

Garnishing Basics

For just about any garnish, keep these guidelines in mind:

✔ Garnishes should be edible.

✔ Keep garnishes uncomplicated and use only a small amount of any one garnish.

> ✔ Use garnishes to add a contrasting texture.
>
> ✔ Use garnishes to add visual contrast and color to a dish.
>
> ✔ Complement, highlight, or accent the flavors in the dish. Remember cultural origins and garnish accordingly. You can check the flavor combos in Chapter 7 for more information.

Ten Spicy Garnishes

Keep it simple — these easy garnishes are fast and many don't require much preparation, just a light hand! Many recipes in the book suggest appropriate garnishes, but here are a few additional ideas.

A trickle of taste

Drizzle spiced oils on the plate or food. Another option is to top food with a slice of spiced butter. Use on plain vegetables; grilled or sautéed meat, such as chops or steak; fish filets; or chicken, pork, or veal cutlets.

A pinch of spice

Lightly dust food with finely ground spices such as coriander, cumin, chili powder, cayenne, white pepper, black pepper, nutmeg, garam masala, cinnamon, allspice, or paprika. Sprinkle lightly with seeds such as poppy seeds, sesame seeds, or fennel seeds. Add a touch of crushed red chile flakes or a few dashes of Tabasco. Make sure you use spices that are in the dish; those that will enhance the flavor and give a color contrast. Top Hummus or Roasted Eggplant Paté (both from Chapter 12) with cumin, cayenne, or paprika.

A sprinkling of fresh spices

Mince or sliver ginger or seeded chile peppers, such as jalapenos or serranos, and dot a dish with the resulting spice. Top Black Bean Dip (Chapter 12) with slivers of chiles or Indonesian Peanut Noodles with Vegetables (Chapter 17) with a little ginger.

A complement of raw vegetables

Accent food with colorful thin strips or tiny cubes of raw vegetables such as cucumbers, seeded tomatoes, bell peppers, and carrots. Sliced scallions or scallion greens also look good. Or try a dollop of fresh salsa. Garnish Yakitori (Chapter 13) with scallions. Use the salsas in Chapter 11 alongside curries, with Grilled Lime-Cumin Chicken Cutlets (Chapter 13), Southeast Asian Fried Flounder or Sole (Chapter 15), or with Coriander-Spiced Burgers (Chapter 14).

A touch of fresh herbs

Sprinkle food with minced fresh herbs such as parsley, cilantro, basil, mint, celery leaves, chives, or snipped dill. Accent with a sprig of fresh parsley, dill, cilantro, basil, or mint. Use an herb that's featured in the dish, complements the flavor, or is associated with the same region the dish originated in (see Chapter 7). Top Spiced Pepperonata (Chapter 12) or Pasta Puttanesca (Chapter 17) with fresh parsley or basil. Use cilantro to top Indian Rogan Josh (Chapter 14) or Black Bean Dip (Chapter 12).

A tasty potpourri

Sprinkle food with chopped nuts, slivered almonds, bacon bits, chopped or sliced olives, chopped hard-boiled eggs, or croutons. Top Spiced Roasted Vegetables (Chapter 16) with olives. Plain vegetables such as green beans can be topped with sautéed slivered almonds, bacon bits, or chopped hard-boiled eggs.

A dash of dairy

Garnish with a dollop of sour cream, plain yogurt, or whipped cream. Top Beef and Bean Chili (Chapter 14) with sour cream or yogurt. Sunset Butternut Soup (Chapter 12) is good with yogurt. Mexican Hot Chocolate (Chapter 19) and Spiced Poached Fruit (Chapter 18) go well with whipped cream.

A hint of cheese

Sprinkle with grated cheese. Parmesan, Romano, cheddar, and Monterey Jack are varieties to consider. Top with a crumbled cheese, such as feta or blue cheese. Garnish Italian pasta dishes with Parmesan or Romano. Use Monterey Jack on Vegetable Bean Chili (Chapter 16). Blue cheese is a nice accent on green salads.

A fruity accent

Garnish food or desserts with lemon or lime, either thin slices or wedges. Add a curl of a thin strip of lemon, lime, or orange zest. Garnish desserts with chopped or sliced fresh fruit (try mangoes, papayas, and strawberries) or accent the dish with whole berries. Garnish Spiced Chocolate Loaf (Chapter 18) with berries. Serve Spicy Crab Cakes with Cilantro Sauce (Chapter 15) with a wedge of lemon or lime.

A sweet idea

Dust desserts or dessert plates with confectioners' sugar, cocoa, cinnamon, or cinnamon sugar. Confectioners' sugar is a lovely garnish for Old-Fashioned Gingerbread or Spiced Apple Cake (Chapter 18).

Chapter 21

Ten Spicy Sources

Spices, chiles, and exotic ingredients are available through many excellent sources, both on the Web and by mail order. Here's my top ten list.

Chile Today-Hot Tamale

Chile Today-Hot Tamale offers dried spices, chiles, and hot sauces.

Web site: www.chiletoday.com

Telephone: 800-HOTPEPPER

Fax: 973-884-4118

Location: 2-D Great Meadow Lane, East Hanover, NJ 07936

Dean and Deluca

Dean and Deluca is not only a source for spices also but a great place to find a range of gourmet foods.

Web site: www:deananddeluca.com

Telephone: 877-826-9246

Fax: 800-781-4050

Location: 2526 E. 36 St. N.Cir., Wichita, KS 67219; stores in New York, California, Kansas, North Carolina, and Washington D.C.

Earthy Delights

Earthy Delights offers spices and unusual ingredients.

Web site: www.earthydelights.com

Telephone: 800-367-4709 or 517-668-2402

Fax: 517-668-1213

Location: 1161 E. Clark Rd., Dewitt, MI 48820

The Great American Spice Company

The Great American Spice Company offers a variety of spices.

Web site: americanspice.com

Telephone: 888-502-8058 or 219-749-8835

Fax: 219-749-7423

Location: P.O. Box 80068, Fort Wayne, IN 46898

McCormick & Company Inc.

McCormick's offers a huge array of spices, both whole and ground.

Web site: www.mccormick.com

Telephone: 800-632-5847

Location: 211 Schilling Circle, Hunt Valley, MD 21031

Melissa's

Melissa's offers spices as well as unusual and exotic ingredients.

Web site: www.melissas.com

Telephone: 800-588-0151

Location: P.O. Box 21127, Los Angeles, CA 90021

Mo Hotta-Mo Betta

Mo Hotta-Mo Betta is a source for hot chiles, hot spices, and hot marinades and sauces.

Web site: www.mohotta.com

Telephone: 800-462-3220 or 912-748-2766

Fax: 800-618-4554 or 912-748-1364

Location: P.O. Box 1026 Savannah, GA 31402

Penzeys

Penzeys is a source for quality spices and spice blends.

Web site: www.penzeys.com

Telephone: 800-741-7787

Fax: 262-679-7878

Location: Muskego, WI. Penzeys has stores in Wisconsin, Minnesota, Texas, Illinois, and Connecticut.

Spice Hunter

Spice Hunter has quality spices, spice blends, is a good source for dried chile powders.

Web site: www.spicehunter.com

Telephone: 805-597-8995

Fax: 805-544-3824

Location: P.O. Box 8110, San Luis Obispo, CA 93403

Vanns Spices

Vanns offers a large range of quality spices and spice blends.

Web site: www.vannsspices.com

Telephone: 800-583-1693 or 410-358-3007

Fax: 800-583-1617 or 410-358-1617

Location: 6105 Oakleaf Ave., Baltimore, MD 21215

Appendix A

Metric Conversion Guide

● ●

***N**ote:* The recipes in this cookbook were not developed or tested using metric measures. There may be some variation in quality when converting to metric units.

Common Abbreviations

Abbreviation(s)	What It Stands For
C, c	cup
g	gram
kg	kilogram
L, l	liter
lb	pound
mL, ml	milliliter
oz	ounce
pt	pint
t, tsp	teaspoon
T, TB, Tbl, Tbsp	tablespoon

Volume

U.S. Units	Canadian Metric	Australian Metric
¼ teaspoon	1 mL	1 ml
½ teaspoon	2 mL	2 ml
1 teaspoon	5 mL	5 ml
1 tablespoon	15 mL	20 ml

(continued)

Volume *(continued)*

U.S. Units	Canadian Metric	Australian Metric
¼ cup	50 mL	60 ml
⅓ cup	75 mL	80 ml
½ cup	125 mL	125 ml
⅔ cup	150 mL	170 ml
¾ cup	175 mL	190 ml
1 cup	250 mL	250 ml
1 quart	1 liter	1 liter
1½ quarts	1.5 liters	1.5 liters
2 quarts	2 liters	2 liters
2½ quarts	2.5 liters	2.5 liters
3 quarts	3 liters	3 liters
4 quarts	4 liters	4 liters

Weight

U.S. Units	Canadian Metric	Australian Metric
1 ounce	30 grams	30 grams
2 ounces	55 grams	60 grams
3 ounces	85 grams	90 grams
4 ounces (¼ pound)	115 grams	125 grams
8 ounces (½ pound)	225 grams	225 grams
16 ounces (1 pound)	455 grams	500 grams
1 pound	455 grams	½ kilogram

Measurements

Inches	Centimeters
½	1.5
1	2.5

Inches	Centimeters
2	5.0
3	7.5
4	10.0
5	12.5
6	15.0
7	17.5
8	20.5
9	23.0
10	25.5
11	28.0
12	30.5
13	33.0

Temperature (Degrees)

Fahrenheit	Celsius
32	0
212	100
250	120
275	140
300	150
325	160
350	180
375	190
400	200
425	220
450	230
475	240
500	260

Appendix B

Glossary of Cooking Terms

Cooking and recipe-writing have their own distinct language. Before you roast a chicken, for example, you need to know what trussing means. To make a soufflé that rises above the rim of the dish, you need to understand whipping and folding egg whites. This appendix gives you a list of basic terms. Most of them are thoroughly described and illustrated elsewhere in the book.

Adjust: To taste the dish before serving and add seasoning (such as salt and pepper), if necessary.

Al dente: An Italian phrase meaning "to the tooth" that describes the tender but still firm texture of perfectly cooked pasta.

Au gratin: A dish, usually topped with buttered bread crumbs, grated cheese, or both, that has been browned in the oven or under the broiler.

Bake: To cook in the dry heat of an oven.

Barbecue: Any food cooked on a charcoal or gas grill. Also refers to the process of cooking foods in a pit or on a spit for a long time.

Baste: To add flavor and moisture by brushing food with pan drippings, fat, or a seasoned liquid as it cooks.

Batter: An uncooked, semiliquid mixture usually containing beaten eggs, flour, liquid, and a leavening ingredient, such as baking soda or baking powder, that makes the batter rise when cooked.

Beat: To mix ingredients briskly in a circular motion so that they become smooth and creamy. A hundred hand-beaten strokes generally equal one minute with an electric mixer, if you're the type who counts these things.

Bruise: To crush or crack.

Beurre manié: A butter-flour paste used to thicken soups and stews.

Bind: To bring together a liquid mixture, such as a sauce, with a thickening ingredient, such as cream or butter.

Blanch: To plunge vegetables or fruits into boiling water for a short time to loosen their skin or preserve their color.

Blend: To mix or combine two or more ingredients with a spoon, whisk, spatula, or electric mixer.

Boil: To bring the temperature of a liquid to 212 degrees for water at sea level, causing bubbles to break at the surface.

Bone (or debone): To remove the bones from meat, fish, or poultry.

Bouquet garni: A package of mixed herbs (often tied in cheesecloth) that is used to season stocks, soups, and stews to impart flavor. A typical combination is parsley, thyme, and bay leaf.

Braise: To brown meat or vegetables in fat and then cook, covered, in a small quantity of liquid over low heat, usually for a long time. The long, slow cooking both tenderizes and flavors the food, especially tough cuts of meat. Braising can take place either on the stovetop or in the oven.

Bread: To coat a piece of food with crackers or bread crumbs to seal in moisture and give it a crisp crust. The piece of fish, poultry, meat, or vegetable is usually first dipped into a liquid, such as beaten egg or milk, to make the crumbs adhere.

Broil: To cook food under a hot oven coil, as opposed to grilling, in which the heat is underneath.

Brown: To cook food briefly over high heat, usually in fat and on top of the stove, to impart a rich brown color to its skin or surface. Food also may be browned in a very hot oven or under the broiler.

Brush: To coat the surface of food with a liquid ingredient such as melted butter, egg, or fruit glaze.

Butterfly: To split food down the center (removing bones if necessary), leaving the two halves joined at the seam so that the food opens flat to resemble a butterfly.

Caramelize: To heat sugar until it melts into a liquid, syrupy state that ranges from golden to dark brown in color (320 degrees to 350 degrees on a candy thermometer). Also, to cook onions and other vegetables until they become soft and brown (the sugars they contain caramelize).

Chile peppers or chiles: Peppers from the of the _capsicum_ family; considered a spice.

Chili powder: A mixture of chile pepper powders often used to make the stew-like dish known as chili.

Chop: To cut food into small pieces by using a knife or food processor.

Clarify: To make a cloudy liquid clear by removing the impurities. For example, you can clarify a stock or broth by simmering raw egg whites or eggshells for 10 to 15 minutes to attract impurities. You then very gently strain the liquid through a sieve lined with cheesecloth.

Core: To cut out the core of a food, usually a fruit or vegetable such as an apple or pepper.

Cream: To beat one ingredient, such as butter, with another, such as sugar, until soft and smooth.

Crimp: To press together with your fingers or a fork and seal the rim of a double-crust pie to form a double thickness of dough that you can then shape into a decorative pattern.

Crumble: To break up or crush food, such as dried herbs or crackers, into small pieces with your fingers.

Cube: To cut food into ½-inch square pieces. Cubed food is larger than diced food. *See also* **dice.**

Curry: A blend of several spices. Though there is no standard formula, curry powder can include cumin, coriander, dried chiles, cardamom, cinnamon, cloves, fennel, peppercorns, mustard seeds, ginger, fenugreek, and turmeric.

Cure: To preserve food such as meat or fish by salting, drying, and/or smoking.

Dash: *See* **pinch.**

Deglaze: To add liquid, usually wine or broth, to a hot skillet or roasting pan and scrape up the browned bits clinging to the bottom of the pan that pieces of sautéed meat, fish, or poultry left behind. You then reduce and season the pan sauce.

Degrease: To skim the fat off the surface of a soup or gravy with a spoon. Also done by chilling the mixture, turning the liquid fat into a solid, which you can then easily lift off the surface.

Demi-glace: A rich, brown sauce made by boiling down meat stock until it's reduced to a thick glaze that can coat a spoon.

Devein: To remove the vein from shrimp or other shellfish.

Devil: To season foods with hot and spicy ingredients such as Tabasco sauce, mustard, or red pepper flakes.

Dice: To cut into small (⅛-inch to ¼-inch) cubes.

Dilute: To thin a mixture by adding water or other liquid.

Disjoint: To sever a piece of meat at its joint, as when you separate a chicken leg from its thigh.

Dot: To distribute small portions or pieces of food (such as bits of butter) over the surface of another food.

Drain: To remove the liquid from a food, often in a colander. Also, to pour off liquid fat from a pan after you brown a food (such as bacon or ground meat).

Dredge: To coat the surface of a food by dragging it through flour, cornmeal, or crumbs.

Drizzle: To pour a liquid such as melted butter, sauce, or syrup over a food in a thin, slow stream.

Dust: To give the surface of food a thin coating of flour or confectioners' sugar.

Fillet: To cut the flesh away from the bones of a piece of meat or fish.

Flambé: To ignite food that is drenched in alcohol so that it bursts into a dramatic flame just before serving.

Fold: To combine a light mixture, such as beaten egg whites or whipped cream, with a heavier mixture, such as sugared egg yolks or melted chocolate, by using a gentle mixing motion.

Fricassee: A white stew in which meat or poultry is not browned before cooking.

Fry: To cook or sauté food in fat over high heat. Deep-fried foods are submerged in hot fat and cooked until crisp.

Fumet: A concentrated fish stock that is used as a flavoring base for sauces.

Garnish: An edible plate adornment, ranging from a simple wedge of lemon to a dusting of chile pepper powder to a fancy chocolate leaf.

Glaze: To coat the surface of a food with syrup, melted jelly, an egg wash, or other thin, liquid mixture to give it a glossy shine.

Grate: To rub a large piece of food (such as a block of cheese) against the coarse, serrated holes of a grater.

Grease: To spread a thin layer of fat, usually butter, on the inside of a pan to prevent food from sticking as it cooks.

Grill: To cook food over a charcoal or gas grill, or to cook on an iron (or other) grill on the stovetop. Relatively high heat is used to sear food and add depth of flavor.

Hull: To trim strawberries by plucking out their green stems.

Infuse: To gently heat a spice in liquid over medium-low heat until the liquid is barely simmering.

Julienne: To cut foods into thin (⅛ inch or less) strips.

Knead: The technique of pushing, folding, and pressing dough for yeast breads to give it a smooth, elastic texture. You can knead by hand or with an electric mixer equipped with a bread hook or a bread machine.

Marinate: To soak or steep a food such as meat, poultry, fish, or vegetables in a liquid mixture that may be seasoned with spices and herbs in order to impart flavor to the food before it is cooked. The steeping liquid is called the marinade.

Mash: To press food, usually with a potato masher or ricer, into a soft pulp.

Mince: To cut food into tiny pieces.

Mirepoix: A combination of finely chopped sautéed vegetables, usually carrots, onions, and celery, that is used as a seasoning base for soups, stews, stuffings, and other dishes.

Parboil: To partially cook foods, such as rice or dense vegetables like carrots and potatoes, by plunging them briefly into boiling water.

Pare: To remove the skin from fruits or vegetables.

Pepper mill: A hand-held grinder for peppercorns.

Pickle: To preserve food in a salty brine or vinegar solution.

Pinch or dash: A small amount of any dry ingredient (between ¹⁄₁₆ and ⅛ teaspoon) that can be grasped between the tips of the thumb and forefinger.

Poach: To cook foods in a simmering, not boiling, liquid.

Pound: To flatten food, especially chicken breasts or meat, with a meat mallet or the flat side of a large knife (such as a cleaver) to make it uniform in thickness. Has some tenderizing effect.

Preheat: To turn on the oven, grill, or broiler before cooking food to set the temperature to the degree required by the recipe.

Puree: To mash or grind food into a paste by forcing through a food mill or sieve or by whirling in a food processor or blender. Finely mashed food also is called a puree.

Ream: To extract the juice from fruit, especially citrus.

Reconstitute: To bring dehydrated food, such as dried milk or juice, back to a liquid state by adding water.

Reduce: The technique of rapidly boiling a liquid mixture, such as wine, stock, or sauce, to decrease its original volume so that it thickens and concentrates in flavor.

Render: To cook a piece of meat over low heat so that its fat melts away.

Rhizomes: An underground stem that produces knobby roots. Ginger and turmeric are examples.

Roast: To cook in the dry heat of an oven.

Roux: A cooked paste of flour and fat such as oil or butter that is used to thicken soups, stews, and gumbos.

Rub: A spice blend that's, uh, rubbed on meat, poultry, or fish before grilling or sautéing.

Sauté: To cook food quickly in a small amount of fat, usually butter or oil, over very high heat.

Scald: To heat milk to just below the boiling point when making custards and dessert sauces to shorten the cooking time.

Score: To make shallow cuts (often in a crisscross pattern) on the exterior of a food (such as meat, fish, or bread) so that it cooks more evenly.

Sear: To brown quickly in a pan, under the broiler, or in a very hot oven.

Season: To flavor foods with herbs, spices, salt, pepper, and so on.

Shred: To reduce food to thin strips, usually by rubbing it against a grater.

Shuck: To remove shells from shellfish, such as clams, oysters, and mussels or to remove husks from fresh corn.

Sift: To shake dry ingredients, such as flour or confectioners' sugar, through a fine mesh sifter to incorporate air and make them lighter.

Simmer: To gently cook food in a liquid just below the boiling point or just until tiny bubbles begin to break the surface (at about 185 degrees).

Skewer: To thread small pieces of food on long, thin rods made of bamboo or metal to hold meat, fish, or vegetables for grilling or broiling.

Skim: To remove the fat and bits of food that rise to the surface of a soup or stock with a spoon.

Steam: To cook over a small amount of simmering or boiling water in a covered pan so that the steam trapped in the pan cooks the food.

Steep: To gently heat a spice in liquid over medium-low heat until the liquid is barely simmering.

Stew: To simmer food for a long time in a tightly covered pot with just enough liquid to cover. The term stew also can describe a cooked dish.

Stir-fry: The Asian cooking technique of quickly frying small pieces of food in a wok with a small amount of fat over very high heat while constantly tossing and stirring the ingredients. The term stir-fry also can refer to a dish prepared this way.

Stock: The strained, flavorful liquid that is produced by cooking meat, fish, poultry, vegetables, seasonings, or other ingredients in water.

Strain: To separate liquids from solids by passing a mixture through a sieve.

Stuff: To fill a food cavity, such as the inside of chicken, turkey, or tomato, with various types of food.

Tenderize: To soften the connective tissue of meat by pounding or cooking very slowly for a long time. *See also* **braise.**

Toss: To turn over food a number of times to mix thoroughly, as when a green salad is mixed and coated with dressing.

Truss: To tie meat or poultry with string and/or skewers to maintain its shape during roasting.

Whip: To beat air into ingredients such as eggs or cream with a whisk or electric beater to make them light and fluffy.

Whisk: A handheld wire kitchen utensil used to whip ingredients like eggs, cream, and sauces. When used as a verb, the term whisk describes the process of whipping or blending ingredients together with a wire whisk.

Zest: The colored, grated outer peel (the colored portion only) of citrus fruit that is used as a flavoring ingredient in dressings, stews, desserts, and so on.

Appendix C

Spice Quantity Guide

*M*ost cooks like to improvise from time to time and give a recipe their own special signature. Whether making a stir-fry from what's in your fridge or adding a dash of spice to a muffin batter, many folks wonder what quantity of a particular spice to use. There's no set formula for how much you should use in a dish. It depends on the quantity you're making and what type of food you're preparing (such sweet baked goods versus savory fare) as well as what combinations of spices you put together.

Spicing is an art that requires some experience. It's really a matter of taste and a bit of trial and error, but the following tables should give you a general idea. The suggestions of spices are for 4 to 6 servings for savory fare, and one standard-size recipe for sweet or baked goods, such as one 8 to 9-inch cake or one 12 muffin recipe or one 9x5 inch loaf. Some spices are used for both sweet and savory dishes, but if they aren't, no quantity is listed for the category. Of course, you'll find recipes in this book and others that use different amounts than those listed here. Use these as a starting point and adjust them to your taste. To use spices as a garnish, simply sprinkle a bit on top of the dish and look in Chapter 20 for ideas.

Dried Spices

Dried Spice	Savory Fare Quantity	Sweets and Baked Goods Quantity	Additional Tips
Allspice	3 to 6 whole berries, pinch to ½ teaspoon ground	⅛ to ¼ teaspoon	Use in combination with cinnamon and/or ginger or in place of ground cloves in baked goods and fruit dishes; add to poaching liquids, marinades, and curries

(continued)

Dried Spice	Savory Fare Quantity	Sweets and Baked Goods Quantity	Additional Tips
Anise or aniseed		¼ to ½ teaspoons	Sprinkle on bread dough or cookies before baking; blend with cream cheese
Achiote (annato)	¼ to ½ teaspoon		Add for color when sauteeing onions and garlic; add to water when cooking rice
Caraway	¼ to ½ teaspoon	1 to 2 teaspoons	Sprinkle on top of bisuits, or mix in bread dough before baking; add to meat stews; good with cheese and potato dishes
Cardamom	2 to 6 whole pods, ¼ to ½ teaspoon ground	¼ to ½ teaspoon ground	Use in place of ground cinnamon in baked goods
Cayenne or ground red pepper	⅛ to ½ teaspoon	pinch to ¼ teaspoon	Add to taste in spicy dishes; sprinkle lightly as a garnish
Celery seed	¼ to ½ teaspoon		Add to cole slaw, salad dressings and stewed tomatoes
Chile pepper powders	heat factor varies by type of chile; use the manufacturer's suggestion as a guide		Use in sauces, marinades, stews, chilis, vegetables and raw vegetable salads.
Chili powder	1 to 3 tablespoons		Use in chilis, meatloaf, or meatballs; sprinkle as garnish

Dried Spice	Savory Fare Quantity	Sweets and Baked Goods Quantity	Additional Tips
Cinnamon and cassia	½ to 1 stick, ¼ to ½ teaspoon ground	¼ to 1 teaspoon ground	Use in marinades, curries and in breakfast breads and desserts; good with fruit dishes; sprinkle as garnish for desserts; often used in combination with ginger, nutmeg, allspice or ground cloves
Cloves	2 to 8 whole, pinch to ¼ teaspoon ground	⅛ to ¼ teaspoon ground	Use whole to stud in ham; use in marinades, curries, stews; use in combination with cinnamon and/or ginger in baked goods
Coriander	½ to 1½ teaspoons whole, ¼ to ¾ teaspoon ground		Use freshly ground for garnish for salads and savory dishes; add to poaching liquid and marinades for poultry, seafood, or fruit
Crushed red chile flakes	pinch to ½ teaspoon		Use for hot flavor to taste in sauces, stews, pasta dishes, sprinkle lightly as garnish
Cumin	½ to 1 teaspoon whole; ¼ to 1 teaspoon, ground		Use in curries, chilis, marinades, sauces; add to savory pies and meatballs; blend with cheese; add to avocado or egg salad, sprinkle as garnish

(continued)

Dried Spice	Savory Fare Quantity	Sweets and Baked Goods Quantity	Additional Tips
Curry powder	1 teaspoon to 3 tablespoons		Add to curries, marinades, and mayonnaise
Dill seed	¼ to ½ teaspoon		Use in salad dressings, with fish and vegetables
Fennel	¼ to ½ teaspoon	1/4 to 1/2 teaspoon	Use in seafood dishes, curry powder, tomato sauce and sausage
Fenugreek seed	¼ to ½ teaspoon		Use in curry blends
Filé powder	1 to 3 teaspoons		Use in gumbo and Cajun stews
Five-spice powder	¼ to 1 teaspoon		Use in marinades, stir fries along with fresh ginger and garlic
Garam masala	¼ to ½ teaspoon		Pinch as garnish for curries
Garlic powder, garlic flakes, and garlic salt	¼ to 1 teaspoon		Use in marinades and salad dressings; use with butter to make garlic bread
Ground ginger		½ to 1 teaspoon; up to 1½ tablespoons for full gingery flavor	Use in baked goods; often used in combination with cinnamon and nutmeg
Juniper berries	1½ to 3 teaspoons		Add to meat and game stews and savory pies

Dried Spice	Savory Fare Quantity	Sweets and Baked Goods Quantity	Additional Tips
Lemon grass and sereh	1½ to 2 tablespoons dried strips; 1 teaspoon sereh		
Mace	⅛ to ¼ teaspoon	⅛ to ¼ teaspoon	Use in baked goods, curries, sauces, and marinades
Mustard seed	½ to 1 teaspoon		Use in curries and with vegetables
Nutmeg	pinch to ¼ teaspoon	pinch to ¼ teaspoon	Use in baked goods, with spinach, ricotta cheese lasagne filling, pumpkin, buttenut, and fruit; use in combination with cinnamon; sprinkle as garnish
Onion powder	¼ to ½ teaspoon		Use in marinades
Paprika	1 teaspoon to 2 tablespoons		Pinch as garnish
Peppercorns and pepper	1 to 3 teaspoons whole, ¼ to ½ teaspoon ground	½ tablespoon cracked peppercorns	Add to or season top savory food and add to savory bread dough
Poppy seed	½ teaspoon to 1 teaspoon	½ to 3 tablespoons	Use in salad dressing; toss with buttered noodles; use in baked goods; top bread dough before baking
Saffron	3 to 4 strands, dissolved in 2 tablespoons liquid	3 to 4 strands, dissolved in 2 tablespoons liquid	Use in rice, stews, seafood dishes, and baked goods

(continued)

Dried Spice	Savory Fare Quantity	Sweets and Baked Goods Quantity	Additional Tips
Salt	½ to 1 teaspoon	¼ to ½ teaspoon	Add to or season savory food; use in baking as directed
Sesame seed	½ teaspoon to ¼ cup	sprinkle liberally	Top savory bread dough; use in sauces and in place of bread crumbs
Star anise and sauces	1 to 2 whole		Use in marinades
Szechuan pepper	¼ to 1 teaspoon		Use in marinades and stir fries
Turmeric	¼ to ½ teaspoon		Use in curries; add to rice while cooking
Vanilla		½ bean split, ½ to 1 teaspoon extract	Use in desserts, cookies, cakes, fruit dishes, dessert sauces, candies

Fresh Spices and Aromatics

There are no exact quantities to use when cooking with fresh spices, but generally the following amounts are good if you're making a recipe that serves 4 to 6 people. If you're cooking for only 1 or 2, use a bit less than what's suggested here.

Fresh Spice	Savory Dishes Quantity	Additional Tips
Fresh garlic	1 to 3 plump cloves, minced	Use in many savory dishes, marinades, sauces
Fresh ginger	½ to 1 inch piece, peeled and minced	Use in Asian-style dishes, curries and stir fries and Caribbean dishes, marinades and sauces

Fresh Spice	*Savory Dishes Quantity*	*Additional Tips*
Fresh chiles	1 to 2 fresh chiles, such as jalapeno, serrano and bird's eye; ½ to 1 Scotch bonnet, seeded and minced	Use in Mexican, South western, Caribbean and Asian dishes, marinades, and sauces
Dried chiles	1 to 2 dried chiles (except Habanero: ½ to 1 only), reconstituted, seeded, and minced	Use in Mexican and Southwestern dishes, marinades, and sauces
Fresh lemon grass	1 to 2 stalks, bruised and/or chopped	Use in Thai and Vietnamese dishes, marinades, and sauces
Fresh lime leaves	1 to 3 leaves	Use in Thai dishes, marinades, and sauces

Index

* *

• *H* •

• *N* •

Discover Dummies Online!

The Dummies Web Site is your fun and friendly online resource for the latest information about *For Dummies* books and your favorite topics. The Web site is the place to communicate with us, exchange ideas with other *For Dummies* readers, chat with authors, and have fun!

Ten Fun and Useful Things You Can Do at www.dummies.com

1. Win free *For Dummies* books and more!
2. Register your book and be entered in a prize drawing.
3. Meet your favorite authors through the Hungry Minds Author Chat Series.
4. Exchange helpful information with other *For Dummies* readers.
5. Discover other great *For Dummies* books you must have!
6. Purchase Dummieswear exclusively from our Web site.
7. Buy *For Dummies* books online.
8. Talk to us. Make comments, ask questions, get answers!
9. Download free software.
10. Find additional useful resources from authors.

Link directly to these ten fun and useful things at
www.dummies.com/10useful

For other titles from Hungry Minds,
go to **www.hungryminds.com**

Not on the Web yet? It's easy to get started with *Dummies 101: The Internet For Windows 98* or *The Internet For Dummies* at local retailers everywhere.

Hungry Minds™

Find other *For Dummies* books on these topics:
Business • Career • Databases • Food & Beverage • Games • Gardening
Graphics • Hardware • Health & Fitness • Internet and the World Wide Web
Networking • Office Suites • Operating Systems • Personal Finance • Pets
Programming • Recreation • Sports • Spreadsheets • Teacher Resources
Test Prep • Word Processing

FOR DUMMIES
BOOK REGISTRATION

Register This Book and Win!

We want to hear from you!

Visit **dummies.com** to register this book and tell us how you liked it!

- Get entered in our monthly prize giveaway.

- Give us feedback about this book — tell us what you like best, what you like least, or maybe what you'd like to ask the author and us to change!

- Let us know any other *For Dummies* topics that interest you.

Your feedback helps us determine what books to publish, tells us what coverage to add as we revise our books, and lets us know whether we're meeting your needs as a *For Dummies* reader. You're our most valuable resource, and what you have to say is important to us!

Not on the Web yet? It's easy to get started with *Dummies 101: The Internet For Windows 98* or *The Internet For Dummies* at local retailers everywhere.

Or let us know what you think by sending us a letter at the following address:

For Dummies Book Registration
Dummies Press
10475 Crosspoint Blvd.
Indianapolis, IN 46256

FOR DUMMIES™

BESTSELLING BOOK SERIES

Cooking with Spices For Dummies®

A World of Flavors at Your Fingertips

Different cuisines favor different spices and herbs. Here's a look at spices and flavorings from around the globe. More details are given inside.

Cajun and Creole

Spices: cayenne, white pepper, black pepper, garlic, chile peppers, celery seed, file powder

Herbs and other flavorings: thyme, sage, parsley, Tabasco or hot pepper sauce

Caribbean

Spices: garlic, ginger, curry powder, allspice, cloves, chile peppers, Scotch Bonnet peppers, white and black pepper, cayenne, nutmeg, mace, coriander, annato, achiote

Herbs and other flavorings: mint, cilantro, thyme, lime juice, rum

Chinese

Spices: garlic, ginger, five spice powder, dried chile peppers, crushed red pepper flakes, sesame seeds, star anise, Szechuan pepper

Herbs and other flavorings: orange zest, soy sauce, Chinese or toasted sesame oil, hot chile oil, sherry, bean pastes, oyster sauce, hoisin sauce, Chinese chile paste

Greek

Spices: garlic, cinnamon, nutmeg, black pepper

Herbs and other flavorings: parsley, oregano, dill, lemon, honey

Indian

Spices: garlic, ginger, garam masala, cinnamon, all-spice, cloves, coriander, cumin, curry powder, turmeric, saffron, fenugreek, fennel seed, black peppercorns, mustard seeds, cayenne, chile peppers

Herbs and other flavorings: bay leaf, cilantro, mint, lemon

Indonesia and Malaysia

Spices: ginger, garlic, chile peppers, cardamom, cloves, curry powder, curry pastes, cinnamon, cumin, turmeric, mace, nutmeg, black and white pepper, crushed red chile flakes

Herbs and other flavorings: bay leaf, mint, cilantro, soy sauce, sambal ulek or chile paste, vinegar, lemon or lime juice

Italian and Southern French

Spices: garlic, coriander, cumin, crushed red chile flakes, paprika, fennel seed, nutmeg

Herbs and other flavorings: mint, basil, parsley, oregano, rosemary, bay leaf, wine, lemon, orange, balsamic vinegar

Japanese

Spices: ginger, garlic, Japanese mustard or wasabi, sesame

Other flavorings: dashi or fish broth, pickled ginger, soy sauce, sherry, mirin and sake rice wines, vinegar, lemon juice or Ponzu, sesame oil

Mexican

Spices: arbol, ancho, cascabel, poblano, jalapeno, habanero, and serrano chile peppers, garlic, cumin, cinnamon, cloves, cayenne, black pepper, sesame seeds, vanilla

Herbs and other flavorings: sherry, lime juice, lemon juice, vinegar, sour orange juice, tomato-based adobo sauce, fresh cilantro, oregano

Cooking with Spices For Dummies®

Cheat Sheet

Middle Eastern

Spices: garlic, cumin, cinnamon, cloves, sesame seeds, black pepper, crushed red chile flakes, chile peppers

Herbs and other flavoring: parsley, mint, basil, dill, lemon, honey

Moroccan and Tunisian

Spices: garlic, ginger, cumin, coriander, cardamom, cinnamon, cloves, crushed red chile flakes, chile peppers, cayenne, turmeric, sesame seeds, saffron

Herbs and other flavorings: mint, cilantro, parsley, honey, orange zest, lemon, harissa

Portuguese

Spices: garlic, paprika, chile peppers, cayenne, nutmeg, black pepper

Herbs and other flavorings: parsley, lemon, port wine

South African

Spices: garlic, ginger, allspice, cinnamon, cloves, cardamom, coriander, curry powder, curry pastes, cumin, mace, nutmeg, turmeric, fennel seed, garam masala, black and white pepper, chile peppers, crushed red chile flakes

Herbs and other flavorings: bay leaf, cilantro, parsley, mint, vinegar, lemon juice, tangerine zest

South American

Spices: garlic, cumin, chile peppers, cloves, cinnamon, black pepper, achiote or annato

Herbs and other flavorings: oregano, cilantro, vinegar, palm oil

Spanish

Spices: garlic, paprika, black and white pepper, saffron, fennel seeds

Herbs and other flavorings: oregano, bay leaf, parsley, sherry, sherry wine vinegar, orange juice and zest

Tex-Mex and Southwestern

Spices: garlic, chile powder, cumin, cayenne, jalapeno, serrano, poblano, New Mexican or guajillo chile peppers, black pepper

Herbs and other flavorings: oregano, cilantro, lime juice

Thai

Spices: lemon grass, ginger, chile peppers, chile paste, red or green curry paste, galangal

Herbs and other flavorings: makrud lime or Kaffir lime leaves, fish sauce or Nam Pla, soy sauce, holy or Thai basil, basil, mint, cilantro, vinegar

West African

Spices: allspice, garlic, chile peppers, crushed red pepper flakes, ginger, black pepper

Herbs and other flavorings: peanut oil, palm oil, cilantro, parsley

For Dummies: Bestselling Book Series for Beginners

26821956R00194

Made in the USA
Middletown, DE
06 December 2015